THE POLYNESIAN FAMILY SYSTEM
IN KA-'U, HAWAI'I

ISBN 1-56647-232-6

Cover design by Jane Hopkins

First Printing, February 1999
1 2 3 4 5 6 7 8 9

Mutual Publishing
1215 Center Street, Suite 210
Honolulu, Hawaii 96816
Telephone (808) 732-1709
Fax (808) 734-4094
e-mail: mutual@lava.net
url: http://www.pete.com/mutual

Printed in Australia

THE POLYNESIAN FAMILY
SYSTEM IN KA-'U, HAWAI'I

BY

E. S. CRAIGHILL HANDY

AND

MARY KAWENA PUKUI

With a concluding Chapter on
the History and Ecology of Ka-'u
by
ELIZABETH GREEN HANDY

and an Introduction by Glen Grant

Mutual Publishing

DEDICATION

THIS STUDY is dedicated with deep affection and respect to two *kupuna* of whom the old Ka-'u saying was true:

> " Our proud heritage is that of the *'Ohana* of Ka-'u: We are like the *'a'ali'i* shrub, which holds fast with its roots to the rocky soil of the homeland, whatever winds may blow."

To an *Ali'i Wahine* learned in sacred lore—

PO'AI-WAHINE
(Na-'li'i-po'ai-moku)

of Waikapuna, Ka-'u; *kama hanai* and *Punahele* of Kane-Kuhia, who was trained as a *Kahuna Pule* in the Temple of Lono at Kealakekua, Kona, Hawaii; wife of The Chief (who preferred to live and work) without-servitors, Ke Ali'i Kanaka-'ole, of Puna, Hawaii.

And to the child of Po'ai-wahine and Kanaka-'ole, who bore the name, " The Laboring Chiefess," our beloved

PA'AHANA

without whose learning and faithful devotion our present knowledge would be more fragmentary; who was *wahine mare* to

HENRY NATHANIEL WIGGIN

from Salem, Massachusetts; *makua wahine* and *Hula makua* of

MELE KAWENA WIGGIN PUKUI;

and warmly remembered *makua wahine ho'okama* of

ELIKAPEKA-HI'IAKA-NOHO-LANI
and
KANE-APU'A HANDY.

Come!
You are welcome, O lehua blossom of mine from the
    upland forest,
A blossom around which the birds gather,
My lehua that bloomed in the Ha'ao rain.
Light comes to our house, for you are here.
Come! Come, we are here!
            —*KAHEA*—a welcoming chant.

FOREWORD

THE island of Hawai'i dominated the culture of the northernmost of the Polynesian groups, even before the High Chief Kamehameha conquered the other islands and formed a united kingdom in the first decade of the nineteenth century. This truly great warrior, diplomat and ruler was born in Kohala, but was reared, trained and toughened for his mission in Ka-'u, the southern and most rugged district of Hawai'i, where his mother, the High Chieftainess Keku'i-a-poiwa, isolated herself to protect her child against the enmity

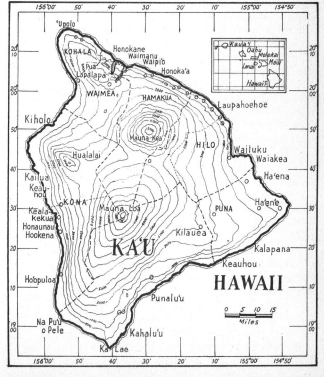

of rival claimants to highest rank and power. The cultural dominance of Hawai'i was doubtless a consequence of size, richness of forests and soils, diversity of environmental conditions and hence variety and quantity of population. The dynamic temperament of the old Polynesian stock of the "Big Island," as it is affectionately called today, was probably partly a consequence of the grandeur of the scene, where the great ocean and the Pacific's greatest volcanoes respectively formed the outlook and the background of every locality in which Hawaiians of Hawai'i were born and reared, lived and loved and hated, laboured, planted, hunted, fished, played, fought and worshipped. Its active vulcanism certainly had a dynamic effect on the culture of this island, and may be presumed to have affected directly the organisms that were the folk who lived intimately with and within and upon the stupendous earth-drama of lava eruptions accompanied by seismic and meteorological disturbance, and the explosive seething of forest and ocean when the molten rivers of *pahoehoe* (flowing lava) and steaming smoking *a'a* (crumbling cooling rubble) poured or crept seaward from pits and vast fissures on the slopes of Mauna Loa. Within the life spans of my colleague, Mrs. Pukui, and of her mother and grandmother, dwelling in Ka-'u, that land has been the scene of eight great flows that have crept from Mauna Loa's barren uplands, through forests and over the inhabited plains, four of them plunging into the sea.

Ka-'u is the most rugged, the most forbidding, of all the areas of habitation in these islands, with its lava strewn coasts, vast windswept plains that are almost treeless, beyond which rise the majestic slopes of Mauna Loa, deeply forested just above the plains, but snow-covered towards the summit in winter months. The toughness of Ka-'u folk was the result of their rugged homeland and hardy life in wresting a living from land and sea. It was affected certainly by the extremes of temperature as between night, when the breezes and winds flow seaward from frosty altitudes, to midday when the black lava of plains and shore is furnace-hot from the sun.

Historically, the people of Ka-'u were the rugged individualists of these islands. There are recorded in tradition repeated episodes in which these tribesmen summarily disposed of their High Chiefs when they were weak or tyrannical. The folk of Ka-'u regarded themselves as one tribe (*maka'ainana*), bred from a single parental stock (*'ohana*). In the words of their tribal slogan:

> Ho'okahi no 'ohana o Ka-'u,
> Mai ka uka a ke kai,
> Mai kahi pae a kahi pae.
>
> Offshoots of one lineage are the people of Ka-'u,
> From the uplands to the sea,
> From border to border.

It is by reason of this tribalism, peculiar in these islands to Ka-'u, that it is of particular interest to compare its institutions with those of the Maori.

Mary Kawena Pukui was born and reared in Ka-'u. Her full Hawaiian name is *Ka-wena-'ula o ka Lani* (The-Rosy-Glow of the Heavens) *a Hi'iaka i-ka-poli-i-Pele* (of Hi'iaka [youngest sister of Pele] in-the-bosom-of-Pele) *na-lei-lehua a Pele* (wearing the crimson *lehua* [*pua rata* in Maori] wreaths of the Volcano Goddess). Her lineage is from the *ali'i* (chiefs) and *kahuna* (priests and craftsmen) of Ka-'u and its neighbouring district of Puna. As the names given reveal, hers is the heritage of the mytho-poetic nature gods of Hawai'i known as the Pele clan or family, which includes Lono-makua (the embodiment of cloud, rain and thunder), Kane-hekili (lightning), Wahine-'oma'o (the "woman clad in green," i.e., the verdure of forests), Laka [Maori Rata] the tutelary god of the *hula* ritual, Hi'iaka (of the rainbow and healing waters), and other minor figures.

The information upon which this and succeeding articles on Ka-'u are built was acquired in 1935, when Mrs. Pukui spent some time in Ka-'u working with the undersigned and his wife, working both there and in neighbouring districts with elder relatives of Mrs. Pukui. In that year there were enough old folk still surviving in Ka-'u, Puna, Hilo, Kona and Honolulu to enable us to reconstruct a truly adequate record of many phases of the local heritage, traditions and culture of her *'ohana*. As we write now, in 1950, there survives in Ka-'u but one elder in this lineage, living in lonely solitude on the windswept plain of Kama'oa.

The proper spelling of Hawaiian names and words is given in the Glossary and Index, and the reader is asked to refer to this in reading this Memoir. We have made every effort to standardize the spelling of words and names throughout the text, but this has been difficult for the following reasons. Although the papers making up the series of articles here collected in one volume were published consecutively over a period of four years, they were actually written over a much longer period, the first in 1936. Before that time the use of diacritical marks and hyphens was rare in Hawaiian spelling and it was not standardized. We commenced using diacritical marks and hyphens in the spelling of certain words in order to make pronunciation and derivation clear. But we were not systematic. Neither of us is trained in modern linguistics.

Furthermore, our collaboration was done under difficult circumstances, often apart, for long periods interrupted by urgent demands and distractions of other work, illness, travel, and the like. Toward the end of the writing of the series, in fact in 1952, Dr. Samuel E. Elbert, Linguistics Professor at the University of Hawai'i, assumed the enormous responsibility and labour of systematizing phonetically Mrs. Pukui's vast word lists which are now in process of preparation for the new Hawaiian dictionary, to be published by the University of Hawai'i. The Glossary and Index here printed will bring our spelling of names and words in Hawaiian into accord with Mrs. Pukui's forthcoming new Hawaiian dictionary as edited by Dr. Elbert, except in the case of a few words in which we reserve the right to differ with Dr. Elbert in the matter of pronunciation.

The publication of this series has been a labour of love, a joint effort at long distance instigated and aided by the interest in our studies manifested by Te Rangi Hiroa (Doctor Peter H. Buck) as far back as the summer of 1931, when we enjoyed together a brief episode of field work on the Island of Hawai'i, his first field excursion in Hawai'i, which took us into Kona, Ka-'u, Laupahoehoe, and Waipi'o.

We tender our thanks to the McInerny Foundation of Honolulu for two grants-in-aid; to the Bernice Pauahi Bishop Museum, its Trustees, Director and Staff; to C. Brewer and Co. Ltd., Management and Staff in their Honolulu office; and Brewer and Co.'s Hutchinson Plantation in Ka-'u, where all personnel, Management and Labor alike, at all levels and at all times and places, have given generous and enthusiastic co-operation; to Drs. Gordon MacDonald and Chester Wentworth, geologists, and Dr. Otto Degener, botanist, formerly of the Research Staff of the

Volcano Observatory and Museum at Hawaii National Park at Kilauea. Also we wish to thank the Dispersed Community of Ka-'u as a whole—too many to name one by one, except and especially Keli'i-hue (our "old-timer"), "Aunty" Pu'uheana Jansen, Deputy Sheriff George Kawaha, Howard Kupakee Hayselden, Uncle Fred Hayselden and Aunt Rachel Hayselden Westcoatt, "Pecky Bob" (Bob Beck), "Uncle Willie" Meinecke and Marian Kelly, and Miss Ben Taylor, Miss Lily Auld and Mrs. Dick (Kalei) Whittington.

And, last but not least, we offer our thanks to Mr. C. R. H. Taylor for his patient and careful editing; to Patience Wiggin Bacon for everlasting understanding and skilled helpfulness; and Berta Metzger, whose loyal aid and expertness as proofreader and typist expedited this little volume in its final stages of production.

—M.K.P., E.S.C.H. and E.G.H.

LIST OF PRIMARY HAWAIIAN REFERENCES

HANDY, E. S. Craighill—" Dreaming in Relation to Spirit Kindred and Sickness in Hawaii," in *Essays in Anthropology in Honour of Alfred Louis Kroeber*, University of California Press, 1936, pp. 119-127.

HANDY, E. S. Craighill—" Perspectives in Polynesian Religion," *Journal of the Polynesian Society*, Vol. 49, 309-327, 1940.

PUKUI, Mary (Kawena) Wiggin—*Hawaiian Folk Tales*, Third Series, Vassar College, Poughkeepsie, N.Y., 1933.

PUKUI, Mary Kawena—" Hawaiian Beliefs and Customs during Birth, Infancy and Childhood." *Bernice P. Bishop Museum, Occasional Papers*, Vol. XVI, N. 17, Honolulu, 1942.

HANDY, E. S. Craighill, Mary Kawena Pukui and Katherine Livermore —" Outline of Hawaiian Physical Therapeutics." *Bernice P. Bishop Museum, Bulletin 126*, Honolulu, 1934.

MALO, David—*Hawaiian Antiquities*. Translated by Dr. N. B. Emerson, Honolulu, 1898.

(Other incidental references appear in footnotes.)

TABLE OF CONTENTS

CONTENTS—Continued

VOICES FROM AN INHABITED HOUSE
An Introduction to
The Polynesian Family System in Ka'u Hawai'i

By Glen Grant

*I wawa ia ka hale kanaka
Nawai e wawa ka hale kanaka 'oke?*

Voices are heard around an inhabited house.
Who hears voices around an uninhabited one?

Who would listen to the voices fading from the Hawaiian house occupied by the native people who survived into the twentieth century? Doomed into oblivion by the political, economic, cultural and social system of the Territory of Hawai'i with the sanctimonious apologia of the Social Darwinists that "survival of the fittest" also applies to nations, the indigenous voices of the Hawaiian house seemed on the surface to be silenced. The village and sacred monuments of the ancient people were being covered with thousands of acres of sugar and pineapple fields. Former fishponds and taro *lo'i* or terraces were being plowed under for housing subdivisions or shoreline resorts. The material culture of a civilization was being catalogued and labeled in the sequestered halls of scientific laboratories or being placed on exhibit for tourists in deathly quiet museums. Archives were becoming the only repository for knowledge about these people of old who were classified lamentably as a "passing race." Except in the musical strains of *mele kahiko* or ancient song or in the precise choreography of a *hula kahiko* or ancient dance which were on rare occasions performed for the enjoyment of a growing visitor industry, it seemed true to the untutored ear that *"kanaka pau,"* the voices of the native people were gone. Their ways had seemingly perished with the Americanization of the Hawaiian islands.

Several years ago, Monsignor Charles Kekumano, retired Roman Catholic priest and chairman of the Queen Liliuokalani Trust, met with a group of *kupuna* who were conducting house tours of Washington Place for former First Lady Lynne Waihe'e. Discussing the overthrow of the Hawaiian monarchy and the life of Queen

Lili'uokalani, Monsignor Kekumano made the observation that for his parent's generation, the U.S. annexation of the Hawaiian Islands at the turn of the century had a devastating impact on the life spirit of the *maka'ainana* or common people. "It is hard to measure the depth of their sadness," the Monsignor noted. "Their very countenance emoted a melancholy that flowed out from the depth of their loss—the loss of their Queen, their nation and the future of their culture."

Who would listen to these sadden voices in their houses dwindling in population, dispersed and neglected in time? And more importantly, who had the heart and the mind to truly understand what these voices were saying?

If in the nineteenth century, Native Hawaiian scholars such as David Malo, Samuel M. Kamakau, John Papa I'i and Kepelino salvaged the heritage of an ancient civilization through their diligent efforts to record the memories of the ancestors, then in the twentieth century the same honor must be bestowed upon Mary Kawena Puku'i for her diligence to hear and preserve the indigenous voice of her own *kupuna* or elders. A remarkably talented woman with an extraordinary ability to capture the poetry, spirit and *kaona* or hidden meanings of the Native Hawaiian language, Mary Kawena-'ula o ka Lani a Hi'iaka-i-ka-poli-i-Pele na-lei-lua a Pele (The Rosy-Glow of the Heavens of Hi'iaka in the bosom of Pele wearing the crimson *lehua* of Pele) Puku'i was born on April 20, 1895 at Haniumalu in Ka'u on the island of Hawai'i to Mary Pa'ahana Keali'i-kanaka'ole and Henry Nathaniel Wiggin of Salem, Massachusetts. Raised in the traditional *'ohana* or family of Ka'u, Ms. Puku'i was also trained in the Christian influenced classrooms of the Hawaiian Mission Academy where she acquired the literary skills which she would later hone as one of Hawai'i's most prolific authors. From her early teenage years, she began collecting and recording the oral traditions of her ethnic heritage, commencing what would be a lifelong task of writing and translating the poetry and folklore of Native Hawaiian people. Her diligent and tireless work with Samuel H. Elbert to compile a more complete Hawaiian-English Dictionary remains the single most important volume to fuel the renaissance of the Hawaiian language, culture and sense of being that has transformed the Islands' cultural landscape during the last three decades of the twentieth century. Recognized by her biographer Noelani Mahoe as "the personification of the evolution of Hawai'i from ancient to modern," Mary Kawena Puku'i possessed "the ability and the power to communicate the essence of Hawaiianness."

In addition to being an author, chanter and language consultant to a younger generation of musicians sometimes unsure of their correct Hawaiian language usage, Ms. Puku'i also taught Hawaiian studies for many years at Punahou School. In 1931 she began work as a translator and cultural consultant for the Bishop Museum, an association which would continue for the next four decades. Through her collaboration at the museum with Dr. E.S. Craighill Handy, Ms. Puku'i began in the summer of 1935 what would become a seminal study of the living oral traditions of the Native Hawaiian community at her birthplace on the island of Hawai'i, in the southernmost district known as Ka'u. Dr. Handy, his wife Elizabeth Green Handy and Ms. Puku'i lived in the community during that year, extensively interviewing the *kupuna* or elders including Ms. Puku'i's mother Pa'ahana and her venerable elder aunt, Keli'ihue. With the precious insights of family members willing to share the deeper truths and sometimes concealed knowledge of the past for the sake of perpetuating their culture for the future generations, the team sought to "reconstruct a truly adequate record of many phases of the local heritage, traditions and culture of her *'ohana.*"

The results of the study were published in five articles which appeared between 1950-1955 under the title "The Hawaiian Family" in the *Journal of the Polynesian Society.* The full compilation of the several articles with a concluding chapter on the history and ecology of Ka'u by Mrs. Handy was first published in 1958 as *The Polynesian Family System in Ka`u Hawai'i.* While providing an ethnographic portrait of the Native Hawaiian community of Ka'u during the 1930's, the study went further by weaving a psychic and culture tapestry of an Hawaiian worldview which few studies before or since have been able to match.

The Polynesian Family System in Ka'u, Hawai'i remains fifty years later an indispensable, highly readable and spiritually insightful introduction to the world of the Native Hawaiian family, community and psyche as it evolved into the twentieth century. While the study attempts to provide an understanding of the ancient *'ohana* system, the traditional relationships of family members, the interconnectedness of social rankings, the rituals accompanying various cycles of life and the dynamic interplay of geography, mythology and personality, it is not merely an historical or clinical treatise of an ancient civilization. The ethnographic materials presented in this study are drawn from the rich anecdotal examples of the living generation of the *'ohana* of Ka'u, illustrating the resilience, adaptability and cultural continuity of the Native Hawaiian extended family system and spiritual values despite genocide, dispossession and disenfranchisement. The voices of the inhabited house had not been quieted—they had only been neglected and undervalued.

The most compelling aspect of this collaborative effort is the loving respect continually paid to the subjects of this ethnographic study. *The Polynesian Family System in Ka'u, Hawai'i* is fortunately devoid of the cold, scientifically objective terminology and intrusive curiosity which is sometimes so offensive in the field of anthropology. The researchers respect the endemic views of their subjects; they are careful not to impose their value judgements or predisposed notions of "reality" upon the rich psychic materials which they present in a language devoid of arrogance or disrespect. As they openly aver, although they are fully acquainted with the jargon of the anthropologist, "we do not conceive it to be our role...to incorporate in this description either terms or interpretative comments which are foreign to the native Hawaiian philosophy and theory of nature and man." The reader is left to make their own interpretations of what meaning the Hawaiian perceptions of life, death, spirit and the cosmos may have for them on a personal level. The unfiltered voices of the indigenous people are allowed to be heard.

As Hawai'i prepares to enter the third millennium, the cultural and spiritual values preserved in this seminal work take on a new importance not only for the Native Hawaiian community, but for anyone who feels attachment for the *'aina*, the land or "that which feeds." If we are to pass on to our progeny a Hawai'i which preserves the time-cherished values presented here as embodied in the *'ohana*, then many challenges await the current leadership in all fields of endeavor. The strengthening of our multicultural points of commonality, including the importance of reciprocity, extended family relationships, spiritual open-heartedness and the prevailing attitude of aloha as a daily practice, not a meaningless slogan, must be our highest priority. In that effort, we must attune our ears to receive the wisdom shared by the many voices from all of our inhabited houses.

I.

THE DISPERSED COMMUNITY

The degree to which the Hawaiians in olden times utilized steep slopes, dry land and localities difficult of access for intensive cultivation, and the complete parcelling out of the coasts in offshore fishing rights comparable to the land titles, indicate a density of population which required the utilization of the native resources of sustenance to a maximum.

This being the case, it is peculiar that density of population did not result in the development of villages or towns as centres of political, religious, commercial and industrial activity. Even in localities, such as Waimea on Kauai, Lahaina on Maui and Kailua or Waipi'o on Hawai'i, where intensive cultivation and good fishing grounds combined to concentrate population, there was no development of village or town communities.

In New Zealand, for defensive purposes, the warlike Maori tribes learned to live in fortified villages. But in Hawai'i distinct tribes and inter-tribal strife did not exist under the feudal system of the *ali'i* (chiefs) and consequently tribal village forts never developed as in New Zealand.

Samoa is more like Hawai'i than is New Zealand, in historic background and in natural environment, although decidedly more tropical. The Samoans live in well-established villages ruled by hereditary chiefs, villages that are aggregations of domiciles housing strongly cohesive families.

But native Samoan life contrasted fundamentally with native Hawaiian life in two ways and these differences represent factors which produce villages in Samoa and prevent their development in Hawai'i:

(1) Due probably to an era of dominance many centuries longer than that of the Hawaiians, the *ali'i* or chiefly caste in Samoa had established a political system which was far more stable in its institutions, permanent in relation to land titles, and which prescribed succession through family heads (*matai*) selected and appointed by the families in accordance

2

with an established traditional convention. In Hawai'i political control was constantly in flux and political institutions were ill defined; land titles were evanescent due to redivision of spoils amongst faithful supporters upon the accession of every new high chief (whether he had acquired power through conquest or election by family council); and the external mechanism of family form and authority was less well regulated, though the family was, internally, completely integrated.

(2) The Samoan population was practically confined to the seashore. Cultivation of the soil never reached a systematic plane. A racial or cultural element in the Samoan heritage, perhaps leading to proclivity for marine rather than horticultural life, combined with ideal off-shore fishing lagoons and on-shore dwelling grounds, presumably offer the reason why Samoans took and still take less interest in their inland areas and are little skilled in horticulture compared with Hawaiians. The Hawaiians, by contrast, cultivated intensively their valleys extending into the heart of the mountains, and the seaward slopes where soil and rainfall were favourable. Consequently dwellings were dispersed throughout agricultural regions, be they valleys like Manoa on Oahu or Waipi'o on Hawai'i, or sloping lands such as Kona, Ka-'u and Kohala; while at the same time the localities along the shore that were suitable for fishing and favourable for clusters of dwellings were extremely rare and far apart, relative to the whole coastline and in comparison with Samoan shores.

THE COMMUNITY.

Because old Hawai'i lacked village units regulated by established institutions such as existed in New Zealand and Samoa, it must not be concluded that the *community* was not a reality and a fundamental factor in the old political and economic order.

The fundamental unit in the social organization of the Hawaiians of Ka-'u was the dispersed community of *'ohana*, or relatives by blood, marriage and adoption, living some inland and some near the sea but concentrated geographically in and tied by ancestry, birth and sentiment to a particular locality which was termed the *'aina*.

The expanded and all-inclusive family or *'ohana,* and the home-land or *'aina,* were two complementary factors which constituted this regional dispersed community. The term *'aina* represented a concept essentially belonging to an agricultural people, deriving as it did from the verb *'ai,* to feed, with the substantive suffix *na* added, so that it signified "that which feeds" or "feeder." Literally, then, a Ka-'u man in speaking of the locality in which he was born and reared and dwelt, was thinking of this native soil as his feeder. Land of birth was also referred to as *kula iwi* (plain of one's bones) or *one hanau* (sand or soil of birth).

The term *'ohana* was likewise a figure essentially belonging to a people who were taro planters. *'Oha* means "to sprout," or "a sprout"; the "buds" or off-shoots of the taro plant which furnished the staple of life for the Hawaiian are called *'oha.* With the substantive suffix *na* added, *'oha-na* literally means "off-shoots," or "that which is composed of off-shoots." This term, then, as employed to signify the family, has, precisely, the meaning "the off-shoots of a family stock."

The evidence of the cultural dominance of the taro, the food plant that was the Hawaiian staple of life, is implicit in the use of the terms *'aina* and *'ohana.* *'Ai* may designate food or eating in general, but specifically it refers to the paste termed *poi* made from the corm[1] of the taro (Hawaiian *kalo*). The Hawaiian diet was built around *poi.* Now the taro differs from all other food plants in Hawai'i in propagating itself by means of *'oha* or sprouts from the sides or base of the main corm (which is termed *makua,* meaning parent or "father"). The planter breaks off and transplants the *'oha.* As the *'oha* or sprouts from the parent taro (or *makua*) serve to propagate the taro and produce the staple of life, or *'ai,* on the land (*'ai-na*) cultivated through generations by a given family, so the family or *'oha-na* is identified physically and psychically with the homeland

---

[1] The starch-filled base of the taro (*Colocasia antiquorum*) is not a "root," "tuber," or "bulb," but a "corm," in botanical teminology. The corm is the base of the stem which swells and fills with starch. The Jack-in-the-Pulpit (*Arisaema triphyllum*) in our American forest lands, whose corm was utilized as food by the American Indians, is a primitive wild "taro," which propagates itself by seeding, a habit or ability retained by several wild varieties of taro in Hawai'i, but not by the superior cultivated taros.

('*ai-na*) whose soil has produced the staple of life ('*ai*, food made from taro) that nourishes the dispersed family ('*oha-na*).

But the family was not conceived of as consisting only of its living members. It included the family forbears, to whom was applied another term that is a figure from the speech of a folk for whom growth, as observed in the vegetable world, is a basic concept. The inclusive term for deceased ancestors and living elders, *kupuna*, as representing the stock from which the '*ohana* spring as off-shoots, was derived from the verb *kupu* " to grow," with the suffix *na* added.

LAND AND SEA.

According to native phraseology the land was spoken of as inland or upland (*uka*), and seaward (*kai*). The '*ohana* dwelt, some inland or upland, and some near or on the shore. It was customary, therefore, to specify those of the '*ohana* living inland as *ko kula uka* (" of the upland slopes ") and those living seaward as *ko kula kai* (" of the seaward slopes "), *kula* signifying the sloping terrain between the forest and the shore.

The land divisions used to be so cut that they constituted segments running from the shore back into the mountains, the larger sub-division being the *ahupua'a*, which was a section of a *moku* (island or district), and the smaller being the '*ili*, which was a segment of an *ahupua'a*. The complete '*ili* was a narrow strip of the *ahupua'a*, continuous from shore to mountain top. But some '*ili* were broken or discontinuous, that is to say, there was a piece near the sea and another disconnected piece inland. Such an '*ili* was termed an '*ili lele*, or " leaping '*ili*." The disconnected '*ili*—the one *ma uka* was referred to as the " '*umeke 'ai* " as it was that which filled the *poi* bowl: that is, taro was planted there. The *ma kai* one was the " *ipukai*," the " meat bowl," where fish could be found. There were also the '*ili kupono* (" '*ili* in established right ") whose owners held perpetual title through some ancient grant.[2] All other '*ili* were subject to reallocation by the Ruling Chief (*Ali'i*), though in practice tenants who were faithful henchmen cultivated the same land generation after generation.

---

[2] In Ka-'u *ili lele* and *ili kupono* did not exist so far as I know. (E.S.C.H.)

The *ahupua'a* or major subdivision was the domain of the *Ali'i 'ai ahupua'a* (" Chief who ate the *ahupua'a* "), he being the feudal chiefling whose tenure was dependent upon the Ruling Chief or *Ali'i 'ai moku* (" Chief who ate the island or district "). Many *'ohana* made up the population of the *ahupua'a*, constituting altogether the *ma - ka - 'aina - na* ([people]-on-the-land).

There was no *Ali'i 'ai 'ili*. It is to be inferred that the *'ili*, with its inland and seaward expanses, was essentially and probably originally the province of a single *'ohana*, those living, cultivating or hunting inland being *ko kula uka* (referred to above) and those to seaward being *ko kula kai*. Inevitably, in the course of inter-marriage between families, the *'ohana* would ramify throughout the *ahupua'a*, and ultimately into neighbouring *moku*; though there would remain a concentration of closest-related *'ohana* in the original *'ili*. This is precisely what has occurred in the case of one *'ohana* belonging to Ka-'u, Hawai'i.

Inshore fishing rights on the coast belonged to the respective *ahupua'a* proprietors and the *'ohana* on their lands.

HOUSEHOLDS.

Within the *'ohana* the functional unit is the household. One term used for household was the word *hale,* house. In inquiring about the number of " families " or domiciles in a given locality, one would ask " *Ehia hale la?*" (How many houses?) *'Ohua* was a term that signified retainers or dependents in the household. In contradistinction to " family " (*'ohana*), inmates who were not kin by blood or adoption were *'ohua*. This word *'ohua* signified passengers on a canoe or ship exclusive of owner and crew. Through the head (*po'o*) of the house the *'ohua* integrated with the *'ohana*. The household included members of the family proper of all ages plus attached but unrelated dependents and helpers. The *po'o* (" head ") or functional head of the domicile was not necessarily the senior member: it was and is specifically the member who assumes responsibility and makes decisions.

Between households within the *'ohana* there was constant sharing and exchange of foods and of utilitarian articles and also of services, not in barter but as voluntary (though decidedly obligatory) giving. *'Ohana* living inland (*ko kula uka*), raising taro, bananas, *wauke* (for *tapa*, or barkcloth, making) and *olona* (for its fibre), and needing gourds, coconuts and marine foods, would take a gift to some *'ohana* living near the shore (*ko kula kai*) and in return would receive fish or whatever was needed. The fisherman needing *poi* or *'awa* would take fish, squid or lobster upland to a household known to have taro, and would return with his *kalo* (taro) or *pa'i'ai* (hard *poi*, the steamed and pounded taro corm). A woman from seaward, wanting some medicinal plant, or sugar cane perhaps, growing on the land of a relative living inland would take with her a basket of shellfish or some edible seaweed and would return with her stalks of sugar cane or her medicinal plants. In other words, it was the *'ohana* that constituted the community within which the economic life moved.

In enterprise requiring communal labour the inland and seaward *'ohana* combined. When *olona* fibre for the fish-nets used to be harvested, scraped and spun, all the *'ohana* joined forces in the shed built near the *olona* plantation in the lower forest zone. If there was to be a *huki lau* (fishing by dragging the shallows), relatives from the upland lent a hand with the *lau* (leaf-drag) and the *'upena* (net), and the catch was divided up amongst all the households that participated. Similarly, a man building a new dwelling was aided by his *'ohana*. When there was a feast to mark the first year of the first-born, to celebrate a wedding, to welcome a returning member or distinguished stranger, all households of the *'ohana* contributed what they had, some fish, some *poi*, or potatoes, or cane; or perhaps, where gifts were in order, mats, gourds or bowls.

Equally the *'ohana* functioned as a unit in external economic and social affairs. The levy of the *ali'i* during the period of collection of tribute (the *makahiki*) or for offerings prior to making war, or in honour of his first-born, used to fall not upon individuals or single households but upon the *'ohana*.

The pivot of the *'ohana* was the *haku* (master, director), the elder male of the senior branch of the whole *'ohana*. The *haku* divided the catch of fish amongst the households of the *'ohana* which had participated in the fishing; he presided over family councils; and in general he had authority over the individuals and households in all such matters as entertaining strangers and welcoming the *ali'i*, in supervising work, worship and planned communal activities. The *haku* was the functioning head of an *'ohana*. The term differs from *ali'i* in that it has no relation to class, politics or occupation. There were *haku*[3] of *ali'i* families, of *kahuna* (priestly) families, of fishing and planting families. *Haku* in general means a " master " in the sense of " director." Thus the man in charge of the composition of eulogistic chants (*mele*) for an *ali'i* first-born was the *haku-mele*; a man in charge of land was *haku-'aina*.

The *haku* headed the councils of the *'ohana*; he was the revered leader; but the old folk, men and women, of strong character were extremely independent in speech and action; consequently the *haku* was no dictator but was subject to the advice and opinion of householders and of all other members of his *'ohana* concerned in or affected by decisions and enterprises.

KAUHALE (Dwellings).

Every Hawaiian household had a group of houses instead of a single house as it is today. A group of such houses was called a *kauhale*.

It used to be customary, in inviting people to come to one's dwelling, to say, " *E ho'i kakou i kauhale,*" or " Let us go to [our] *kauhale.*" A person accustomed to go from house to house is said to be " *ma'a i ka hele i kauhale.*" This word, *kauhale*, was used for a dwelling place until recent times when it changed to *ka hale*, the house, to fit the modern residence. A large group of *kauhale* or family houses was called a *kulana-kauhale*, the word for village. The word *kulana-kauhale* is still in use, for town, city, or village. Today, towns are called *kaona*, a word that is Hawaiianized from the English. A large village was a *kulana-kauhale nui* and a small one was a *kulana-kauhale 'u'uku.*

The *kauhale* in the olden days were widely scattered, wherever a living could be secured—on the beaches for the fishermen's family and in the upland for the farmer's. No

---

[3] It seems best to translate *ali'i* generically as "noble" and specifically as "chief"; *kahuna* generically as "adept" and specifically as "priest," "master-craftsman," "witch," "doctor," according to function; and *haku* as "master," "director," or "lord," according to context.

head of any family would build without first consulting a *kuhikuhi pu'uone* (one-who-points-out-contours), a person skilled in picking good sites. For instance, if a man wanted to build a family dwelling at Nalua, he would go to a man who was skilled in studying the land and let him look over the location. The latter would look it over carefully and point out to him just where the house should stand, where to face and what he should do.

The picking of a good site was imperative, as a bad one brought trouble to the family. Much has been told among the Hawaiians about this which was later regarded as superstitious. It was not superstition in most instances but common sense, for a *kuhikuhi pu'uone* knew that a home should not stand at the base of a cliff where there was danger of a land slide; should not stand between two ponds where there was a danger of keeping the house constantly damp and cold; where it was open to draughts and so on. Even if the home was built right, the location and surroundings should be right also, therefore the home builder was told not to have trees directly before the doorway. Such things as trees, houses and so on before the doorway of a house were called *'alai* or obstructions preventing blessings from entering the house. The entry should have light and no obstructions.

A home wrongly built drew comments termed *ho'oiloilo*, that is, a foretelling of unpleasant experiences to befall those who dwell there, such as sickness, a going away, constant misfortune or death. A home, to the Hawaiians of yesterday, was not just a place to live in, but there was a certain personal quality acquired by each home that either held the family in a warm, friendly, loving embrace, or pushed and repulsed them and others who came within its boundary. Therefore the *kuhikuhi pu'uone* was always consulted, so that the grounds and home and family would form a happy unit, instead of an unhappy one.

In Ka-'u and in some places in Puna, many of the dwellings were built on old lava beds, thus reserving the good tillable soil for food growing, but these lava bed sites should present a friendly attitude for the family *kauhale*, even if they appeared rough and forbidding. Those who had good lands to live on often laughed at those whose homes were on old lava beds as " *po'e noho pu'u 'a'a* " or " dwellers on heaps of lava rocks " but none could deny that the " rock dwellers " were as healthy and as happy as they.

The *Mua* or men's eating house was a sacred place from which women were excluded. It was the place where the men and older boys ate their meals and where the head of the family offered the daily offerings of *'awa* to the family *'aumakua.* Here men and family gods ate together, and that was why women, who were periodically unclean, were not allowed to enter here. The daily offering was never omitted and if the head of the family was unable to perform his duty, he appointed some one to do it. The prayers were for the welfare of the ruling chief and for the family itself.

When a serious problem arose, such as a new venture to be attempted or sickness in the family, the head of the family slept in the *Mua*, where the family gods would give him directions as to what to do.

Thus the *Mua* served both as a place for the men to eat and a meeting place with the family gods.

The women had their own eating house, the *hale 'aina*. Here the women, girls and small boys ate together. From infancy to about five or six, the boys remained with their mothers or foster mothers. They wore no *malo*. In describing a very small boy, it was said: " *'a'ohe i pa'a ka hope i ka malo,*" or " the back side is not yet covered with a *malo*." He was still in the stage called *poke'o*, too young to join the men. There were prayers in the women's eating house for the family *'aumakua* to bless their food and to come and partake, but the presenting of offerings belonged to the men in the *Mua*. After a ceremony called " *ka i Mua* " or " expulsion to the *Mua*," which usually occurred in the sixth year of a boy's life, he was permitted to wear a *malo* and join the men in their eating house. He was then a man. The word *ka* in the expression " *ka i Mua* " is like a violent thrust, a quick and complete push out of the women's house into the men's and so a boy was never more allowed to return and partake of food with the women of the family. This has been termed a " weaning," but a weaning from the breast was an *ukuhi*, and a separation of a boy from eating with the women was called " *ka i Mua*," which was not regarded by Hawaiians as a " weaning." Both the *ukuhi* and *ka i Mua* were ceremonially performed.

Everybody slept in the *Hale Noa* (House freed of

kapu), where no restrictions were placed on the men and women sharing it together. This house was for sleeping and no eating was permitted there. In sleeping, there was a set pattern which was kept up until private bedrooms became common. A man slept beside his wife, and next, but not too close, to her might be her sister. Next to the sister might be the sister's husband. A man never slept between two women, unless both were his wives, nor did a woman sleep between two men. A young son might sleep next to his mother but not after he had grown up—likewise, with a daughter and father. Whole families and guests, too, slept together in the sleeping house but always with the thought of who was sleeping next to whom. Several men might sleep near each other, and so might several women. Thus confusion and mix-up of wedded pairs were avoided. In the olden days, no one slept with head close to the wall where there was danger from the thrust of an enemy's spear through the thatching.

The *hale noa* was divided into a sleeping place and a sitting or walking place. The sleeping place was raised and covered with finer mats. When unused for sleeping, no one was allowed to walk, sit or play on it. It was strictly *kapu*. The lower floor division was also covered with mats, but plaited with a wider mesh than that used for the sleeping mats. Here, the family and guests sat and talked and the children played quiet games, like riddling and guessing games. No running and leaping about were allowed in here or in the eating house, and children were reminded to keep their lively games out-of-doors. In the daytime the making of string figures was allowed, but not at night, being suggestive of death, since the dying interlace their fingers and raise them to the mouth—motions typical of making string figures.

The women had another house that was built near but not too close to the other houses of the *kauhale*. This was the *hale pe'a*, a small comfortable thatched house where the women of the family retired when menstruating and remained until the period was completely over. The woman was restricted by the *kapu* from taking part in any outside activities, thus forcing her to take care of herself during that period. But it did not restrict her from repairing the mats in the *hale pe'a* or making new ones in there for her own comfort during the time of retirement. Men were not allowed to set foot on the area around it or on the *paepae* or raised platform on which the house was built, nor to enter under penalty of death. Food was brought to the door by a woman relative, so that the person or persons within did not lack nourishment. This woman wore a green *ti* (*Cordyline terminalis*) leaf *lei* to protect her from the result of defilement.

Every woman kept her old worn-out skirts for use as pads at this time. When a skirt was no longer fit to wear as a garment, it was rinsed in water, dried in the sun and taken to the *hale pe'a*. Only skirts, being worn below the waist, were used. Any other article of clothing, worn above the waist, was *kapu* for this purpose. Each woman used her own worn-out skirts and nobody else's. *Pulu*, the soft cotton-like substance gathered from the *hapu'u* fern was used as padding. When her period was entirely over, the woman buried the soiled pads outside of the *hale pe'a*. (That was why there was a restricted area outside, around the *hale pe'a*, for that was where soiled pads were buried. Such things were never burned as it was believed that blood was a life sustaining substance, *he ola ke koko*, and should not be destroyed by fire.) After all the pads had been disposed of, she went to take a bath before rejoining her family.

The other houses depended on the activity of the adult members of the family. A fisherman had a *halau* or long thatched house where he kept his canoe, fish-nets, and other paraphernalia. *Kapu* were enforced there also, for no women were permitted to handle the large nets, nor was anyone allowed to step over the lines, hooks or nets. Women had their own nets, usually small ones. They made their own scoop nets and fish basket traps. Women helped to twist the *olona* (*Touchardia latifolia*) fibres into lines, but once a large net was made and dedicated with ceremonies, women were not allowed to handle it.

A canoe builder also had his *halau* where the canoes were finished with added parts, such as dash boards and outrigger. No one was permitted to enter except the helpers who worked with the expert on the canoes.

An inland dweller would have a house to keep his implements and store his crops until needed. A house in which to store the crops was a *hale papa'a*.

A chief had, among his houses, a *hale papa'a* or store house. (The word *papa'a* in this case should be hyphenated to *pa-pa'a*, a solid enclosure.) Here were kept his extra mats, tapas, nets, dried fish and whatever else he might have. It was usually built up on posts to prevent dogs and pigs from getting in after the food. A very prosperous chief had several of these *hale papa'a*, with stewards to watch over his property.

Tapa makers had a thatched shed, called a *hale kuku*, where they pounded the inner bark of *mamaki* (*Pipturus* spp.) or *wauke* (*Broussonetia papyrifera*) into *tapa* cloth. Sometimes there was a *pa kaula'i*, a drying pen where the *tapa* could be dried without animals running over them; it was made of stone or sticks.

If the mother of the family was a skilled maker of mats she too, had a shed with thatched roof, the *hale ulana*, where she plied her art and stored her materials.

There was also the *hale kahumu* (*kahu-umu*), a thatched shed where cooking was done in bad weather and cooking materials were stored. The men had one, and the women had theirs, until the *kapu* on eating was abolished. In good weather, cooking was done in outdoor *imu*, one for the men and one for the women; but in rainy weather, or if there was not a quantity of cooking to do, the *hale kahumu* was the place to go. Some of these were small but many were large enough to include the storage of the utensils and implements. Even when the cooking was done out of doors, the *hale kahumu* was still used for storage. There is an account by a Kohala man who wrote that old and worn-out mats were used for *imu* covering in cooking. That was not done by Ka-'u people, who had a contempt for covering food with something that was sat and walked on. As the food in the *imu* was intended as offerings to the *'aumakua* as well as nourishment for the people, the use of old and worn-out mats was defiling. Thick, coarse mats were purposely made for the *imu* and when the cooking was over, these were rinsed to free them of soil, spread out to dry and kept in the *hale kahumu*. The *hale kahumu* rarely had thatched walls, as these might ignite from the *kapuahi* (*kapu* meaning restriction and *ahi*, fire: a restriced place for fire). Many were walled with stone, with a roof of thatching. Some were just posts and a roof, with the windy sides covered with plaited coconut leaves, or strips of bark. Wood (*wahie*) and kindling (*pulupulu*) had their own storage corner in the *hale kahumu*. The *kapuahi* was not a deepened pit like the *imu*, but was built on the ground or with a very shallow depression. It was just a circle of stones to keep the fire confined and an opening for the addition of fuel. Broiling or cooking in bundles of ti leaves could be easily done here but when more cooking was required the addition of more stones of the right size could quickly convert it into an *imu pao*.

The *kauhale* was the permanent home of the family, where they lived most of the year but some families had other dwellings besides.

A farmer who did much of his planting in the upland forest often had a *papaʻi* or small house there, where he could stay occasionally. These were often built with walls and covered with *ukiuki* grass, ti leaf (*la-ʻi*) or sugar cane leaves (*la-ʻo*). As forests were often rainy, a *papaʻi* or small house was built on a *paepae* or platform of stone, to keep it off the wet ground. Smaller stones were scattered on the large ones of the *paepae* to level the floor, then over this went layers of *hapuʻu* or *ʻamaʻu* fern leaves and last of all a mat. Perhaps, on one side of the room, more fern leaves were laid and then a smaller mat, and there was the bed.

Canoe makers sometimes made temporary houses in the forest, roofed with tree bark spread out and overlapping on a wooden frame. They were good dry houses, for the tree bark kept the water out. Thick layers of fern leaves inside kept the occupants from sleeping on the damp earth. A temporary house like this was called a *kamala*. It was tent shaped. The rafters came right to the ground. There was still another type of *kamala* in Ka-ʻu, the *kamala pohaku*, composed of one long back wall flanked by two side walls a little longer than a tall man. These were used mostly in the dry summer months when salt could be gathered and *ʻohua manini* (spawn of *Hepatus triostegus*) appear by the million at the beaches. All that was needed to convert each of these stone-wall enclosures into comfortable sleeping quarters were two long poles across the top and a layer of coconut leaves.

Some people built *papaʻi* or small houses on the beaches just as the upland farmers did in the forest, that is, if they were to be used only for short periods. Otherwise shore dwelling families had their *kauhale*.

Another kind of vacation dwelling, if it might be called that, was a *hau* (*Hibiscus tiliaceus*) tree. Large spreading *hau* trees were chosen, then some of the inside branches were cut away to make room, and a low opening through which one could enter stooping. The spreading branches kept the sleepers protected from the winds and from the warm sun in the daytime. '*Ilima* (*Sida* spp.) branches spread thickly on the ground over which a pandanus (*lauhala*) mat was spread, served as comfortable beds. Cooking was done outside in the open.

There were also caves (*ana* or *lua*), some with wide ledges, that served as temporary homes for vacationers. One much lived-in cave at Pa'ula had a pond in the centre that provided its inhabitants and neighbours round about with drinking water.

Some caves that were always cool through summer and winter were never used as dwellings but as places in which to prepare *hala* leaves for plaiting. These leaves are best prepared in the early morning, on a cool night or rainy day. The warmth of the sun has a tendency to make them brittle and hard. Women used to take their *lauhala* into these cool caves to prepare and to store. The cave, being cool prevented the leaves from becoming brittle. Very dry caves were good places to store the surplus salt in thick *lauhala* baskets. Deep and long caves with several openings, in the upland and at the beaches, with a good draught in places where smoke of fires would be quickly dispersed by the wind, were used as places of refuge in time of war. There were places inside of these where sweet potatoes were stored in preparation for just such happenings. These were kept renewed from time to time, so that when war came, all could find refuge and sustenance. Fuel was kept in readiness near fireplaces, and salt for the fish or meats. The location of these caves of refuge was not talked about to outsiders. Burial caves were not used as dwellings or for storage; they were only for the dead and their possessions. These were kept secret by the caretakers. Ka-'u was sometimes referred to as " *Ka lua huna o na ali'i* " or " Secret burial place of chiefs," for many chose that as their last resting place, even some who were born and had ruled elsewhere.

DISINTEGRATION.

Partly as a consequence of the sudden abandonment of the *kapu* (legal tabu) system in 1819 (see Handy: " Cultural Revolution in Hawaii," *Institute of Pacific Relations*, 1931) ; partly due to the influence of foreign education imposing from the outset Euro-American principles, conceptions and ideals of marriage, relationship and duty: but chiefly as a secondary consequence of the marriage of Hawaiian women to white and Oriental men (often for the sake of economic security under the new system), the *'ohana* system has lost its integrity. With its slow disintegration over a period of 150 years the individuals belonging to disarticulated *'ohana* have had recourse to two means of personal and social adjustment: some, especially those who have clung to planting and fishing, in other words to the old means of subsistence, and certain families in whom, despite removal from their native milieu, the instinct of loyalty to their Hawaiian progenitors has remained very strong, have clung to their *'ohana* and its inclusive obligations and privileges. Others, particularly those most affected by intermarriage and by American education, or by city life, have chosen whole-heartedly to adhere to the American system. Most Hawaiians nowadays adhere in some degree to both the old Hawaiian system and the American. Oriental Hawaiians generally combine, with the Hawaiian-American, many habits and conventions derived from Chinese or Japanese life as a result of social and personal ties with Oriental relatives, transference of habits and conventions.

Along with the disintegration of the *'ohana* and concurrent economic changes has gone the removal from *'aina* or land of birth. When a Hawaiian woman married a man of another race it was not only likely to remove her and her children somewhat from the *'ohana*, but also from the *'aina*. Other influences, in Ka-'u as elsewhere, potent in separating individuals from homeland have been: in the early days the recruiting of native sailors for whaling; the establishment of the sugar plantations; ranching, which inevitably had the effect of disrupting native agriculture; the taking over of commercial fishing and favourable fishing localities by Orientals; the substitution of rice for taro in irrigated land (*lo'i*), and of Oriental for Hawaiian labour where taro continued to be grown; and last but by no means least the steady flow of Hawaiians to Honolulu, the able-bodied men seeking work on the waterfront, in the public services and government offices, both sexes being drawn thither for purposes of being taught and of teaching, elders coming to be with their young folks, and many lured from the country by the excitement, sociability and conveniences of city life.

But a great proportion of the Hawaiian people still have their roots in the country, even those who reside in the city; and attachment to the soil and the sea that nourished them is a profound instinct met with amongst all true Hawaiians and Polynesians everywhere.

Equally, attachment to blood relatives is with most Hawaiians a deep and unchanging instinct. One has to know intimately country Hawaiians, or city Hawaiians who remain Hawaiian at heart, to realize the inner depth and strength, and the outer importance in current living, that blood relationship has today.

CONCLUSION.

The *'ohana* still exists as a vital factor in Hawaiian life. Modified and adapted to modern conditions, and shorn of onerous and archaic features, is it desirable that it be perpetuated as a social institution and force? If desirable, can it be perpetuated where it still prevails; and can it be revived where it has lapsed? Modern urbanism, education, economic life, individualism and intermarriage with other races are all against it.

It is in the country districts that the spirit and institution of *'ohana* is still alive today as a cohesive force. Certain relationships which still regulate personal, social and economic intercourse offer a striking contrast with the isolated Hawaiian household typical of Honolulu, Hilo, etc. The country *'ohana* still constitute, as the old *'ohana* did, mutual benefit associations, and manifest genuine community spirit; while the typical town household is apt to be distinguished by rampant disruptive selfishness and irresponsibility.

The intimate relationship existing between the *'ohana* and the land has been made clear in the early part of this paper. One of the chief motives behind the generous but unwise granting of individual title to lands on the part of the *ali'i* in the Great Mahele (division of land in 1848) was the hope of keeping Hawaiians on their land. It may be that one reason why that hope has not been realized was because the titles were granted to individuals. Country Hawaiians in the middle of the 19th century had little understanding of the meaning of private ownership. But they had a very strong sense of *family rights and responsibilities.* It is interesting to speculate on what might have been the outcome of the Mahele had the grants been as *'ili* or sections allocated to *'ohana,* represented legally by their respective *haku,* instead of as parcels (*kuleana*) in fee simple to individuals. Probably in most instances the *haku* would have been guided in decisions, planning and action by interest in the welfare of the whole *'ohana*: he would at least have been subject to the advice of the family council and of shrewd and hard-headed elders in particular.

The role of the *'ohana* as an economic community in ancient times deserves further study. Since the time of the *Mahele,* Hawaiians have repeatedly attempted corporate enterprise in what are termed *hui* (" groups "). These have for the most part had to do with co-operative agricultural and fishing enterprises and practically without exception they have been dismal failures because those responsible for them were completely lacking both in business acumen and experience necessary for dealing with whites and Orientals, and in the sense of personal responsibility. There have been, however, several successful fishing *hui* on the islands of Kauai and Maui. In each instance these are family *hui,* and it seems likely that it is this that has made them succeed. It would be interesting to compare with the old *'ohana* as an economic community, the relationship of certain family groups today, as economic units, to the industrial and social structure of modern Hawai'i.

Finally, it would certainly be instructive to consider the possibility of carrying the *'ohana* principle into the recent and current homesteading movement. Up to this time homesteading has been planned and attempted, not too successfully, on the individual basis. By selecting some of the country districts where a number of households still retain the *'ohana* relationship, it might be possible to try the experiment of creating a modern co-operative enterprise that would adapt the old principle of the *'ohana* to current circumstances and needs.

II.

THE PHYSICAL ENVIRONMENT

The unique physical environment of. Ka-'u was a potent factor in conditioning, if not determining, the form and nature of the dispersed community (*'ohana*) described in the first section of this present study. Actually, the cultural pattern conforms to the traditional Polynesian form. It may be said, therefore, that the physical environment *conditions* the functioning mechanism of adjustment: but it would be incorrect to say that the physical environment *determines* the form or pattern. Nevertheless, the particular form which the Ka-'u community manifests, as a variant from the basic norm (if there be a norm) of an old Polynesian community as an aggregate or complex of families, can not be brought into true focus except against the background of the Land (*'Aina*). The *'Ohana* as a functioning social mechanism operates within the *milieu* of sea, shore, coastal and inland slopes and uplands, subject to weather, sun and moon.

The physical environment, in its specific factors and phenomena, is also the material upon which and out of which the legendary drama of Ka-'u is wrought with the patterns of inherited traditional Polynesian lore. This legendary setting must likewise be understood in specific detail as a factor affecting the functioning of the *'ohana*. Shark, caterpillar and gourd, certain rock formations, trees, volcanic and meteorological phenomena are *kupuna* (forbears) of particular families and persons: relationship, tabus, in fact every phase of personal and family life, are contingent upon affinity arising herefrom.

The dispersal of the households comprising the extended family (*'ohana*), the types of structure constituting the domiciles, the means of livelihood and exchange of products of sea, land and handcraft between individuals and households were all affected by topography, rainfall and vegetation, the nature of the shore and the sea offshore, by climate and weather and the cycle of the seasons. Readers not intimately acquainted with rugged and windswept Ka-'u

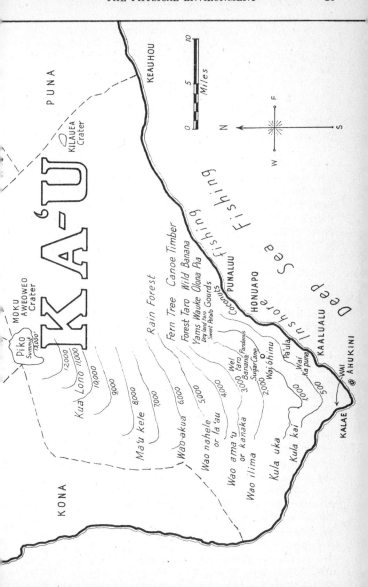

—and few today, even in the Hawaiian Islands, know this district of the Island of Hawaii well—will have an entirely false picture of this unique country if they conceive it to be like any other part of the Hawaiian Islands or any other area in Polynesia.

The accompanying figure gives a cartographic sketch of the nature of this southern segment of Hawai'i, where vulcanism is still in its most active phase. The various zones of sea and land and their uses are indicated.

TERRAIN.

A deep-sea fisherman's view of the southern flanks and "foreland" (Ka Lae) of Hawai'i looks over a white line of surf breaking against abrupt lava walls along the whole coast. Along this shore (*kahakai*) there are occasional minute indentations—Wai-o-'Ahukini, Ka-'Alu'alu, Wai-ka-puna, Honu'apo, Punalu'u, Keauhou hardly deserving the name of bays, flanked by short narrow beaches of black smooth lava pebbles or black sand. There are no coral reefs, there is no white sand. Near the bays and beaches are coconut trees, houses, canoe sheds. Beyond the shore the immediate landscape is one of rough irregular exposed black lava interspersed with small bushes and sparse tufty grasses, green from December till May, dry for the rest of the year. In the old days many footpaths meandered seaward through this wide wasteland from the higher slopes miles inland, where there was soil enough for gardens. The scattered homes and gardens of this lower zone of habitation were those " of the seaward slopes " (*ko kula kai*), where sweet potato and gourds were cultivated, but little else. These households had relatively easy access to the sea and consequently depended on shellfish, seaweed and inshore fishing, and had these for exchange with relatives living farther up the slopes.

Moisture increases and evaporation decreases with altitude here, so beyond the *kula kai* (the lowest habitable zone) were the dwellings " of the upland slopes " (*ko kula uka*), less accessible to the sea, but increasingly favourable for gardening. In addition to sweet potato, dry land taro of the variety called Paua was planted, and sugar cane flourished. (This is the zone of super plantations today.) Beyond this the open slopes (*kula*) become fern lands, then gradually merge with the lower forest (*wao*). In this zone where fern, bushes and small trees prosper other varieties of upland taro requiring more water were cultivated, under mulch to keep in the moisture. This continued right back into the lower forest. Here were the wild bananas, wild yam (*Dioscorea*), arrowroot (*pia*); and tree fern (*Cibotium*), whose starchy core was eaten, extending down into this zone from the rain forest.

These zones were not fixed as to altitude. On the east, the wet uplands were wetter and extended lower than on the west, which was both beyond the range of heavy precipitation from trade winds and cut off somewhat by the shoulder of Mauna Loa running to Kalae.

Quite distinct from the rest of Ka-'u is the valley of Waiohinu, which is flanked in such a way by the mountain side that it escapes the violence (and evaporation power) of both trade and southerly winds, while receiving a generous share of rainfall. This was the locality chosen by the chiefs (*ali'i*) for their residence.

William Ellis gives a good description of this choice locality as he saw it in 1819.[4]

"Our path running in a northerly direction, seemed leading us toward a ridge of high mountains, but it suddenly turned to the east, and presented to our view a most enchanting valley, clothed with verdure, and ornamented with clumps of *kukui* and *kou* trees. On the south-east it was open toward the sea, and on both sides adorned with gardens, and interspersed with cottages even to the summits of the hills. A fine stream of fresh water, the first we had seen on the island [they had landed at Kailua, in Kona] ran along the centre of the valley, while several smaller ones issued from the rocks, on the opposite side, and watered the plantations below . . . then continued our way along its margin through Kiolaka'a, walking on toward the sea until we reached Waiohinu . . .

"Our road, for a considerable distance, lay through the cultivated parts of this beautiful valley. The mountain taro, bordered by sugar-cane, and bananas, was planted in large fields on the sides of the hills, and seemed to thrive luxuriantly. On leaving the valley, we proceeded along by

[4] *Journal of a Tour Around Hawaii*, Boston, 1825, pp. 103-105.

the foot of the mountains in a line parallel with the sea, and about a mile and a half from it. The country appeared more thickly inhabited, than that over which we had travelled in the morning."

Beyond the zone of habitation of this land of wide spaces on a clear day, the eyes of our deep sea fisherman will see the heavily forested zone (*wao akua,* jungle of gods), where his great *koa* (*Acacia koa*) trees cut for canoe hulls are growing. Beyond that the verdant rain forest, frequently swathed in cloud. And on up beyond, the bare, sweeping majestic curve of the bare flanks of the great active volcano, Mauna Loa. In January and February snow may be seen mantling the summit. And when the volcano is erupting, this summit, in fact all the forests of Ka-'u, may be shrouded in a pall of smoke, and at night the lurid red of Moku'aweo-weo's fountains and rivers of molten lava illumine the whole sky above these slopes.

It is profoundly significant that the Hawaiians of Ka-'u did not fear or cringe before, or hate, the power and destructive violence of Mauna Loa. They took unto them this huge Mother mountain, measured their personal dignity and powers in terms of its majesty and drama. They named their land " The Breast " (*Ka-'u*). They loved Pele, whose home was their land: they endured her furies, and celebrated the drama of creation with which they lived so intimately in the songs and dances of the sacred *hula,* which dramatizes the myth of the " Woman of the Pit " (the crater, Kilauea) and her " family," embodied in cloud, thunder and lightning (Lono), in the forest and verdure (Wahine 'Oma'o, " Green Lady ") in Hi'iaka " of living waters," the healer, and other cosmic terrestial forces that encompassed them.

We have gone thus fully into the description of the extended, fragmented terrain of Ka-'u because this explains the *dispersal* of the extended *'ohana.* There could be no greater contrast than between the compact Samoan village or the Maori *pa,* composed of households of interrelated kinship groups, and the dispersed community of *'ohana* in Ka-'u. All are basically Polynesian. And Ka-'u, for all its uniqueness, is typical of the Hawaii Islands. There were no true villages in Hawaii. Yet the Hawaiian is essentially " old Polynesian." The tendency to close community of domicile in New Zealand was, we presume, due to the early stage of pioneering which existed, and to tribal rivalry, which ultimately would have given way to alliances and larger areas of continuous settlement held together under dominant leadership, comparable to Hawai'i. Were there tendencies in this direction in late pre-"discovery" Maori history?

THE SEASONS.

The season of storm and rain was termed Ho'oilo, including roughly the period of November through March. It commenced with 'Ikuwa (October-November) whose name means " Loud-voice," when Lono's thunder resounds over uplands and plain. Now the long drought of summer, when the intense heat of radiation of sun on black lava combined with the steady tradewinds made the *kula kai* seared and dry as a black tropical desert and the *kula uka* brown and arid, gives way to moisture-laden southern warm fronts pressing inshore, as tradewinds lapse. November is a noisy month with variable strong winds; and with the winds comes the roaring and pounding surf on Ka-'u's lava-walled shores and small steep beaches. Commencing now, and continuing through the rainy months until March, there was and is little deep-sea fishing, and inshore fishing depended on those occasions when the sea was not too rough. Equally, in olden days, upland work, such as cutting timber, stripping bark for cloth and fibre, collecting wild foods, hunting birds, was gradually abandoned because of the rains. *It was a time of the indrawing* of households into their respective homesteads: a time for work that could be done under a roof and out of the wind.

Welehu (November-December) commences the period of southerly (*kona*) storms.

O Welehu ka malama, kau ke po'o i ka uluna:
Welehu is the month to lay the head on the pillow.

Women occupied themselves with making baskets and mats: salt baskets of double pandanus leaf, with lids; lighter baskets, with lids, for dried fish; small thick mats for drying salt, broad-strand mats for floors, finer mats for bed space, rough mats for covering the oven. Most of the spinning of cord, with fingers rolling coconut or *olona* fibre on the thigh, was done by womenfolk. Men repaired their

houses, and in the *Mua* (men's house) or outside, worked on
weapons, fishing and hunting gear, made utensils of coconut-
shell (cups), gourd, wood, or stone. Men also spun cord and
made their nets for fishing, for carrying food containers.

The names of the months in their order throw light
on the round of the year and the family's seasonal activities:

'Ikuwa (October-November)—"Loud voice": This is
the time of thunder in the uplands, wind in the lowlands, and
crashing surf along the shore. (A child born in this month
will be a loud talker.)

Welehu (November-December)—The "ashes" (*lehu*)
of fires for cooking, warmth and drying, "sift" (*we*), as
the wind swirls about the eating and work sheds.

Makali'i (December-January)—The "little eyes"
(*makali'i*) or shoots of yams, arrowroot, turmeric, looking
like points or eyes (*maka*), are showing.

Ka-'elo (January-February)—"The (*ka*) drenching"
(*'elo*) times, as the rainy season and southerly winds cul-
minate and subside, as northrly winds push in. This is the
month when migrating birds are fat and greasy (*'elo'elo*).

Kaulua (February-March)—"Two together" (*ka*, the,
lua, double), i.e., partly cold and partly warm: alternating
cool and warm spells. *Kaulua* means also "of two minds,"
"indecisive": the weather is "undecided," so people are
uncertain whether to go *mauka* or *makai*, to go out or stay in.

Nana (March-April)—The word means "animation."
Life in plants shows vigour, young mother birds (*kinana*)
are on the move, fledgelings (*punua*) are trying to get out of
nests.

Welo (April-May)—"Vining out" (like a tail, *welo*):
The sweet potatoes, yams, morning glory and other vines
are spreading with little shoots like tails.

Ikiiki (May-June)—"Warm and sticky," uncomfort-
able: Now there is little wind and it is humid.

Ka'aona (June-July)—"Pleasantly (*ona*) rolling along
(*ka'a*)." The serenely moving puffy clouds (*ka 'alewalewa*)
roll along mountain and horizon. *Ona* means lure in fishing:
figuratively, then, attractive, alluring.

Hina-ia-'ele'ele (July-August)—"Dark (*'ele'ele*) clouds
inclining (*hina-ia*) mountainwards."

Mahoe-mua (August-September)—"The twin before
(first twin)."

Mahoe-hope (September-October)—" The twin behind (second twin)."

These two months, in weather, are as alike as twins. Rains and wind alternate with good weather.

Let us return now to our description of living and work of the seasons in the old days. With the ground well soaked, and with the ending of the heavy rains that wash out the tilled soil on slopes, every household turns in February and March to the planting of their taro, sweet potato, gourds (in the lowlands), paper mulberry and *olana* (*Touchardia latifolia*) for fibre (on the upper slopes), yams and arrow-root in the upland. But this season of planting is a time of scarcity of land foods: last year's supply has been consumed and this year's crops but newly planted. Yams (*Dioscorea*) or *Uhi,* and arrowroot or *Pia,* are in the early stage of growth. There was in normal years enough wild banana and tree-fern pith. Consequently this is the season when those of the upland households (*ko kula uka*) go into the lower forest for tree-fern starch and banana; while those to seaward (*ko kula kai*) are busy with the inshore fishing, and the collecting of shellfish and seaweed. It is a time when the intra-familial commerce of exchange between households is actively revived. This is a spreading-out time: mountainward, and seaward, a time of mobility and intercourse, of work and sport.

During April, gardens are tended; by May plants both domesticated and wild are growing vigorously, and in May quick-growing varieties of sweet potatoes can be eaten, and wild yams and arrowroot are coming to maturity and can also be eaten. They come into their prime in late May and June. Now we are in the early hot season (Kau—pronounced like " cow "). This is the time when women are working at making bark cloth (*kapa*) at home. Men are active hunting in the forest, fishing at sea, busy with their nets, canoes and gear at the *halau* (shed) by the sea. By June, wild foods are abundant in the forest, potatoes plentiful. Inland women-folk migrate to the shore, and there live in caves and shelters. With their fishing baskets (*hina'i*), salt and fish baskets, mats and utensils, they catch small fry like *manini* spawn, collect and store salt that has dried in the pools in black lava depressions by the shore.

Summer is the time for deep-sea fishing in particular. (In the old days inshore fishing was restricted during spawning season, from February to late May.)   In July gourds (and, after introduction, melons) ripen on the *kula kai*. It is increasingly hot and dry. Upland farmers have mulched their taro and potato patches with dried grass and fern. August is hot, but some dark clouds appear and bring showers: as they fall, the mulch is turned back from plants, then replaced when the rain has soaked in. At the shore in caves, and at home, salt and dried fish and octopus are stored in quantity, against the rainy season.

Then come the twin months, September-October, Mahoe-mua (Twin-before) and Mahoe-hope (Twin-behind, or after), with increasing showers and rough seas alternating with fine weather. The wild ground growths in the uplands are dying down; it is time to harvest potatoes ere the heavy rains come; it is the time to be industrious at deep-sea fishing on good days, ere the winter storms commence. Great pieces of the larger firm-fleshed fishes (bonito, tuna, albacore, swordfish, dolphin) are sun-dried to preserve them till eaten. Sweet potatoes are likewise preserved by cooking and sunning.

III.

THE LEGENDARY SETTING

The cycle of the seasons, the unique climate and natural habitat, and the physiographic and geologic formation of their land, compassed by oceans and the heavens, make up the dynamic Natural Setting of the native cultures of Ka-'u. The core of this culture is the family.

The legendary drama of their forebears must be pictured against the background of this natural setting, of which it was a part, and with which the folk identified it and were identified. The ocean, the underworld of vulcanism, the terrain and the heavens all harboured and brought forth elemental Persons embodying natural forces or phenomena and generic forms of life. There were first and foremost the clan of Pele, embodied in terrestrial and associated meteorological phenomena of vulcanism. There was Kua, the ancestral shark-lord, who came from Kahiki, a high-chief and warrior in the ocean's depths. There was Ku, from whose voluntary self-immolation for the sake of his children comes the breadfruit tree. Niu-loa-hiki, the "Far-going-coconut," like Pele and her clan, was an overseas ancestral link with Kahiki.

Believed to be local in origin were other forebears: that one from whose navel grew a great gourd vine, originating in a certain cave, which spread over and peopled seven districts of Ka-'u; another ancestor, identified with a particular hill, who appeared in the form of the caterpillars that feed upon the foliage of sweet potatoes, the staple of life in these districts. And there were countless other things, some of which we would call "inanimate" and others "animate," all part of the natural scene of everyday life, which were forms assumed by individual spirits ancestral to particular families.

To give some impression of the depth, the variegated patterning of this heritage of mental-emotional projection of thought and feeling that we call "legendary," it will be necessary briefly to review these living, dynamic so-called "legends," for there is no stereotyped pattern—each is different, each has its peculiar setting, time and relationship to locale and persons and families.

It is hard for the modern intellectually regid and extroverted mind to sense the subjective relationship of genuine Hawaiians to Nature, visible and invisible. But without in some degree *sensing the feeling* that underlies this quality of consciousness in those who live intimately in a condition of primary awareness and sensitivity on the plane of subjective identification with Nature, coupled with perceptions and concepts arising therefrom—without some comprehension of this quality of spontaneous *being-one-with-natural-phenomena which are persons, not things,* it is impossible for an alien (be he foreigner or city-hardened native) to understand a true country-Hawaiian's sense of dependence and obligation, his " values," his discrimination of the real, the good, the beautiful and the true, his feeling of organic and spiritual identification with the *'aina* (homeland) and *'ohana* (kin).

If Pele is not real to you, you cannot comprehend the quality of relationship that exists between persons related to and through Pele, and of these persons to the land and phenomena, not " created by " but *which are,* Pele and her clan. A rosy dawn is not merely a lovely "natural phenomenon ": it is that beloved Person named " The-rosy-glow-of-the-Heavens," who is " Hi'iaka-in-the-bosom-of-Pele," the youngest and most beloved sister of that greater (and loved though awe-inspiring) Person, Pele-honua-mea (Pele-the-sacred-earth-person), whose passions express themselves in the upheavals of vulcanism, whose " family " or " clan " are the terrestrial and meteorological phenomena related to vulcanism and the land created by vulcanism, as actively known in Ka-'u. The stories that we are about to review are not archaic " legends " to a true native of Ka-'u: they are living, dynamic realities, parts of an orderly and rational philosophy, now obscured and superseded by the new dynamics and the chaotic values of the sugar plantation, with its mechanical and industrial modernism and concomitant ethnic, social, economic, political, religious and other " new ways." These " new ways " are not a New Order for the country Hawaiian, and never will be: for they have exterminated him. He was engulfed and drowned in the tidal wave of Progress which inundated his land, his folks, his life and his spirit.

THE VOLCANO GODDESS.

The most important *kupuna* for all *'ohana* of Ka-'u, greatly loved in spite of her bad temper, was Pele-honua-mea (Pele-the-sacred-earth-person). The Volcano Goddess was also called Wahine-o-ka-Lua (Woman of the Crater) because she made her home in the depths of Hale-ma'u-ma'u and other craters on the slopes of Mauna Loa. To the island of Hawaii she had come by way of Maui where, as recited in the chants of her epic, she formed the vast crater of Hale-a-ka-la (House of the Sun). All extinct craters in these islands are spots where she dug with her staff Paoa, seeking a dry place for her eternal fires. Before coming to Maui she dug on Oahu the craters called Kohe-lepe-lepe (" Koko Crater "), Leahi (" Diamond Head "), Pu'u-o-waina (" Punchbowl "), Alia-pa'akai (" Salt Lake "). To Oahu she had come from Kauai, and to Kauai she had made the migration from Kahiki, accompanied by brothers and sisters and other relatives.

HER CLAN.

Chief navigator on these voyages was Pele's brother Ka-moho-Ali'i, the King of Sharks. There is a cliff at the Crater of Kilauea (island of Hawai'i) named Pali-kapu-o-Ka-moho-Ali'i. Smoke rolling from Pele's lava will blow in every other direction, but never against that cliff: in that direction it blows straight up without touching it. That is because of his *kapu*; he was her elder and best-loved brother.

Ka-uila-nui-makeha (the-great-flashing-lightning) is another brother. Kane-'apua was the youngster (*poki'i*) having a shark body: he succoured the spirits of those lost at sea (*'apua* is a kind of fish basket).

Ka-poha-i-kahi-ola is the brother who makes explosions (*poha*, burst, in the place, or *kahi*, of life, *ola*).

Kuku'ena-i-ke-ahi-ho'omau-honua (The-burning-hot-one-in-the-eternal-fire-in-the-earth), is a younger sister who always prepared Pele's *'awa* (beverage brewed from the root of *Piper methysticum*). She was also the maker of *lei* or flower garlands.

Kapo-'ula-kina'u was a sister of Pele who came to Hawai'i from Kahiki before the migration of Pele and her following. Kapo was a patron of sorcery. She also came via Kauai to Maui, and ultimately settled on Molokai.

Na-maka-o-Kaha'i, an older sister of Pele, had a violent quarrel with Pele while still in Kahiki.

With Pele came also Pele's father Kane-hoa-lani (male-friend-of-Heaven), and her mother Haumea. Kane-hoa-lani is a great headland on Oahu's windward coast; Haumea had many bodies, one of which was the low lying breadfruit tree.

HER BENIGN YOUNGER SISTER.

The most poetic figure amongst the nature spirits, and perhaps the one most loved, was Pele's younger sister, Hi'iaka. This benign yet powerful being is described with many epithets indicative of her many roles in nature. The great sequence of chants which as a whole made up the cycle of the consecrated dance-ritual of the *hula*, recounting the drama of Pele and her family, depicts Hi'iaka as dancer; as voyager seeking the stricken Lohi'au, Pele's beloved slain by her own jealous passion, whom Hi'iaka revives; as healer and guardian; as spirit of ocean, of cloud forms, of the uplands.

Seen in the heavens was Hi'iaka-noho-lani (-dweller-in-the sky) who was the same as Hi'iaka-i-ka-maka-o-ka-'opua (-in-the-face-of-the-rainclouds). In righteous anger she could be Hi'iaka-wawahi-lani (-who-breaks-through-the-heavens), a flash of lightning. As healer she was Hi'iaka-i-ka-wai-ola (-in-the-water-of-life), and as beneficent guardian and fosterer, Hi'iaka-i-ka-poli-i-Pele (-in-the-bosom-of-Pele). In her search for Lohi'au, this saviouress knew the ordeals of flagging strength, hardship and tribulation. There are, therefore, implications of sympathy for the feeble and distressed in these names: Hi'iaka-kuli-pe'e (-whose-knees-are-weak) and Hi'iaka-pokole-waimaka-nui (-little-one-greatly-tearful).

Fishermen were warned of dangers from wind and wave by Hi'iaka-makole-wawahi-wa'a (-the-red-eyed-who-smashed-canoes), seen in the short red rainbow standing at sea-level and foretelling storm; and also in the bright red-orange coloured fruit of the *hala* (pandanus), which blooms in the spring when seas run high. This voyager along the seacoasts was also described as Hi'iaka-i-ka-'ale-'i (-in-the-running-billows) Hi'iaka-i-ka-'ale-moe (-in-the-low-billows), Hi'iaka-i-ka-'ale-kua-loloa (-in-the-long-backed-billows), Hi'iaka-i-ka-'ale-hako'iko'i (- in - the - agitated

billows), Hi'iaka-i-ke-au-miki (-in-the-receding-current),
Hi'iaka-i-ke-au-ka (-in-the-pushing-current), Hi'iaka-'au'au-
kai (-the-sea-bather), and Hi'iaka-noho-lae (-dweller-of-the-
capes).

In the uplands this spirit was seen in the lovely *lehua*
pompoms of the forests bordering the volcano, as Hi'iaka-i-
ka-lihilihi-o-ka-lehua (-in-the-fringes-of-the-*lehua*), which
were favourites for *lei* (garlands) for high chiefs; where-
fore she was also Hi'iaka-lei-'ia (-the-beloved-garlanded) and
Hi'iaka-lei-lani (-the-heavenly-garland) or Hi'iaka-lei-mau-
ia (-garland-ever-beloved). Likewise of the uplands she
was Hi'iaka-kolo-pupu (-the-creeper), the same as Hi'iaka-
kolo-pali (-who-creeps-about-cliffs). Was this perhaps the
vine *maile* (*Alyxia olivaeformis*), also beloved for garlands?
Or might it be, more poetically, the rosy sunlight seen at
dawn creeping along the uplands, described in another of her
names: Hi'iaka-i-ka-pua-'ena'ena (-in-the-glow-of-the-rising-
sun—literally, -in-the-burning-blossom)?

LONO THE THUNDERER.

The most important male *'ohana* in the Pele clan was
her uncle, Lono-makua (Maori Rongo-matua). The name
means Lono-the-elder. Lono (resounding) probably refers
to thunder. It was he who kept the sacred fire of the underworld under his armpit. Vulcanism in Ka-'u is associated
with heavy rain, thunder and lightning. Rain clouds were
referred to in chants as " bodies (*kino*) of Lono." The
sweet potato, whose culture on the semi-arid *kula* (lower
slopes) of the volcano's flanks in Ka-'u and Kona was
dependent upon the winter rains, was identified with Lono
in his hog form as Kamapua'a (Hog-child): this earth-god,
who plays a dramatic role in the cycle of Pele chants as
tempter and taunter of that passionate Lady of the Pit, in
humbler moments roots up the earth of the potato patch as
the tubers grow, and sometimes, humorously, the humble
'u'ala were referred to as " droppings " of Kamapua'a.

It was Lono-makua to whom offerings of food and other
products of the land were presented in the annual Makahiki
festival during November, December and January (the
months of southerly winds and rains). On the altars at the
borders of the districts, where the offerings were collected,
Lono was represented by a wooden carving of the head of a

hog—the word for district boundary was *ahu-pua'a* (altar-of-the-hog). In the royal procession through the districts, when the harvest tribute was accepted and the land and crops were blessed and released from *kapu*, the high-chief (Ali'i-nui) acted as deputy to Lono, his ancestor, who was represented by a symbol remarkably suggestive of the sail of a square-rigged ship: a tall staff with a small carved figure at the peak, having a cross-piece near the top from which hung a square of white bark-cloth (*kapa*).

Lono was believed to come annually from Kahiki when the Pleiades first appeared over the horizon at dusk (late October or early November). His landing place was Keala-kekua (the-path-of-the-god) in Kona district, westward along the coast from Ka-'u. Here was the temple dedicated to this seasonal god " from overseas " (Kahiki). From this locality, at the end of the festival of offering tribute to Lono-makua, a canoe to which was attached a basket containing every variety of food, was set adrift in a southerly direction. This floating altar was called " Lono's canoe."

By an extraordinary coincidence of time and place, Captain James Cook was led to put in at Kealakekua Bay to provision his ship at the season of Lono's festival. He was received and worshipped as Lono-makua. Subsequent events unhappily disillusioned the Hawaiians, and the great navigator suffered death on the shore called " The path of the god," where for centuries Lono-makua had been believed to come ashore each year, bringing rain and plenty.

KU THE ERECT.

Another lineage, and yet one related to that of Lono-Pele-ma (*-ma* as a suffix means " -and family ") is that of Ku (Erect). A living descendant today of the old high-chiefly line of Ka-'u is Ku-pa-'ai-ke'e (striker-out-of-flaws), embodied in the adze obliquely hafted for hollowing the canoe hull. Ku of the forest and uplands, where the great trees erect their trunks, patron of canoe builders, was also addressed in chants as Ku-moku-hali'i (-island-bedecking), Ku-mauna (-of-the-mountains), Ku-ka-ohi'a-Laka (-of-Laka's-hardwood), meaning *Metrosideros*, the crimson-blossomed *Ohi'a-lehua*, or Maori *Pua-rata*).

Many were the names of Ku in the uplands. On the *kula* slopes some planters invoked him as Ku-ka-o'o (-of-the-digging-stick), as Ku-kulia (-of-dry-planting), Ku-ke-olo-walu (-of-wet-planting). As Ku-'ula (Red Ku), represented by a stone wrapped in red cloth, he was traditional patron of deep-sea fishing. As Ku-ka-'ai-moku (-eater-of-islands) he was war-god of the land-hungry chieftains. But for the householder and his family there were intimate beneficent attributes that made precious this ubiquitous forebear. Ku and his wife Hina (Grey, Silvery—presumably the Moon anciently), were invoked by a man and his wife as personal guardians and helpers, in all work, in sickness. The *ti* plant (*Dracaena terminalis*), protective and purifying, planted near the home, useful in countless domestic ways, was Ku. So likewise was the *noni* (*Morinda citrifolia*), whose medicinal uses were many. Of the lineage of Ku also were the coconut, the eel and the sea-cucumber.

It will make more real to our readers the feeling of his worshippers toward Ku if we end this summary reference to him with a resumé of a Hawaiian story of the origin of the tall-growing breadfruit tree of Puna (Pukui, 1933, p. 127). Ku once took to himself as wife a woman of this land. She bore him children. A time of famine came and Ku saw his children starving. "Let us go into the garden," he said. There, after bidding his wife farewell, he stood on his head (compare with the Maori conception that Kane as forest god stands head down). Slowly he sank into the ground until he disappeared entirely. His devoted wife watched the spot day by day, watering it with her tears. One day a sprout appeared. It grew, became a tree, and bore great fruit—the breadfruit. The women and children ate to their hearts' content. Later, when other sprouts shot up they were given to others for planting. This was the gift of Ku to his people.

KANE THE PROCREATOR.

More distant, more widely "pantheistic," and more exalted and possibly more ancient, is Kane, the primordial "Male" (*kane*), who dwells in Eternity (*i-ka-po-loa* in-the-everlasting-night). He is Ka(ne)-'onohi-a-ka-la (-eye-ball-of-the-sun), and Ka(ne)-wai-ola (-water-of-life, i.e., sunlight and fresh water in rain or streams, as life-giver and healer). Ka(ne)-huna-moku (or Moku-huna-a-Kane) is the "Hidden-land-of-Kane" to which his worshippers go if worthy, the land seen in the magnificent, sun-lit, billowy cloud-continents that float by majestically on distant windward horizons in the seasons of the trade-winds. As Kane-hekili, he is lightning, the same as Kane-wawahi-lani (-splitter-of-the-sky). Countless are his forms: he is Kane " in-the-whirlwind," " the-great-wind," " the-little-wind," " the-peaceful-breeze "; " in-the-rainbow " of many types of clouds variously described, " in-the-heavenly-star," "in-the-great-outpouring-of-water," "in-the-little-out-pouring "; " of-the-mountain," " the-precipice," " the-out-cropping-stone." Erect stones, natural or set up, were termed " stones-of-Kane." In the sea Kane is coral of many sorts. For the planter he was, as embodied in fresh water for irrigation, *ka-wai-ola-a-Kane*, water-of-life invoked in taro planting. In Ka-'u there still remain the vestiges of a shrine of Kane, near the lands where taro was planted. The family bowl of *poi* (starch staple made from taro) in the household was sacred to Haloa, who is Kane, an ancestor in the line senior to man, in the genealogical records of the generations born of the Heavens (Wakea, " wide-spread-whiteness or light ") and the Earth (Papa). The bowl of *poi*, sacred to Haloa, occupied in the Hawaiian household a place not unlike that of the hearth for the Latin and Greek ancestor worshippers, or the sacred fire in the Hindu home. For the healer, *popolo* (*Solanum nigrum*), a ubiquitous plant in ancient Hawaii, had many beneficent uses: *popolo* is sometimes referred to as the foundation (*ke-kumu*) of Hawaiian therapy; it is one of the embodiments of Kane as healing force.

KANALOA, LORD OF OCEAN.

Kanaloa was lord of ocean and ocean winds, and as such embodied particularly in the octopus and squid. But he had land forms (*kino*) also, particularly the banana, and certain other plants of similar habit. An interesting group of local legends identified with freshwater sources in various localities of the Hawaiian islands describe Kane and Kanaloa as travelling companions in ancient times, moving about the land and opening springs and water holes for the benefit of men. In these tales Kane and Kanaloa are, like Pele and her " family," described as coming from " Kahiki."

NAMES THAT CONFER STATUS.

The significance of these Persons for *ali'i* of old Ka-'u and still in our day is, that these names, given and spoken with a sense of potency and prestige, even today perpetuate the sense of the reality and sanctity of these Persons, when borne by living descendants of these lines. Lono and Ku, Pele and Hi'iaka and many other *'aumakua* (ancestral Persons embodied in Nature) have their namesakes amongst living descendants of their lineage. Sometimes the names are selected and given as a matter of choice. But in many instances such a name or a figurative compound name which describes a particular attribute of an *'aumakua,* is *inoa po,* a name-out-of-night, a term which refers to the receiving of a name to be given by an elder relative in a dream or vision. A person receiving such a name in childhood and honouring it is believed to be protected and blessed: but if the elder fails to bestow the name, or if it is dishonoured, woe betide both elder and child! Of this we shall say more in a section on the psychic phase of *'ohana.* (For considerations relating to this custom see Handy, 1936 and 1940, in the list of references.

ANCESTRAL SPIRITS EMBODIED IN ANIMAL AND PLANT FORMS.

Of a somewhat different order of ancestry from these lords of primordial elemental forces are various other more recent legendary beings from whom certain families of Ka-'u trace their lineage and who continue to act as *'aumakua* or guardians to their descendants. One such important being was Kua.

Sharks.

Kua, the *mano ali'i* (shark chief), described in a local Ka-'u *mele inoa* (name chant) in praise of him as " the red shark, huge and thick-skinned," came directly to Ka-'u shores from " Kahiki " as leader of a great company of sharks, several of his male relatives being his lieutenants. As the Hawaiians of old were versed in symbolic speech, it is our belief that Kua and his company have historical significance, not actually as fish of the deep but as a raiding party of fierce warriors (" sharks ") on war canoes. As the dramatic chant of Kua describes his arrival, there were probably nine single canoes or four double canoes, each under the command of a valiant leader whose name remains celebrated in the chant of praise.

One unusual feature of the story is that Kua brought with him his favourite sister, " riding on his back," a sister having human form, and this sister, marrying a chief of Ka-'u, became the ancestress of many of the Ka-'u 'ohana. Kua, the shark chief, also became a direct ancestor through mating in spirit form with a descendant of his sister: a son, Kua-opio (Young Kua) otherwise called Pakaiea (meaning a certain green seaweed), and a daughter, were the results of this union, the son having fish form; but of the daughter and her descendants it is said there were no shark-like physical characteristics except rough skin between knee and ankle, called 'i'ili-a-mano (shark skin). The son is said to have been the progenitor of more than one mano-kanaka (shark-man) in his line, most famous being Kalani, recognized by the inhabitants of Ka-'u as part shark and part human. This term mano-kanaka was used by Ka-'u folk to designate sharks who were related to them by blood, and such people described themselves as " na mamo i ka halo o Kua " (children of the bosom of Kua), having the blood of Kua flowing in their veins.

To these Ka-'u 'ohana Kua was and is a guardian and an omen of good. His territory stretches along the coast of Ka-'u from 'Ahukini to 'Apua, and there were places of worship dedicated to him at Kalae, Wai-ka-puna, Pa-'ula-kai and Na'alehu. He is known also as Ka-wohi-ku-i-ka-moana (the chief-who-stands-guard-in-the-ocean), and there are many stories of specific warnings and rescues attributed to this great red shark. His shark son Kua-opio, or Pakaiea, has also been recognized as a benefactor through the years. The latter is recognizable by his deep brown skin and green markings, the patterning of the green limu pakaiea (seaweed) in which he was wrapped at birth by his human mother and carried to his father Kua in the sea.

Within the memory of a living descendant this shark Pakaiea has been seen accepting first offering of fish from the fishing spear of an elder kinsman who told her this story of his brother's rescue at sea. His canoe broken by a storm, the brother was near exhaustion on his long swim homeward, when a body rose beneath him and carried him to shore. It was the shark Pakaiea. The grateful man rewarded him with banana and *'awa* and the two became lifelong friends, aiding each other in fishing and sharing food. At the man's death, Pakaiea continued in the guardianship over the younger brother who in old age pointed out the family benefactor to the child.

Because of the shark relationship, the colour red (Kua's colour), the *pakaiea* seaweed, and shark's flesh of any kind are all *kapu* (forbidden) to all natives of Ka-'u who claim Kua or his sister as progenitor.

Caterpillar.

Another Ka-'u *'aumakua* was Kumuhea, a son of Ku, who came from "Kahiki" first to Molokai and thence to Ka-'u on the island of Hawai'i. He fell in love with a girl there who returned his affection, and when he became her husband he took her to the top of a hill, now called Pu'u-Enuhe (Caterpillar Hill) to make their home. He had never visited her or her relatives except at night, and now after marriage he always vanished in the daytime, returning at evening bringing sweet-potato greens for their provender. An exclusive diet of greens soon reduced his wife to skin and bones, and when her brothers came to see her they were shocked at her appearance and went to a relative who was a *kahuna* to discuss the matter. It was revealed to the *kahuna* that the young man was a *kupua* (nature spirit) whose other form was the caterpillar that feeds on sweet-potato foliage. The God Ku, whose son it was, was called upon for help, and Ku came and put an end to his son's assuming human form.

Nevertheless Ka-'u remained the permanent home of Kumuhea, and because of the marriage relationship that had existed no native of the place would deliberately destroy a caterpillar. It is still remembered, from the childhood of living persons, that precautions were taken to avoid stepping on them even when the roads were covered with them during unusual and pestilential visitations. When natives planted their sweet potatoes they called upon Kumuhea to help himself to the leaves but not destroy the plants or harm the tubers, and the plants were left unharmed; but should newcomers or careless natives set about to kill off the "pests," more and more would appear until his vines would be utterly consumed. Kumuhea could be a friend, but he could also be a bitter enemy.

Another form which Kumuhea assumed was the *loli* (*Holothuria*), or sea-cucumber, a soft-bodied large slug found under stones near shore, plentiful in Ka-'u waters. Though liked and eaten freely by most natives of Hawai'i, they were *kapu* to those *'ohana* of Ka-'u for whom Kumuhea was an *'aumakua*. Instances are cited of young folk who have scoffed at the warning of the elders against this *kapu* food as " deadly poisonous " to the family, and who have sickened and died after eating *loli* in a spirit of reckless defiance. It is said that the whole body swells painfully, until death releases the sufferer.

Another story like the above in which the caterpillar and sea-cucumber are forms of the same *kupua*, casts sea-cucumber and eel as companions who come up out of the sea at nightfall and, turning into handsome men, make love to two girls who have come to the beach to bathe. (Pukui, 1933.)

Bitter Gourd.

Among the distant legendary ancestors of one Ka-'u *'ohana* were twin sisters who were said to have been born from a bitter gourd (*ipu-'awa-'awa*) that grew out of their dead mother's navel. A young couple, because of parental disapproval of their marriage, eloped and made their home on Kamao'a plain. Many who loved them followed, and thus began the peopling of that plain. When the young wife was about to become a mother she died and was borne to a cave where she was lovingly laid to rest. Unknown to her people, a vine sprouted from her navel and grew very rapidly. It travelled far, crossing seven *ahupua'a* (land sections) before it fruited, back of a fisherman's home, close to the boundary between Ka-'u and Kona. The fisherman was pleased at finding such a fine gourd growing beside his house, and would frequently thump and pinch it to see if it was ready to pick. The spirit of the dead woman visited her husband in a dream and complained of soreness from being thumped and pinched. When the husband wakened he went to look at her body and found the vine growing out of her navel. This vine he traced to its fruiting end beside the fisherman's house. An argument ensued over the ownership of the gourd, which was settled by establishing the vine's source, and the husband took the gourd home, where he kept it carefully on a bundle of fine *kapa*. In time the gourd cracked open and out fell two seeds which developed into identical twin girls, who became famous in later life as robust and powerful fighters as well as prolific mothers.

Because of the gourd relationship, it became *kapu* amongst this large *'ohana* of Kamao'a plain to burn any fragment of gourd, since " to burn the bones of an ancestor " was an insult. Midwives placed a gourd at the head of a woman in difficult labour, with a request for ancestral help in delivering the child.

This story has an interesting symbolism. The gourd is a symbol of Lono, god of agriculture. As a very close relative was often referred to as one's " navel," this, we believe, implied that the people of Kamao'a plain claimed very close relationship, through his priesthood, to Lono. The miraculous growth of the vine refers to the rapid spread of the population in this area, extending across seven *ahupua'a* from Kamao'a to the Kona boundary, and so arose the saying of that *'ohana*: " We are the people of the seven *ahupua'a*," referring to their descent from the woman out of whose navel the gourd vine grew. It is also noted that since the birth of the gourd sisters, twins have been a common occurrence from generation to generation in this *'ohana*.

Psychic Aspect of Community Relationship.

The psychic phase of relationship of *'ohana* to *'aumakua* (ancestral forbears who concern themselves with nature and man) and *kupua* (nature spirits that choose at will human, animal and vegetable forms as means of physical incarnation) will be described in a subsequent section. It is necessary to comprehend this psychic phase, against the background of Hawaiian religious experience, beliefs, practices and concepts, if family relationships, duties, *kapu* and ethical principles are to be understood. No one can comprehend the so-called " lore " and " beliefs " relating to *'aumakua* and *kupua* without knowing a great deal about the aspects and features of the locale and natural environment with which *'aumakua* and *kupua* are identified. Equally, persons and *'ohana* in their human relationships can be comprehended only in the context of natural setting and " lore " *in terms of the psychic relations subsisting between Nature and its phenomena, ancestral and nature spirits, and native mankind in old Ka-'u.*

IV.

THE KINSHIP SYSTEM

Kinship in Hawai'i extends far beyond the immediate biological family. The terminology of kinship must be thought of against the background of the whole community of kith and kin, including in-law, and adoptive categories.

In the first section of this treatise we spoke of the fact that the Hawaiians of Ka-'u on the great island of Hawai'i considered themselves all offshoots ('*ohana*) of one stock.

That the inhabitants of other of the ancient ethnic divisions in the Hawaiian Islands, like Ko'olau Poko ("Short Windward") and Ko'olau Loa ("Long Windward") on Oahu likewise considered themselves, and in fact were originally, '*ohana* seems certain. In the semi-mythical era of Oahu history in which Lono (Maori Rongo) as Thunderer and Rain God and progenitor of the sweet potato ('*u'ala*) manifested himself in the form of the legendary giant "Hog-child" (Kama-pua'a), the whole of windward Oahu (Ko'olau Poko and Ko'olau Loa) was the land (Moku) of 'Olopana (Maori Koropanga, Tahitian 'Oropa'a) whose Ilamuku (Body Guard, Constable and Executioner) was Makali'i (Pleiades, Maori Matariki).[5] Ka-'u likewise had

[5] Throughout the Hawaiian Islands the first appearance of the Pleiades on the horizon at sunset (October-November) marked the commencement of the winter season (the month named 'Ikuwa, "Noisy") of southerly winds and drenching rains. Then war was forbidden. The High Chief (Ali'i Nui), on behalf of his ancestor Lono, in the pageant of the Makahiki festival accepted offerings of food placed before wooden carvings representing a hog's head on altars called "Hog-shrines" (Ahu-pua'a) which were erected at the border of each district (the land division which was likewise termed Ahu-pua'a). Rain prayers were chanted to Lono: "Your bodies, O Lono, are in the heavens, a long cloud, a short cloud . . .", etc. The people frolicked with sports, boxing, dancing and bathing, as the rains subsided (February). Then, the land being thoroughly soaked, and sunny days assured, every household turned to preparing the fields round about their homes and planting sweet potatoes, taro, banana, sugar cane, gourds. It was only after these four months devoted to the important business of livelihood that the warlock *Ali'i* turned their thoughts and the energies of their people to mobilization of resources, priests and warriors in the royal sport of warfare, to fight—while the weather was pleasant—for glory, for land and wealth or for revenge.

its legend of Makali'i as a local hero, but not of 'Olopana. Lono, the thunderer and rain god, and Kamapua'a, are intimately related to the vulcanism of Ka-'u.

There are ample indications that in this legendary era pioneering Hawaiians were tribal groups, under individual chiefs, many of whom came from islands south of the equator, generically referred to as "Kahiki" (generally meaning "a land overseas"). From the point of view of Polynesian history, a study of these evidences, scattered through legends, myths, chants and genealogies, is capable of yielding rich rewards, in interest and in scholarly returns.

In historic times, compact communities, segregated by natural boundaries such as Kalalau, Hanapepe, Waimea on Kauai, the great valley communities of West and East Maui and of Windward Hawai'i, such as Waipi'o and Waimanu, were certainly tribal in tradition, like Ka-'u; and like Ka-'u they were presumably descendants of the founding pioneer group, infiltrated by marriage and adoption from neighbouring communities.

As we see it, an essential and needed step toward a true comprehension of the pre-discovery Hawaiian society and polity, is to break through and reject the facade of "a unified kingdom," with political concepts comparable to those of monarchial Europe, a fantasy which the British and French explorers, and the American and French missionaries, projected after the conquest of all the islands by Kamehameha. There was in Hawai'i, as in Samoa and Tonga and Tahiti, the institution of genealogically superior High Chief. There was no "King" until Vancouver, and Kamehameha's English advisors Young and Davis, "indoctrinated" that great warrior.

Dr. Buck writes (*The Coming of the Maori*, p. 338): "All members of a Maori tribe are related to each other by blood descent, and the record of a common tie is preserved in the family genealogies. . . . The kinship terms in use are capable of expressing the relationship between any two members of the tribe . . ."

By way of introduction to the discussion of the particularities of Hawaiian kinship terminology we feel that the most interesting entry to that rather dry field of linguistic archaeology may be by way of a comparative table giving both the Hawaiian and the Maori terms. With Sir Peter's kind permission, we are adapting the systematic tabular presentation of the basic Maori system printed on page 339 of his *The Coming of the Maori*, modifying and adding to this as needed for the presentation of our Hawaiian terms.

TABLE 1.

Kinship Terms, Hawaiian and Maori.

Generations	English	Hawaiian	Maori	Collaterals
— 2	Grandparents	kupuna	tipuna, tupuna	
	Grandfather	kupuna kane	tipuna tane	grand uncle
	Grandmother	kupuna wahine	tipuna wahine	grand aunt
— 1	Parents	makua	matua	
	Father	makua kane	matua tane	uncle
	Mother	makuahine	whaea, whaene	aunt
0	Elder brothers of male	kaikua'ana, addressed as kua'ana	tuakana	cousins
	Elder sisters of female	kaikua'ana, addressed as kua'ana	tuakana	
	Younger brothers of male	kaikaina, addressed as kaina	teina, taina	
	Younger sisters of female	kaikaina, addressed as kaina	teina, taina	
	Brother of female	kaikunane, addressed as kunane	tungane	
	Sister of male	kaikuahine, addressed as kuahine	tuahine	
+ 1	Children	keiki, kama (s.) kamali'i (pl.)	tamaiti (s.) tamariki (pl.)	tamaiti keke Iramutu[G] (Maori), nephews and nieces
	Son	keiki, kama	tama, tamaroa	H. nephew
	Daughter	kaikamahine	tamahine	H. niece
+ 2	Grandchildren	mo'opuna	mokopuna	
	Grandson	mo'opuna kane	mokopuna tane	grandnephew
	Granddaughter	mo'opuna wahine	mokopuna wahine	grandniece

[G] Ilamuku (in Hawai'i)—the trusted bodyguard of the *Ali'i*—an uncle, nephew, half-brother. He sometimes had authority to speak for the *Ali'i*.

RELATIONSHIP.

A system of relationship existed whose apparent simplicity in " classifying " according to generations is somewhat misleading. Actually there were three primary factors determining relationship, duty and status.

1. Horizontally, the family is stratified by generations: grandparents, parents, brothers and sisters, sons and daughters, grandchildren.

2. Precedence or status was determined by genealogical seniority, not by generation or age, or by sex: persons stemming from a genealogically elder branch outrank older generations of junior branches.

3. Vertically, sex cuts through the generations: male children are claimed by the father's " side " ('ao'ao kane), female by the mother's (ao'ao wahine). Within a generation, all males have one term for each other, likewise females; males and females have distinct terms for each other. This is a part of the systematic segregation of the sexes, which prevailed throughout every phase of Polynesian life.

When Holoholoku, the foster-parent of Maihunali'i, came to Oahu from Kauai (as he was instructed to do in a dream) to seek the wife chosen for his ward, he found her grandmother at Makapu'u. The girl, Malei, was sent for and before she left for Kauai the grandmother expressed her thoughts to Holoholoku. If a daughter should be born of this union of the Oahu chiefess and the Kauai chief, then she (the grandmother) would want to rear her here on Oahu—but if the child was a boy (like his father) then he was to be reared by those of his father's side of the family. Should there be no daughter born, then after death Malei must be brought back to her old home for burial.

Biological relationship then was ordered or defined in terms of the three factors: generation, genealogical seniority and sex.

No elaborate rationalizations seem called for to explain the inclusive terms for generations: it is a logical consequence of regarding the extended family as a unit while recognizing genealogical sequence. The generations are not age groups, but genealogical strata. Regard for seniority is the logical corollary of the principal of genealogical sequence.

The system of sex segregation, in the opinion of the co-authors, is explicable in Hawaiian life in terms (a) of the segregation of males when engaged in the essentially masculine activities of livelihood and labour, namely, fishing, planting, canoe- and house-building, and fighting; and (b) of the segregation of females due to the actual and imagined offensiveness to men and gods of their uncleanness in menstruation and parturition.

Marriage (ho'ao), adoption (ho'okama) and fostering (hanai) introduce three secondary categories of relationship whose basis is social rather than biological.

Apart from the words for brother and sister, which serve as terms of address, all the Hawaiian relationship terms are purely descriptive. A Hawaiian spoke to his sister as "Sister" but did not address his male parent as "Father." Commonly, relatives, whatever their relationship, addressed each other by name. Today "Mama" and "Papa" are commonly used as in English, and children address a beloved grandparent or elder of either sex as *tutu* or *kuku*, a contraction of the word *kupuna*.

In union of common folk, which was termed *noho pu* ("just settling in"), the boy would ask permission of his grandparents or parents (whoever had reared him), who would then go and consult the girl's grandparents or parents and ask their permission for their boy to marry their girl. Or the reverse might be true, the girl's "folks" going to the boy's "folks." Then there was a period of probation when the boy had to bring taro, fish, etc., to show that he was a provider. If acceptable, the boy or man went then to live with the girl's folks: never the girl to her husband's.

Maikai ka hanai kaikamahine he noho mai, he hanai makua honowai ke keiki kane.

"It is good to have a daughter to feed who continues to dwell with the parents: a feeder of the parents-in-law is the son."

On the girl's side, the mother had for each child made a dowry of *kapa* (bark cloth): these remained with the girl. The boy would bring his *kapa* with him. Since *kapa* making has lapsed, quilted bedspreads (*kapa lau*) have been made for the same purpose and serve the same function.

GRANDPARENTS AND GRANDCHILDREN.

The term *kupuna* signifies grandparents and all relatives of the grandparent's generation; and is also the term for known forbears and related folk who have died, or distant forbears in genealogy or legend. It is a contraction of "*kupu ana*" meaning "process of growing" (*kupu,* to grow; *ana,* present-participial suffix).

A grandparent is called a *kupuna;* a great-grandparent is a *kupuna kua-lua* or two generations back from the parents; a great-great-grandparent is a *kupuna kua-kolu* or three generations back; a great-great-great-grandparent is a *kupuna kua ha* or four generations back, and so on.

Kupuna hanauna (contraction of *hanau ana*) signifies all cousins belonging to the grandparent's generation. *Makua hanauna* are all cousins belonging to the parent's generation.

The correct term of address for a grandparent is *kupuna,* a dignified term. *Tutu* or *kuku* is commonly used as a term of address today, but the term is equivalent of "Granny" in English, and has not the dignity that *kupuna* has. (Since neither *tutu* or *kuku* appears in the dictionaries, we assume that these terms are relatively recent innovations.)

Hulu kupuna is a term for one of the few remaining of the living blood relatives of the grandparent's generation. They are as precious, as dearly loved as the choice feathers (*hulu,* a term of dignity and beauty) woven into a feather cape. *Hulu makua* is the precious elder of the parent's generation. (*Lei,* wreath, is the term for the precious person of the same generation or one younger: one whom one would embrace with the arms, like a *lei*).

Mo'opuna is grandchild; *mo'opuna kua-lua,* great-grandchild; *mo'opuna kua-kolu,* great-great grandchild; and so on down. Grand-nieces and grand-nephews are *mo'opuna* equally with grand-daughters and grandsons; and the word is used inclusively by elders for all children two generations or more below who are related by blood to the speaker.

Mo'opuna hanauna distinguished the grandchild of my brother or cousin from my own biological grandchild (*mo'opuna*). *Mo'o* is a general term used in referring to lineage. *No ka mo'o kahuna* means of the line of priests, while *mo'o-ku'auhau* means genealogy. *Mo'opuna* meaning grandchild is doubtless connected with this wider meaning of the word *mo'o.* Sometimes a grandparent may say of a grandchild merely: "*Ku'u mo'o keia*"—"This is my descendant."

The first child of any union was *mua,* the term which generically refers to the prow of the canoe or anything "ahead" or "in front." Those after the *mua* were *hanau muli,* those "born after." *Muli* is the stern of a canoe or the thing coming after in place or time.

Poki'i is a general term applied to younger brothers, sisters, cousins, individually or collectively. It is used as a diminutive when addressing small children affectionately. In particular it means the youngest member of a family (*ka hanau muli loa*—"The one born farthest behind") or the younger of two children of the same sex. *Poki'i kaikaina,* applied to a younger brother or sister, is also a term of endearment. In the chants that recite the legend of Pele, Hi'iaka, the youngest and most beloved sister of the goddess, is lovingly referred to as Pele's *poki'i.* And Kamehameha figuratively called his men affectionately "younger brothers" when he exhorted his warriors, "*I mua e na poki'i a inu 'i ka wai 'awa'awa*"—"Forward my brethren. Let us drink the bitter waters (of death)!" Although the first-born is actually the *haku* or head of a family, a beloved *poki'i* may be playfully called *haku* because the elders like to carry the little one around on their shoulders, which ceremonially was an honour accorded to the first-born. *Hapu'u,* a word meaning "to abound," is often used in referring to a small child. *Eia a'e ku'u hapu'u* —"Here comes my child," figuratively implying "Here is the token of my fertility."

Punahele—spring or source (*puna*) that goes on (*hele*) —is a term meaning favourite or precious child, one chosen by a *kupuna* for strict rearing and special training in traditional arts and lore.

Any beloved child may be referred to as *ku'u lei* (my wreath) ; or by an older brother or sister as *ku'u lei poki'i* (little wreath).

In families of rank the special word applied to the first-born reflects the southern derivation of the Hawaiian *Ali'i.* *Hiapo* in the Marquesas and Tahiti refers to the bark cloth made from the banyan tree, with which the loins of the first-born child of rank were girt.

Makahiapo, generally shortened to *hiapo* in current usage, was applied to the first-born in Hawai'i, whether male or female. Although the banyan tree was not found in Hawai'i, *keiki hiapo* nevertheless continued to signify first-born son, and *kaikamahine hiapo* first-born daughter. This word designates status in the lineage, but also has the implication of a relationship term when used in such a phrase as *ku'u hiapo,* meaning my first-born, or *ko makou hiapo,* meaning the first-born of our family. The male *keiki hiapo* was expected to be the head, or *haku,* of his family. In the case of a ruling *Ali'i,* he was addressed in person by kinsmen as *ku'u haku kaikunane,* but only within the family circle, lest it seem boastful.

When a mother died in bearing the *hiapo,* it was said, " *I pa'a i ka hiapo 'a'ole e puka mai na poki'i.*" (The *hiapo* closed [the womb], no younger children could come forth.)

Descendants in general are referred to as " seedlings " or *pulapula.* " *I ka'u po'e pulapula aku* " means " Unto my descendants."

Pua and *mamo* are poetic terms of dignity which the people used in speaking of the descendants of chiefs. *Pua* means a flower, and the spawn of fish, while *mamo* is the name of the little black and yellow bird (*Drepanis pacifica*) whose brilliant yellow plumage adorned the mantles worn as symbols of prestige by ranking chiefs. *Pua ali'i* and *mamo ali'i* thus mean descendants of chiefs. The expression " *O kana mau pua ia* " means " Those are his descendants "; or " *Na mamo kela a Kua* " means " Those are Kua's descendants."

Ewe, a word which really means " family characteristic," is also personified to mean descendant, in the sense that (embodied in a child) it represents a family type. *Ewe* also means, besides family characteristic, the birthplace of one's people. *Welo* is another term for a pronounced family trait, seen widely in a certain family today whose members are noted for their patience; or *welo* may mean " generation after generation " (as, *he welo mai na kupuna mai*—" a trait inherited from the ancestors ").

Pili ma na kupuna (" adhering-by-way-of-forbears ") means " related through ancestors "; that is, a more distant relationship which belonged to the grandparents' generation or before.

BLOOD TIE.

Pili koko means the blood (*koko*) tie (*pili*), or adhering because of blood relationship. Other phrases meaning the same thing are: *wehena 'ole* (cannot be untied or unwrapped), *'i'o pono'i* (own flesh) and *pilikana* (closely related).

Another way of expressing it is, *He iwi, he 'i'o, he koko*, or " Bone, flesh, blood," like the Biblical " bone of my bone and flesh of my flesh."

No kahi ka malo, na kahi e hume, or " The loin cloth of one can be worn by the other," is another expression referring to relationship, that is, they are so closely related that one could wear the other's loin cloth.

Even among relatives there is a " skin kapu " (*kapu 'ili*) which forbids the wearing of each other's clothing unless the relationship is very close. *'A'ohe i like ka 'ili*, or " the skin is not the same," is said of a relationship that does not allow the wearing of each other's clothing. In explaining near kinship a *kupuna* would say, *Nou ka malo, nana e hume; nona ka malo, nau e hume*, or " Your *malo* he can wear; his *malo* you can wear." Even so, one does not wear the other's clothes unless they were given to him or when circumstances make it absolutely necessary, but the saying is accepted as meaning blood kin.

The *Ali'i nui* (High Chief) of a Moku (island or district) or the *Moi* (Sovereign, Supreme Chief) was so *kapu* that under no circumstances could his clothing be worn by any except himself and not even his closest relative could eat his left-over food.

Some women of *ali'i* blood were so *kapu* that they could not rear children, not even their own. Such women were said to have *'uha kapu* or *kapu* laps. Should they attempt to rear children, the children either died or became crippled. This was a personal idiosyncracy, not a consequence of exalted breeding or rules of chiefly *kapu*. There is a case of a woman from Maui who was unable to rear children. Only the three daughters that she gave away to relatives lived to grow up. Another instance is told of a neighbour who was warned by an elder relative that she would never be able to rear sons as she was *kapu* to male children. Her devoted efforts to raise her sons were all in vain: they died in infancy. Then, to save the life of her youngest son, she gave him away to a relative at birth. He is now a healthy young man, married, with children. Had she kept him, it is said, he would have died. This is not *'uha kapu*. There is no special term for this peculiar condition. Inability to rear children is not uncommon among the Hawaiians: the *'uha kapu* is accepted as a matter of course. The explanation given for this is as follows: The woman who is *'uha kapu* is precious to an *'aumakua* (guardian spirit). The *'aumakua* does not want the person who is precious (a matter of affection) to be soiled by urine and faeces of an infant. Consequently the *'aumakua* depletes the woman's children's life force and they die. The only way to save them is to give them away to relatives to rear. In the case of the woman who could not raise sons, this was an instance of a male *'aumakua* who was jealous, as a husband may be jealous of sons. Another case of the *'uha kapu* was that of the chiefs whose persons were considered sacred. Should a child accidentally wet a chief, that child was killed or automatically became his foster-child. Children were usually kept away from an *Ali'i*, unless the chief himself wished to see them and insisted on holding them, in which case the parents were not held responsible for the accidental wetting that made the child the property of the chief. This did not apply to the children of the commoners, only to those of his personal attendants who were usually of chiefly blood. Only those of chiefly blood and of the same lineage ever came close enough to the chief to attend to his personal needs.

When a serious disagreement arose to disrupt the family relationship, it was called *moku ka piko* or *mo ka piko* ("the umbilical cord is cut"), to indicate the ruptured relationship. Relatives did not declare the "umbilical cut" unless the offense was a very serious one, such as assisting a sorcerer to destroy a member of the other's family, cruelty to or heartless neglect of the child or parent of the other, or other offences of similar nature. If one had offended the other beyond his endurance, he would say, "*Ua mo ka piko*," meaning that love was cut off between them. All privileges and obligations of relationship ceased, and there was no more mutual help nor voluntary assistance in time of need. The offender was ostracized. The only way to reinstate himself was to go to an older and trusted relative, preferably a *kahuna*, with a gift of a pig. The two together would then go with the pig to the offended party to ask his pardon and that of the family ancestral guardians ('*aumakua*). This going before an offended relative with a pig is called *me ka ihu o ka pua'a* or " with the nose of the pig." The relative could not refuse to forgive him then, lest the family '*aumakua huli kua*, or " turn their backs " on him for being unforgiving. The pig was killed and eaten by both parties. The *kahuna*, by means of releasing prayers (*pule kala*) recited over the pig before it was killed, asked the '*aumakua* to forgive the offender for the evil he had done to a blood kinsman. The feast was naturally an occasion for rejoicing and merriment and the night was spent together under one roof. If the offender took very sick as a result of his sin (*hala*), due to holding fast to his grudge (*ho'omau hala*) and was unable to go of his own accord but was willing to forgive (*kala*, to untie, unbind and let go), then members of his household prepared a feast and sent a messenger to bring the offended party. The messenger was always the *kahuna* who had seen that the illness arose out of sin against a kinsman; or the *kahuna* would send a message. If the offended relative was *pono* (upright, in good order), he accompanied the messenger to his relative's house and there would forgive him, but if he was obstinate *pa'akiki*, hard), or an evil person (*kanaka 'ino*), and continued to bear malice (*ho'omau hala*), he would refuse and let his offending relative die. He was under no obligation to go to his relative's house, for it was he who had been insulted. If the relative came to him, then, unless he dared the displeasure of his '*aumakua*, he must forgive and become his blood brother again.

In case of people for whom pork was *kapu*, the fish called *pua'a kai* or " sea hogs," such as the '*ama'ama* (mullet) or the *kumu* (red " goat fish "), served as a substitute offering.

If a relative disregarded the " *mo ka piko* " and did not go to ask pardon of his relative, he carried the consequence on his own head. If he did go, it was not enough to say, " Brother, I have done wrong to you; please forgive me," but he had to offer the prescribed sacrifice to him and to their mutual '*aumakua*.

When a man (or woman) had hurt his relative beyond endurance no forgiveness took place and neither the relative nor any of his household went near his dead body when he died nor contributed to the food supply of the mourners according to the usual custom.

Among the relatives of an informant were a brother and sister who had a falling-out. It was believed that he was jealous of his sister's favourite daughter and obtained the services of a sorcerer to cause her death. As a sorcerer or his employer never went to see or mourn the victim lest the malicious influence (*mana'o 'ino*, evil thought) sent out fasten itself upon them (the senders), the evidence of complicity and malpractice was strengthened by the absence of the brother at the funeral of his niece. The sister declared a "*Mo ka piko*" and for years she would have nothing to do with her brother. When he died, all of the other relatives came to the funeral, but not his sister; nor did any of her children or grandchildren. The *mo ka piko* applied only to the guilty person and not to his descendants, but the children of the offended party did not go to the house of the offender until a year or more after his death. After that, the remaining relatives resumed the old relationship. *Ho'i hou i ka iwi kuamo'o* ("to return to the backbone") or *ho'i hou i ka mole* ("to return to the taproot") are the two Hawaiian figures of speech descriptive of a return of loyalty to kith and kin.

Here is another instance of *mo ka piko*, in an *Ali'i* lineage. When Ke-kua-o-ka-lani (Liholiho's first cousin, the son of Kamehameha's sister) rebelled and refused to give up the old order of *kapu* between the sexes after the establishing of the *'Ai-noa* (Eating-in-common), when Liholiho (Kamehameha's son and heir, as *Moi*, or "Sovereign") did away with the *kapu* by eating publicly with the women, Ke-'opu-o-lani (Liholiho's mother) tried to mend the breach between the two cousins, Liholiho and Ke-kua-o-ka-lani. Failing in that, she said "*Mo ka piko la, e na hoa hanau*" ("Severed are the umbilical cords, O cousins"). She knew then that strife was inevitable.

HUSBAND AND WIFE.

Husband and wife are designated simply by the words *kane* and *wahine*, meaning male and female. The husband or wife of an intimate friend may be referred to as *kane* or *wahine*, but this usage is a matter of familiar and friendly reference, not a designation of relationship. The term *kane* is applied by a woman to the husband of a sister or cousin and the term *wahine* is applied by a man to the wife of his brother or cousin. These are terms of courtesy to designate the affinal relationship.

As in the case of the word for parent, the term *makua* for elder or *'opio* for younger is appended to indicate whether a person referred to is husband (or wife) of an older or younger brother (or sister). *Kane ho'omoe* is husband who had been acquired by the procedure of "matchmaking" (*ho'omoe*), when an intermediary arranged for the marriage. *Wahine ho'omoe*, wife acquired by "matchmaking."

Kane ho'ao and *wahine ho'ao* are terms used to distinguish the husband and wife who have been united by ceremonial marriage (*ho'ao*), according to old Hawaiian custom.

Kane ho'opalau or *wahine ho'opalau* was in olden times applied to the boy and girl formally betrothed, later to be joined by the ceremony of *ho'ao*.

The Andrews-Parker Dictionary gives as a meaning for the word *kama*: " Name given by women to former husbands by whom they had borne children." This is a shortening of *hanau kama* (*hanau*, birth; *kama*, child), referring to the husband who fathered a woman's children.

PATERNITY.

There has been some discussion in ethnological literature as to whether certain Melanesians know that conception is directly caused in a woman by male insemination. The question has been asked, " How can you prove that the pre-missionary Hawaiians had more than a vague notion of the role of the father?"

That the Hawaiians comprehended the fertilizing function of the male in coition is proven by the practice, termed *ho'omau keiki* (to fix or insure offspring), that in Hawai'i was the means by which high chiefs sought to perpetuate their lines and increase rank by lineage, marrying a high chiefess to her brother or cousin. The fragmentary account of this that is given by David Malo (*Hawaiian Antiquities*, pp. 179-80) is significant not only because it proves understanding of the principle of paternity and that of preserving purity of " blood " strains, but because it indicates a rational conception of the relationship of the menstrual flow to time of fertility, and also because it has bearing on the bilateral concept of succession.

Malo's description of the ceremony of *ho'omau keiki* is as follows:

> " In the case of high chiefs the affair was conducted as follows: A high chief of the opposite sex was sought out and, after betrothal, the two young people were at first placed (*ho'onoho*) under keepers in separate establishments, preparatory to pairing for offspring, the purpose being to make the offspring of the highest possible rank . . .
> " When the princess had recovered from her infirmity and had purified herself in the bath, she was escorted to the tent made of tapa which had been set up in an open place in the sight of all the people . . .
> " When the princess has returned from her bath, the prince goes in unto her and remains in her company perhaps until evening, by which time the ceremony called *ho'omau keiki* is completed. Then the prince takes his leave, the princess returns home, the people disperse, the *kahunas* depart, the chiefs retire and the tent is taken down. This ceremony is enacted only in the case of the very highest chiefs, never those of inferior rank.
> " If after this it is found that the princess is with child, there is great rejoicing among all the people that a chief of rank has been begotten. If the two parents are of the same family, the offspring will be of the highest possible rank."

In a footnote, Dr. Emerson says that when the union was fruitful neither the mother nor the father involved in the *ho'omau keiki* was permitted to have further sexual intercourse until after the child had been born and the mother had been purified.

Further evidence of the understanding on the part of Hawaiians of the principle of physical paternity lies in the term *ku'u luau'i makua kane*—" my father who begot me." The truth is, the whole system of preserving genealogies in which father is named with mother stands in evidence of ancient recognition of paternity—or else the whole theory of genealogy, so tenaciously adhered to by Polynesians, must be declared a fiction, which would be ridiculous.

Myth and legend are replete with evidence of the knowledge of physical paternity. The point is elaborated here, because it has direct bearing on Lewis H. Morgan's fiction of primordial group marriage as the source and origin of the Polynesian and Hawaiian "classificatory" system of relationship, which is discussed later in this section.

Another clear evidence of Hawaiian conception of paternity lies in an interesting custom known as *hua-'e* (" a-different-seed "). This well-known though relatively rare practice, resorted to in order to obtain living offspring, known as *hua-'e,* may best be explained by recounting an instance. A certain woman on Hawai'i was married, and had borne four children, all of whom came stillborn. The husband consulted her grandfather who was a famous *kahuna* and was told by him that his wife would bear him no living children until she had been given a *hua-'e* by another man. The husband then consulted his own mother, who was very desirous of having grandchildren, and together they concocted a plan to bring about the desired event. There was a certain man living in that region who was notorious for seizing any woman who took his fancy. The husband, on one pretext or another, several times sent this man to his house when his wife was alone, and the desired episode occurred without the woman's wishing it, for she was ignorant of the plan. She told her husband, in fact, what was happening to her and he pretended to tell the man to keep away. In due course she bore a son, from the *hua-'e,* and the child lived. That was the end of her relationship to the other man, but thereafter she bore her true husband two children, both of whom lived, exactly as the *kahuna* had predicted.

Po'o lua (po'o, head; *lua,* two) refers to " double parenthood," believed to occur amongst *ali'i.* Kamehameha I considered himself to have been sired by both Keoua-kupu-a-pa-i-ka-lani-nui (brother of Kalani-opu'u, *Ali'i Nui* of the Moku of Kona and Kohala) and the famous warrior and High Chief of the island of Maui, named Kahekili. He acknowledged both as father. This again, whatever biological science may say of it, is a concept clearly proving knowledge in old Hawai'i of the biological role of the male as inseminator.

ADOPTIVE PLATONIC MARITAL RELATIONSHIP.

Closely related to the *ho'okama* relationship of parent to adopted child is that which establishes an adoptive platonic marital relationship between persons of opposite sex. A boy or man may take a great fancy to a girl or woman, married or unmarried. He tells her or his parents that he wants her as his "adoptive wife" or *wahine ho'owahine*. This does not imply having the sexual husband-wife relationship, but a sort of brother-sister relationship. If the proposal is acceptable, the parents or relatives of the person who first broach the plan make a feast, roasting a small pig. This is called *make ka pua'a* or "killing of the pig," to cement the relationship.

The boy or man is called *kane ho'okane* and the girl or woman *wahine ho'owahine*. Sometimes a girl suggests that a certain man or boy become her *kane ho'okane*. The *kane ho'okane* and *wahine ho'owahine* treat each other with great respect and affection.

Here is an example of such an incident. Hoeawa of Puna became the *kane ho'okane* of a prominent Hilo-pali-ku woman named Hela. Both were married. Hoeawa and Hela were as good to each other as brother and sister. Hoeawa's niece used to go to Hela's with her cousin, Hoeawa's daughter, and both were treated like own nieces. Hela died many years before Hoeawa. She used to give him gifts to take home, and his wife used to make fine mats for him to take to his *wahine ho'owahine*. Such *wahine ho'owahine* and *kane ho'okane* never made love to each other.

Sometimes the "*wahine*" may be but a child of six or seven while the "*kane*" is an adult farmer or fisherman; or the "*kane*" may be just a little lad while his "*wahine*" is a mature housewife.

This story, told by an informant and friend, is a case in point: "I've always liked fishing and dancing and have learned to plait mats, sew, keep house and to plant. I did not know that someone was watching me until a man came to my father's house with his daughter. As soon as I got home with some fish that I had caught that morning, I was called in by my father who told me that I was wanted to be the girl's husband. I looked at her. I had not seen her before. She was well built, homely, but had a sweet disposition. Still I did not want to marry her and leave my father alone. I said, 'I am poor and unable to buy shoes for myself. How could I support a lovely wife like this maiden? Let her be my *wahine ho'owahine* instead.' The father was satisfied and I think the girl was glad, too. For

years we were the best of friends, this girl and I. I caught
fish for her and carried her gifts whenever I could and she
always treated me like her own brother until she died twenty
years ago. Her husband was a good man."

PLURAL MATING.

Punalua is a term of reference and appellation which
cannot be simply translated into English because it is
applied to what for English-speaking people are various
categories of relationship or no relationship. In other
words, it embodies a cultural concept lacking in the social
and personal relationship of English-speaking peoples.

Punalua is a relationship between first and secondary
mates, not a word descriptive of a type of family relationship.

In Hawaiian custom in pre-missionary times it was
permissible for a man to have several wives or for a woman
to have multiple husbands. In such circumstances the two
women or the two men were to each other *punalua*. The
punalua had joint responsibility for the children in the
family.

Persisting in modern usage, when two men are married to sisters (or cousins), the men are *punalua* to each
other. This is also true of two women who are married to
brothers (or cousins).

The younger sister of a man's wife is conventionally
called *wahine ʻopio* or " younger wife " and the older sister
wahine makua or " older wife." These were merely terms of
relationship. These terms are also applied to his female
cousins-in-law, the *makua* or *ʻopio* term depending on
whether they were descended from the older or younger
branch in the family genealogy.

The younger brother (or male cousin) of a woman's
husband is her *kane ʻopio* or " younger husband " and the
older brother or cousin is her *kane makua* or " older husband." These terms carry no implication of plural marriage
relationship.

The fundamental applications of *punalua* extended to
less tangible relationships, which are best explained by concrete examples. Before he was married, Kai had a sweet-
heart named Lana, who bore him a son. Lana later married
another man. Kai subsequently married Mele who bore him

a daughter. Mele (his wife) and Lana (his old sweet-heart) are therefore *punalua*. Mele out of courtesy ought to—and in this instance does—accept Lana's son by Kai as she would a son, addressing him as "son." Equally Lana should regard Mele's daughter as she would her own. In this particular case, Mele had an old Hawaiian upbringing in accordance with a code which regarded jealousy of a *punalua* as disgraceful. She was always courteous and kind to Lana and her son. Lana, pleased with her *punalua*, told her mother about her. Some years later, Mele went to the village where Lana's mother lived and when the old lady heard that her daughter's *punalua* was there, she came to seek her and to extend her hospitality. Mele was always addressed by the old lady as daughter (*kaikamahine*); any reference to her grandson was always as "the son of you two" (*ke keiki a 'olua*) and to Mele's daughter as "the daughter of you two" (*ke kaikamahine a 'olua*). Unfortunately, in these modern times of deculturation and social dissolution, spite and jealousy are frequently rampant in similar relationships.

A further extension is the following: Hana (female) and Kimo (male) establish the "platonic" relationship of *wahine ho'owahine* and *kane ho'okane*. There is no sexual relationship between these two: it is a lasting deep friendship only, in English parlance. Hana's husband Luna accepts Kimo as his *punalua* and the two men will be like brothers. Kimo will treat the children of Hana by Luna as kindly as he would his own.

It seems, then, that the true purpose of *punalua* as an institutionalized principle of relationship defined by a special term was the safeguarding of children arising out of or involved in a triangular relationship of two men to a woman or two women to a man. It marks, in other words, a recognition of the social and psychological consequences of the frictions characteristic of the "eternal triangle."

That spite now characterizes such relationship in Hawai'i as elsewhere is proven by the current modern expression "She treats me like a *punalua*," said by a woman of another who feels toward her *lili punalua* or "*punalua* jealousy." Nevertheless, though Hawaiians were prone enough to personal jealousy where love of one man by two women was involved, it was considered bad manners

(*maikai ole*, " not good ") for a *punalua* to hold spite or
malice in their hearts towards each other. The very existence of the formal relationship, its recognition and responsibilities (which have been abolished under the introduced
American-Christian code of ethics and relationship) worked
against ill-feeling, whereas this now is usual when *punalua*
relationship is either neglected or said to imply something
shameful. A nephew may say of an uncle, " *He lili punalua
kona*," meaning " He is as jealous as a punalua "; which
usage would seem to imply both that jealousy is typical
(even though disgraceful) and that it is regarded as
unwarranted.

Anciently, in the case of a family in which a man had
two wives who were unrelated (i.e., are not elder or younger
sisters or cousins), the children of the same sex born to
both the women and fathered by the mutual husband were
kaikua'ana and *kaikaina* according to precedence in birth,
and the first-born was the man's *hiapo*, while the first-born
respectively of each of the two wives was to each her *hiapo*
in relation to herself and her relatives. Obviously, the child
of the woman who gave him his *hiapo*, being *hiapo* to both
in common, would outrank the first child borne by the other
woman: therefore this woman had superior prestige. This
would compensate her, perhaps, in those cases where a man
took a second wife because he was fonder of her than of
his first wife. It would also put into secondary position a
sterile first wife who consented to her hubsand's taking a
second for the sake of offspring.

Keopuolani and Ka'ahumanu were *punalua*, both being
the wives of Kamehameha. Ka'ahumanu was a good mother
to Keopuolani's children, Liholiho (Kamehameha II),
Kauikeaouli (Kamehameha III) and Nahienaena. *Ali'i*
women quite commonly had *punalua*. Of course, in the
matter of succession and prestige, the *hiapo* of the betrothed
(*ho'opalau*) and formally married (*ho'ao*) mate took precedence: unless the unlikely event transpired whereby the
punalua of an *ali'i* taken after the *ho'oa* should outrank the
first mate. Under such circumstances the *hiapo* of the
second would outrank the *hiapo* of the first, for genealogical
precedence and not the *ho'ao*, or priority in marriage or
birth, prevailed.

Punalua relationships also commonly occurred amongst

simple fishing or farming folk living in isolated localities, as a matter of convenience and in consequence of natural circumstances. They still occur occasionally, despite modern condemnation.

The following are examples from personal experience related by a friend: " When I was in boarding school, there was among my school-mates a Kauai girl. A woman used to come to see her very frequently. I thought she was her mother or aunt because she was so good to the girl. When I asked the girl, she told me that it was her father's first wife. She herself was the daughter of the second wife."

" Among my friends are two women who were *punalua*. The first wife has a son and the second has two sons and two daughters. When one was ill the other nursed her. The children of one were to each other like those of the other. The first wife died a few years ago, after the death of their husband."

" One of my cousins went to another district in his youth, married and had a daughter by his Gilbertese wife. This girl was *hiapo* to both. Later they separated and he took another wife from Puna, a Hawaiian. The eldest daughter moved to Honolulu with her mother and there she married. My cousin's wives often visited each other during vacations and the younger brothers and sisters always looked up to the eldest as the *hiapo* of their family."

In actual practice, then, and to recapitulate: *Punalua* is a relationship between two wives of a man or two husbands of a woman; the husbands of two sisters are by courtesy called *punalua*; similarly, the wives of two brothers or the husbands or wives of cousins.

There are of course plenty of instances of jealous, vicious *punalua*. Tales are told of cases in which one got rid of the other through sorcery or actual murder arising out of *lili punalua*. In speaking of a violent hatred a Hawaiian may say, *He punalua 'ino au iaia*, or " I am hated by her (as if I were a) *punalua*." A man may hate his own sister with a bitter hatred, in which case that sister is figuratively referred to as "*punalua 'ino*."

Illegitimate children today are called *po'o-'ole* (headless) or *manuahi* (free) because of the lack of a male parent, but in the pre-missionary days such terms were unknown. When a man had a passing affair with a woman, those involved did not bother to consider each other as *punalua*. It was only when cared for sufficiently to be taken as one of his wives that the women looked upon each other as *punalua*. True *punalua* received each other as sisters and accorded each other the same treatment as one would a relative.

Here it seems that we must make an exception to our policy of keeping this study of Hawaiian relationship strictly within the bounds of our own research in the field.

Critique of Morgan's Interpretation.

Lewis H. Morgan in his *Systems of Consanguinity and Affinity* and his classical work *Ancient Society*[7] misinterpreted the term *punalua*. We feel we should correct this error. Morgan, having misunderstood the word, proceeded to employ it as a term for an hypothetical primordial and universal form of Polynesian marriage. Then he universalized and compounded his error by naming stage 2, in a supposed sequence of marriage forms in human history, "the Punaluan." The "successive stages of development" of the family have been (*Ancient Society*, p. 384): 1. The Consanguine Family; 2. The Punaluan; 3. The Syndyasmian or Pairing Family; 4. The Patriarchal Family; and 5. The Monogamian Family. To quote his description of type 2:

The Punaluan Family.

[A.] It was founded upon the intermarriage of several sisters, own and collateral, with each other's husbands, in a group; the joint husbands not being necessarily kinsmen of each other. Also, on the intermarriage of several brothers, own and collateral, with each other's wives, in a group, these wives not being necessarily of kin to each other, although often the case in both instances. In each case the group of men were conjointly married to the group of women (p. 384).

The most primitive system of consanguinity yet discovered is found among the Polynesians, of which the Hawaiian will be used as typical. I have called it the Malayan system. Under it all consanguinei, near and remote, fall within some one of the following relationships: namely, parent, child, grandparent, grandchild, brother, and sister. No other blood relationships are recognized. Beside these are the marriage relationships. This system of consanguinity came in with the first form of the family, the consanguine, and contains the principal evidence of its ancient existence. It may seem a narrow basis for so important an inference: but if we are justified in assuming that each relationship as recognized was the one which actually existed, the inference is fully sustained. This system prevailed very generally in Polynesia, although the family among them had passed out of the consanguine into the punaluan. It remained unchanged because no motive sufficiently radical had occurred to produce its modification. Intermarriage between brothers and sisters had not entirely disappeared from the Sandwich Islands when the American missions, about fifty years ago, were established among them (p. 385).

Under the Malayan system a man calls his brother's son his son, because his brother's wife is his wife as well as his brother's and his sister's son is also his son because his sister is his wife (p. 391).

Among the Hawaiians and other Polynesian tribes there still exists [1907] in daily use a system of consanguinity which is given in the table, and may be pronounced the oldest known among mankind (p. 403).

The simple and distinctive character of the system will arrest attention, pointing with such directness, as it does, to the intermarriage of brothers and sisters, own and collateral, in a group, as the source from whence it sprung (p. 407).

At the time the American missions were established upon these islands (1820), a state of society was found which appalled the missionaries. The relations of the sexes and their marriage customs excited their chief astonishment . . . they found the punaluan family, with own brothers and sisters not entirely excluded, in which the males were living in polygamy, and the females in polyandry (p. 414).

In Morgan's table (pp. 419-22), entitled " System of Relationship of the Hawaiians and Rotumans," we find this humble word *punalua* translated " intimate companion " and included as a term of relationship meaning " wife's sister's husband " and " husband's brother's wife." With little knowledge of Hawaiian marital customs, he extracted it from the context of the culture, in which it is a secondary, not to say insignificant, linguistic item, and, having extracted it, elevated it first as a name for presumed but probably never existing principle of consanguinous-collective, or communal-family, sex relations in Polynesia as a whole. In this exhilarating flight of fancy, by utilizing our humble Hawaiian word *punalua* as his boot strap, he infers the applicability of his neat rationalization to all " Malayans," thence to all Oceanians, and ends by dignifying and making it immortal, in the academic cosmos—a service for which Hawaiians should doubtless be grateful!—as the embodyment of a " universal " stage 2 in his evolutionary series through which the human family is supposed to have passed.

Such are the consequences of intellectual fantasy and intoxication induced by conjuring with words extracted from their cultural context without pinning the term to concrete meanings in relation to actual use and practice.

Morgan is not wholly to blame for the original sin of inference. In fact he shows repeatedly in remarks *en passant* that he assumes the Hawaiians to be a more moral people in their actual living than some of the early missionaries considered them to be. Morgan's references with respect to the sources of his information about *punalua* places the responsibility for the inferential error at first on his information. But Morgan might have been shrewd enough not to accept what was patently inferential rather than evidential. Since he capitalized the error and compounded it, with him we must rest the sentence of irresponsibility.

The original responsibility for the inference as to the significance of *punalua*, it seems, lay with Lorrin Andrews, the compiler of the Hawaiian Dictionary, whose authoritative knowledge of Hawaiian language is not to be questioned, but who was certainly indulging in a reckless and inaccurate generalization and inference in the following statement, quoted by Morgan (p. 427) in giving his authority for his own assumptions:

> In 1860 Judge Lorrin Andrews, of Honolulu, in a letter accompanying a schedule of the Hawaiian system of consanguinity, commented upon one of the Hawaiian terms of relationship as follows: " The relationship of *punalua* is rather amphibious [sic]: It arose from the fact that two or more brothers with their wives, or two or more sisters with their husbands, were inclined to possess each other in common; but the modern use of the word is that of *dear friend*, or *intimate companion*."

Note that Andrews says the brothers or sisters in question " were inclined " to possess each other in common. He by no means commits himself to the statement that such a consanguinal group marital relationship was the rule, was common, or was even approved. But Morgan has no hesitation in imparting this meaning to Andrews' rather vague generalization. Writes Morgan (p. 427) :

> [B.] That which Judge Andrews says they were inclined to do, and which may have been a declining practice, their system of consanguinity proves to have been once universal among them.

Actually, Morgan's reasoning contains its own refutation: the joint consanguinous family is assumed to have arisen out of group marriage (A.); group marriage is inferred from the vague statements about *punalua* in Hawai'i (B.); and *punalua* is proven to have been once universal by the (inferred) existence of consanguinous joint families in old Polynesia. Assumption (A.) is proven by assumption (B.), and assumption (B.) is triumphantly declared to be proved because of the declared existence of assumption (A.).

Evidently Morgan's conscience was uneasy, for, in addition to quoting Andrews' remarks to justify his assumptions with respect to the implication of *punalua*, he substantiates his ground by several other wholly vague generalizations quoted from other writers on Hawai'i. The Reverend Artemus Bishop is quoted as writing (p. 427): " This confusion of relationship is the result of the ancient custom among relatives of the living together of husbands and wives in common." An *Historical Sketch of the Missions, etc., in the Sandwich Islands,* by Bartlett, is quoted (p. 428) as reporting that " Husbands had many wives and wives many husbands, and exchanged with each other with pleasure." We suspect that the source of this vague statement in the *Historical Sketch* is Rev. Hiram Bingham's *Sandwich Islands,* in which that pioneer missionary wrote (as quoted by Morgan) that polygamy " implied a plurality of husbands and wives." Referring to this, Morgan writes (p. 428), " the same fact is reiterated by Dr. Bartlett " (whose source was probably Bingham). Finally, let us examine Morgan's own reference to Bingham, whom he quotes as follows (p. 428):

> " The union of brother and sister in the highest ranks became fashionable, and continued until the revealed will of God was made known to them."

Now it will be perfectly plain to everyone acquainted with Hawaiian custom that here Bingham is speaking of the practice of inbreeding to the degree of brother-sister marriage peculiar to ranking families in Hawai'i, limited in Hawai'i to rare occasions of purposeful and conscious inbreeding for scions of supreme rank and in no way a general custom of the Hawaiian people. It exists in Polynesia, so far as we know. nowhere else, even among chiefs.

This quotation, then, which Morgan takes as authority for his generalization with respect to a " universal " custom of brother-sister marriage, in itself refutes Morgan's generalization, for Bingham's reference to this practice of " the highest ranks " describes, as Bingham of course knew, a custom *limited to* a few individuals of a small class of nobles in one island group in the Pacific.

It is certain that if in Hawai'i group marriages involving consanguinous relationship of the sort Morgan assumed were typical or even common, early missionary writers like Ellis and early chroniclers inspired by missionaries, like Malo, would at least have mentioned it: almost certainly so striking a phenomenon would have been especially remarked. Yet the early, as well as subsequent literature describing Hawaiian life at first hand, is completely silent on the subject.

The whole system of genealogical precedence conflicts with and disproves Morgan's belief in group marriage involving brothers and sisters, necessarily of different ages unless all were twins or quintuplets. If it were unknown whether a woman's child was fathered by an elder or younger brother, how could the child be classed genealogically as of *kua'ana* or *kaina* derivation? And yet, such classing of every child is universal, absolutely fundamental, and primary, not only in Hawai'i but throughout Polynesia, determining precedence, function, inheritance, etc. This law of genealogical precedence alone suffices to disprove Morgan's assumption.

Apart from the authority vested in the false inferences analysed above, Morgan's assumption rests in last analysis quite simply on the fact that a man calls his wife's sisters *wahine,* while a woman calls her husband's brothers *kane.* But these terms are applied to cousins of opposite sex in the same generation, to a vast array of collateral and affinal relatives. If the term is authority for assumed marital relationship, then Morgan should have assumed sexual communism to be existent throughout each generation. A Polynesian reading Elizabethan literature would be equally justified in presuming that the fact that any man in England might address any woman as " good wife " proved that promiscuity was the rule in " Merrie England "; or that the same is true of American Indian tribes in which all children address all elders as " grandfather."

Considering the matter on psychological grounds, any-one who understands the individual particularity of Poly-nesians in mating, their freedom of choice, and the loyalty to the single mate typical of most Polynesians, all of which are thoroughly attested (or, should one say, projected in retrospect?), for ancient Polynesia in folklore, legend and mythology, will have some difficulty in envisioning the primordial joint consanguinous promiscuous sexual group upon which Morgan erected his pyramid of inferences, and which in 1907 " still exists in daily use among the Hawaiians and other Polynesian tribes."

Now, having thrown out of court Morgan's grandiose generalizations, let us make friends with his ghost and send it on its way cheerfully by admitting that, since *punalua* meant secondary or casual mate in actual marital relation-ships, its application by a man to his wife's sisters' husbands and by a woman to her husband's brothers' wives perhaps implies that formerly sexual rights with these in-laws were countenanced in Hawai'i as they are said to have been in the Marquesas. (See Bishop Museum Bul. 9, p. 67).

BLOOD AND ENGRAFTED RELATIONSHIPS.

Pili koko (*pili*, adhering; *koko*, blood) refers to those closely related by blood. The expression is *Ku'u iwi, ku'u 'i'o, ku'u koko.* " My bones, my flesh, my blood," is an old Hawaiian expression which finds its parallel in the Biblical " Flesh of my flesh and bone of my bone," a text that Hawaiians have learned to love.

Pili kamau (*kamau*, to add on) refers to an " added-on " relationship, when one who was no relative in actuality was accepted as a member of the family in consequence of his attaching himself to the family.

SONS AND DAUGHTERS, NEPHEWS AND NIECES.

The words commonly used signifying son and daughter are respectively *keiki kane* and *kaikamahine*. If it is a question of designating my true son or daughter, the word *pono'i*, meaning true, is added.

Keiki means children in general or offspring in general (and in this latter sense may be applied to adults), but in common parlance *keiki*, used of an individual, means a male

6

child. When a parent says *ku'u keiki*, " my son," he may mean either true, adoptive, or foster son.

Kama (the equivalent of *tama*, the usual term for child and son throughout Polynesia) standing alone is never applied in Hawaiian to children in general or to a son or male child. *Kama kane* means male child or male children in general, but is not applied to individuals. Thus one might reply, if asked a question concerning certain children, that they are *kama kane*, male children; but if asked " Who is that child?" one would not reply: he is " *ku'u kama kane*," my male child, but " *ku'u keiki*," my son. Similarly, *kamali'i* (or less commonly *kamaiki*) means little children in general, but is rarely applied to individuals, though sometimes it is used as a word of endearment.

Kaikamahine is the word for girls in general, but is used to signify daughter. The Andrews-Parker dictionary makes the following comment (p. 243) :

> According to analogy this word for daughters should be keikiwahine, after the analogy of keikikane, but Hawaiians do not use it so.

Kai is a prefix, the same as Maori *tai*. *Kamahine* is Maori *tamahine* (daughter or girls in general). Evidently this is an old word that is widespread and hence there is no need for the derivation *Keikiwahine*.

In the context of family relationship the words for son and daughter will be applied to nephews and nieces throughout the range of blood, adoptive, fostering and in-law connections. *Kaikamahine hanauna* refers specifically to the daughter of a cousin.

An older child was called *mua* (before) and a younger child *muli* (or after) ; the youngest child was called *muli loa*. Sometimes the first-born or *hiapo* was spoken of as *mua loa*. The full descriptive form for indicating senior or junior birth is *hanau mua* or *hanau muli*. *Ko'u mua a'e* means the child born before me, *ko'u muli iho* the child born after me

BROTHERS, SISTERS AND COUSINS.

As between males (or as between females) an elder brother or male cousin (or sister or female cousin) is termed descriptively *kaikua'ana*; a younger, *kaikaina*. These are descriptive relationship terms.

Corresponding to the general rule that relationship terms are descriptive merely, it is only the basic forms of these two words, namely, *kua'ana* and *kaina*, that are used as terms of address between the individuals so related: a boy will refer to his older brother as *kaikua'ana*, but will address him as *kua'ana* (older brother). The younger brother is referred to as *kaikaina* and addressed as *kaina*.

Similarly, a person's first cousin whose related parent is an older brother, sister or cousin of that person is that person's *kaikua'ana*, to be addressed formally as *kua'ana*; and so on, always, in the collateral relationships, referring back to the original genealogical elder or younger relationship where the genealogy converges to a single parent or two parents.

Discrepancies in age between individuals have no relationship to the use of these terms in this connection. For example, Keli'i is over fifty years old, while Pa'a is thirty years old; yet Pa'a is *kaikua'ana* to Keli'i because her grandmother was the older sister of Keli'i's grandfather.

Hanau mua also is applied to all members of the genealogically senior branch of the living family, and their genealogical antecedents.

A girl or woman refers to her brother or male cousin as *kaikunane* and she will address him as *kunane*; while a boy or a man speaks of his sister or female cousin as *kaikuahine* and will address her as *kuahine*.

PARENTS, UNCLES AND AUNTS.

Makua is a general term referring to parents, and to the brothers, sisters and cousins of parents. As a matter of courtesy, the term may also be applied to close friends of the generation of father or mother in the same way that " uncle " or " aunt " occurs in modern usage.

The specific designation for males in the parental generation (i.e., parents, brothers and male cousins) is *makua kane*, and for the parents' sisters and female cousins the term is *makuahine*.

When preceded by the word *luau'i* (*lua*, two; *i'i*, youthful), *makua* means own parents, conveying a sense of young parenthood. Thus: *Ku'u luau'i makua kane* means my true father, and *ku'u luau'i makua'hine* my own mother. *Luau'i* alone, omitting the qualifying terms, means " own parent," either father or mother.

The specific term for " uncles " who are cousins rather than brothers of either father or mother is *makua kane hanauna*, and for " aunts " in the same category *makuahine hanauna*.

When followed by the word *makua* (here meaning elder), the terms *makua kane* and *makuahine* refer respectively to older brothers or sisters (or cousins) of father and mother; and when followed by the word *'opio* (meaning younger) they refer to younger brothers or sisters or cousins of the father or mother. Thus, *ku'u makuahine makua* means my aunt who is the older sister of my father or my mother; and *ku'u makua kane 'opio* means my uncle who is the younger brother of my father or my mother. These terms as used here, *makua* for elder and *'opio* for younger, also designate respectively cousins of my father or mother who belong to genealogically senior or junior lines. For example, a male cousin who is the son of my grandfather's elder brother or sister is referred to by me as *ku'u makua kane makua*.

The term *makua* may also be used figuratively for anyone who takes care of another " like a parent," regardless of actual relationships.

The term for foster parents who have reared a child from infancy (*makua hanai*) and for adoptive parents (*makua ho'okama*) are discussed respectively under *hanai* and *ho'okama* relationships. The terms for parents-in-law are discussed under *hunowai* and *puluna*.

Hulu makua (*hulu*, literally " feathers," figuratively " precious ") signifies one of the last few surviving blood relatives of the *makua* generation.

Inoa makua characterizes a distant relative in the parent's generation, or a relative by marriage in the category termed *puka-a-maka*, described later, when the said relative belongs to the *makua* generation. The brothers, sisters and cousins of my step-father or step-mother are all termed by me *inoa makua* (" parents in name "). This term would also be applied by me to close friends of my parents.

The term for step-parent is *makua kolea* (plover parent). The *kolea* or plover is a migratory bird which comes to Hawai'i in the fall to feed but leaves in the early spring and breeds elsewhere. No plover in Hawai'i has off-spring born there; hence for the children in a home a step-father or step-mother is likened to a plover. The term is a figure of speech and is used rightly without any implication of mockery.

In the olden days children called their parents or those of their parents' generation by name. If the mother's name was Hina, her children called her Hina, and if the father's name was Kenoi he was Kenoi to his children.

When asked, a child would answer, " I am La'anui, son of Hina and Kenoi."

After the coming of foreign teachers, the natives were taught to say Mama for Mother and Papa for Father. Soon all the uncles and relatives of the parents' generation were Papa and all the females Mama.

RELATIONSHIP THROUGH MARRIAGE.

Hunowai. The term *hunowai* or *hunoai* describes the parents-in-law: thus the father and mother of my spouse are termed by me respectively *makua hunowai kane* and *makua hunowai wahine*; and the same terms refer to the brothers and sisters of the parents-in-law. Cousins of parents-in-law are *inoa makua hunowai,* " so-called parents-in-law " or " parents-in-law in name." *Hunowai,* alone or qualified descriptively, is not used as an appellation or form of address, as are the terms for brother and sister-in-law described next.

Hunona is applied specifically to son- (*hunona kane*) or daughter- (*hunona wahine*) in-law. It was descriptive, not a term of address. It was applied by parents-in-law and brothers and sisters of parents-in-law.

Puluna. The respective parents of a married couple refer to and address each other as *puluna* (*pu,* together; *luna,* above; collectively, the " in-laws " of the generation above, as a group). All the " uncles " and " aunts " (elders of parents' generation) of the wife are *inoa puluna* to the " uncles " and " aunts " of the husband, and vice versa: they are the " together above " (*pu-luna*) nominally (*inoa,* in name) related. To be nominally related is almost equiva-lent to " blood " relationship. When the first child comes, this is the *puka a maka,* " the face " (*maka*) that "appears" (*puka*). Then the relationship is complete, as described following.

Hehi i ka pili, or *ke'ehi i ka pili*. When a married couple had no child, then, if and when one of the couple died, the *Puluna* relationship could be dropped or rejected if so desired by the family of either the deceased or the survivor. If rejected, the act and attitude was termed *hehi i ka pili*, "to step (*hehi*) on the relationship (*pili*)," or *ke'ehi i ka pili* (*ke'ehi*, to stamp on).

Kuleana. The word *kuleana*, meaning part, portion, right, interest or claim, is applied to the relatives through whom a person lays a claim to relationship by marriage. Thus, since Kai *kane* married Mele *wahine*, anyone in his family claiming relationship with anyone in hers would refer to Mele as their "claim" or "stake," *kuleana*. Equally, with Kai's family, Kai is Mele's *kuleana*.

Puka a maka. The relationship between two families consummated through a marriage is, however, sealed (*ua pa'a ka pili*) only by the birth of a child or children to the couple. *Puka a maka*, which appears to mean "appearing or entering of, or by, face," refers to a mutual relative whose birth cemented the relationship between two families. (*Kuleana* may also be used as a synonym of *puka-a-maka*.)

For instance, Heana, a woman of Ka-'u, married Keau, a man of Ewa. To them was born Lei, a daughter. Lei was the *puka a maka* that cemented the relationship between the two families.

If no *puka a maka* is born or lives to maturity the relationship may break up after the death of the *kuleana*. The relatives of one may then, if they wish to, deny their relationship to the other. This denying is called *hehi i ka pili* (stepping on the relationship) or *ke'ehi i ka pili* (stepping hard on the relationship), as previously indicated.

Ko'eke and *Kaiko'eke.* A man employs the appellation *ko'eke* to designate his wife's brothers and male cousins, and designates these *kaiko'eke*; while a woman applies these terms to her husband's sisters. (The man's sisters-in-law are to him *wahine*, the woman's brothers-in-law are to her *kane*.)

Many Hawaiians today use the terms *kua'ana* (elder of the same sex) and *kaina* (younger of the same sex), depending on age of the person in relation to the spouse, instead of *ko‘eke*, but this is not in accordance with correct old Hawaiain usage.

FOSTERING AND ADOPTION.

The child that is taken into the household and reared is known as *kama hanai* (feeding child) and the man and woman who give it hospitality, that is, who foster it, are *makua hanai* (feeding parents). The " feeding child " may be a mere waif taken in out of kindness, who in the course of time automatically assumes a tacitly accepted role of servant in relation to the family and to the true children of its " feeding parents." This is said to be " *hanai ‘ai i kanaka*," or reared to serve the true children of the family. It may be, on the other hand, an orphan or the child of a relative or dear friend, formally adopted and for whom the " feeding parent " comes to have affection that may be as great as that for the biological offspring. Under such circumstances the " feeding child " comes to feel more active affection for the family that raises it and in whose home it spends its childhood than for its true parents; consequently, in later years, when the " feeding child " is grown and the " feeding parents " are ageing, the deepest devotion is oft-times felt and shown on both sides in this relationship.

Quite different from the " feeding " relationship is that of " making " someone else's child one's own (*ho‘okama*) through informal adoption because of love between the adopting parent and the child. The adopting parent becomes to the child *makua ho‘okama* (literally " parent making child his own "), while the child is known as *kaikamahine ho‘okama* if it is a girl, or *keiki ho‘okama* if a boy. The relationship comes about as a result of mutual affection and agreement, at first tacit, then unobtrusively discussed, between the child and the older person; the part of the child's true parents, if living, is normally negative; although if there is strong dislike for the would-be adopting parent the true parent is capable of interfering. This is a relationship involving love, respect and courtesy, but not necessarily responsibility of any sort, and rarely a change of residence.

The establishing of this relationship is not confined to children, for it sometimes happens that an elderly person will take a liking to a younger adult, who reciprocates, whereupon the *ho'okama* relationship will be established. It sometimes happens that one party to a tentative *ho'okama* relationship is cold to the desire of the other, in which case no relationship is fixed by word. *Ho'okama* may come about as between the same or opposite sexes.

Sometimes a child was asked for by a friend or relative before it was born, with the idea of thus cementing the friendship through the care of the child, but not if it was the eldest. (The eldest belonged to the grandparents; a boy to his paternal grandparents and a girl to her maternal grandparents. The children that followed after might be adopted by a relative or friend.) According to some Hawaiians, it was the wrong thing to ask for a babe unborn —while it was *ma kahi haiki* (" in an uncertain place "); better to wait until after it was born, or *ma kahi akea* (" in a wide space ").

Children could not be adopted without the full consent of both true parents, lest some misfortune befall the child, and when consent had been given the child was handed to the adopting parents by the true parents with the saying, " *Ke haawi aku nei maua i ke keiki ia olua, kukae a na'au* " (We give the child to you, excrement, intestines and all). This was as binding as any law made in our modern courts. The child became the child of the adopting or "feeding parents," and only under rare circumstances did the biological parents attempt to take the child back unless the adopting parents died.

If a disagreement did arise between the adopting and biological parents, so that the biological parents tried to recover their child, it was believed that the child would fall prey to a sickness that might result in death. Such a disagreement between the two sets of parents was called *hukihuki* (pulling back and forth). So it was well for adopting parents and biological parents to keep on good terms with each other for the sake of the child.

Unlike the modern way of concealing the true parentage of an adopted child, he was told who his biological parents were and all about them, so there was no shock and weeping at finding out that he was adopted and not an " own " child. If possible, the child was taken to his true parents to become well acquainted with them and with his brothers and sisters if there were any, and he was always welcomed there.

CATEGORIES OF FRIENDSHIP.

Pili aikane (comradely relationship), *pili hoaloha* (relationship of devoted friendship) and *hale kipa* (house lodging) describe intimate friendship. Two women, Kuku and Kama, were devoted friends. Each called the other " *Aikane* " (abbreviated to " *kane* "). This relationship can exist, and is called by the same term, whether between man and man, or women and women; but not between man and woman. The genuine *aikane* relationship is never homosexual. Kama was like another daughter to Kuku's mother. Kuku's father, mother, aunts, uncles, cousins of the parent's generation were to Kama, *inoa makua* (" parents-in name "). *Inoa* as used here indicates that the relationship is not a blood tie. Both *aikane* are equally welcome in each other's home, hence the term *hale* (in the house) *kipa* (to receive). *Hale aikane* refers to hospitality extended to one's *aikane*. *Hoaloha*, meaning devoted friendship, is a descriptive general term, not used as a designation, whereas *aikane* designates the person who is the companion. *Hoaloha* means neighbour, associate, any friend. Kuku in the course of her life had three *aikane* whom her relatives all loved as well as they did their own blood kin. A strong bond still continues amongst the descendants of these *aikane*.[8]

The equivalent of what we refer to in English as " platonic friendship " was not uncommon in Hawai'i. This was the *wahine-ho'o-wahine* (" woman made-wife ") and *kane-ho'o-kane* ("man made-husband") relationship already described.

Makamaka means a relative or a friend whose home welcomes one and whom one welcomes equally. A total stranger may come and be welcomed in somebody's home and treated well: his host or hostess is then referred to as his *makamaka*. We have experienced this frequently in the field, when we have been received and accepted as though we were relatives. The word is equivalent to English host and

---

[8] A homosexual relationship is referred to as *moe aikane* (*moe*, lie with or sleep). Such behaviour is said to have been known amongst some idle and debauched *ali'i*, as it is found amongst similar unfortunates the world over. The vulgar and contemptuous term for male homosexuality was *upi laho* (*laho*, scrotum). *Upi* described the cleaning of the squid or octopus in a bowl of water or salt to rid it of its slime. Homosexuality was looked upon with contempt by commoners and by the true *ali'i*.

hostess, but it connotes a more intimate interest; and it implies definitely a more or less permanent obligation in the matter of exchange in friendship and hospitality. A bond of *aloha* has been accepted, and by acceptance becomes enduring if cherished. *Ho'omakamaka* means to make friends by extending hospitality.

In 1935 in Ka-'u, Nali'i was to Kawena her *makamaka*, for K. was her guest; but to K.'s travelling companions who were camping nearby she was *kama'aina*, for she was the native " daughter of the land " (*kama'aina*) who took the strangers (*malihini*) to see places of interest. So we who were not her guests say of her, *Ko makou kama'aina ia o Ka-'u*—" She was our local resident " (literally " child of the land ") in Ka-'u. Any local resident of long standing may be called a *kama'aina*, but in this instance the possessive pronoun implies an established relationship in referring to THE *kama'aina* who is OUR special friend, OUR *kama'aina*. Equally, the visiting strangers were HER *malihini*. A friend of Nali'i might ask, *Nohea mai kau mau malihini*—" Whence come those strangers who are your friends?"

Kupa is another word that means native son, a *kama'aina kahiko* (ancient *kama'aina*). *Kupu 'ai au* is given in the dictionary as meaning " a native-born who eats (enjoys) the land " (*au*, poetic for *'aina*). *'Apa'apa'a* is another word for one descended from a first settler. A chief of the land descended from the original *ali'i* line of the land was termed *Apa'akuma* (*pa'a*, solid; *kuma*, a contraction perhaps of *ku mau*," " standing always ").

V.

THE LIFE CYCLE

It may be of some value to summarize certain points of fundamental importance relating to the Hawaiian conception of the individual in the frame of family, points which emerge with great clarity in the description of the life cycle:—

The continuum of individual and group: the first born and later born are links in a chain of heredity and heritage from " ancestors " (kupuna) before, and in their turn, after death, will become " ancestors."

From the prenatal period, throughout life and beyond death the individual is regarded as a free, whole, independent entity.

Everything relating to this individual is within the matrix of 'ohana: an individual alone is unthinkable, in the context of Hawaiian relationship.

Rigorous concern for soundness of body is a primary consideration throughout physical life, especially before and during infancy. Coition or physical breeding as a means of perpetuating the 'ohana, was even more important than personal health.

Beauty and physical grace are equally important, and systematically cultivated: the infant was treated like a malleable form whose features and form could be modelled, as a sculptor moulds clay.

Aloha (affection), prestige, hospitality and a good time; social, economic and psychic security; and the solidarity of living 'ohana, the kupuna (ancestors), and 'aumakua (guardian spirits), were the considerations affecting all family ceremonials.

Protecting from evil, blessing with good things, prestige, well-being and happiness, were the purposes of the rituals.[9]

---

[9] In the descriptions that follow, small type is used for lengthy direct quotations. Where not otherwise indicated by specific reference, these quotations are verbatim from Mrs. Pukui's own voluminous notes and published writings, translations, etc.

Our colleague, Miss Margaret Titcomb, has generously shared with me her notes, culled over a period of twenty years, relating to Hawaiian Ceremonial Feasts.—E.S.C.H.

CONCEPTION, GESTATION AND BIRTH.

Hawaiians understood the relationship of coition (ai) to conception. This we discussed at some length in the previous chapter on relationship, with respect to paternity. *Hua* means seed, ovum and offspring.

We are to describe in this chapter the life cycle of the individual, in particular that of the first-born (*hiapo*). The prenatal period will be considered only with respect to practices and incidents believed to affect or be an expression of the child growing in the womb. Psychic and physical aspects of pregnancy, with respect to the mother, and parturition, are properly subjects to be studied and described as phases of native hygiene and therapy. As such, we have written about these elsewhere.[10]

The expectant mother avoided certain foods which it was believed would injure the baby she was carrying. Foods with strong flavour, like onion; hot foods like chili pepper (not ancient) ; *pupu 'awa* (genus Thais, a shellfish with a tart flavour from the gall), were avoided as it was believed that they would injure the eyes of the child in the womb. The expectant mother was encouraged to eat greens such as *popolo* (*Solanum nigrum*), *lu'au* (young taro leaves), *palula* (young sweet potato leaves), as these would build up the child's body; and certain herbals were favoured as mild medicine (*la'au*), such as *'aheahea* (*Chenopodium alba*), *ko'oko'olau* (*Bidens* sp.), and blossoms of *akiohala* (*Hibiscus youngianus*). These were prescribed, as it was said, " to make whole and firm the body of the child by means of greens and herbs " (*i pa'a ke kino o ke keiki i ka la'au*).

Ho'okauhua referred both to pregnancy and to a pregnant woman's craving for some particular food. These cravings were thought to be an expression of the desire and hence of the character, of the child in her womb. For the child's sake the craving should be satisfied. Longing for *manini* fish (*Hepatus triostegus*, Linnaeus), foretold the coming of a child, affectionate and home-loving, shy and

[10] Hawaiian Beliefs and Customs during Birth, Infancy and Childhood," by Mary Kawena Pukui. *Bernice P. Bishop Museum, Occasional Papers*, Vol. XVI, No. 17, Honolulu, 1942. " Outline of Hawaiian Physical Therapeutics," by E. S. Craighill Handy, Mary Kawena Pukui and Katherine Livermore. *Bernice P. Bishop Museum, Bulletin 126*, Honolulu, 1934.

retiring like the *manini* which shelters timidly in holes and small rocky pools by the shore. A mother longing for squid (*he'e*) expressed the desire of a child who would cling like the squid and flee (*he'e*) from danger as the squid swiftly flees. Desire for *hilu* (*Anampses cuvier*), a small bright fish that feeds busily about coral heads, foretold a quiet, industrious child. But if the expectant mother were seized with a lust for the eye of a tiger shark, as was Kamehameha's mother, she would give birth to a ferocious fighter.

The child's nature and character were influenced by the behaviour of the parents while the baby was in the womb. If mother and father were busily occupied with work the child would be industrious and hardworking. So likewise with psychic attributes. Jealousy in either parent would be reflected in a jealous disposition. Breaking *kapu* might mar, cripple or kill the child.

As pregnancy advanced, the wearing of *lei* by the expectant mother was prohibited, lest at birth the umbilical cord strangle the child (*lei i ka piko*). Sewing or cordwork was not permitted: a kink in the thread or cord might cause a kink in the umbilicus. Stringing fish for drying was prohibited, lest a fish spoiling affect the child with a disease of the nose which during certain months of the year caused a discharge of mucus with an evil odour like spoiled fish (termed *i'a kui*, strung fish).

An expert in delivery (*kahuna pale keiki*) could detect the sex of the expected child by various means: by clairvoyance, by dreaming; or more simply at times by asking the mother to extend one hand: if she held out the right it would be a boy; if the left, a girl.

When the time for delivery came, many relatives were on hand. If the mother-to-be was seized with a longing to see a particular relative or friend, this was termed *kau ka maka* (the eye alighting [on someone]). It showed that the child longed to see and would be fond of that person. If the person were absent, a stone was put at the door with a loud exclamation, " Here is so-an-so!" Later the stone must be thrown into the sea or put in the crotch of a tree or elsewhere, where it would be out of harm's way.

The Umbilicus and Navel.

The umbilicus was tied with a string of *'olona* (*Touchardia latifolia*) about two inches from the navel and in the old days severed with a bamboo knife; a little of the mother's milk was rubbed around the navel, and a strip of soft bark cloth bound around the child's body over it. Not until the cord dropped off was the baby bathed. If it came off too quickly it was a sign that the child would feel hunger easily; but if it was seven days or more before it fell off of that child it would be said, "The stomach is firm" (*pa'a ka 'opu*), and it would be a child that could pass a whole day without acute pangs of hunger.

The bit of cord that fell off must be carefully put away where no rat would gnaw it, for this would give the person a thievish nature. *Piko-pau-'iole* (navel-consumed-by-a-rat) was a term for thief. A hole in a rock, which could be plugged with a pebble was a good hiding place.

If the parents wanted a son to be a seafarer, the cord was taken out and dropped into the ocean. Until opportunity came to dispose of the *piko* of children as was desired, they were sometimes put away and kept in a safe place in a small container, of gourd or bamboo.

The Placenta.

The proper disposal of the placenta, termed *'iewe*, required that it be washed: sore and weak eyes were thought to be a consequence of neglect in this matter. Then it must be buried, preferably under or in a hole cut in the trunk of a tree, where it would be protected by the growth of the tree, which henceforth was *kapu* to and identified with the person whose *'iewe* it guarded. In Puna where the thorny *hala* grew near every house a high branch in a pandanus tree (*hala*) to which rats would not climb because of the spines on the leaves, was a favoured place, for neither animal or man would be likely to climb there, which could be said of few other places in Puna with its slopes of broken lava and sandy shores. People of Ka-'u sometimes banteringly called Puna people *maka kokala* ("prickle eyes"): as babies, their eyelashes were said to stand out prettily like the spines along the leaves of *hala* (pandanus) that shielded the *'iewe*.

INFANTICIDE.

When they found Hawaiians practising infanticide, the moral stigma attached to it in Christian ethics shocked early explorers and missionaries to such an extent that they condemned it in general terms without taking the trouble to understand it, thereby giving the impression that it was a universal practice of a " benighted " people devoid of a true sense of the sanctity of life.

Infanticide was occasionally practised as an easy way out of a difficult personal impasse, as by a woman who might fear retaliation from jealous relatives or husband. In general, however, it was countenanced only as a way of preventing adulteration of the purity of *ali'i* blood lines, when, as was not uncommon, a low caste woman bore a child fathered by an *ali'i*, or an *ali'i wahine* gave birth to a child sired by a man of low caste.

" Was infanticide a general practice?" is a question I have been asked time and time again. Hawaiians loved children and were adopters, taking the children of others to rear as their own. Why then should a mother wish to destroy the child she had borne? Stories of lazy, pleasure-loving mothers who did not want to be hampered with children are unknown to me.

My people did not destroy for laziness' sake, for as soon as a woman mentioned the fact that she did not want the child in her womb, relatives and neighbours would beg for it and no matter how large a family there was always room for one more.

Infanticide was practised so that there might be no low-born person to claim blood relationship to the chiefs. High chiefs sought for mates for their children from among high chiefs, at least for the first marriage, that the *hiapo* or first born be high in rank. Should a chief find a mate a little lower than himself in rank the child was not destroyed but would serve as one of the lesser chiefs in the court of his ruler, but should the chief mate with a low commoner, the child was most likely to be destroyed by the *ali'i* who did not like to have a tie of blood-relationship between high and low. The death of the child, or connecting link, was the solution. Sometimes a medical *kahuna* was consulted, one who knew the right concoction of herbs to bring on an abortion, or the mother-to-be underwent violent exercises in an attempt to end pregnancy. This was called *'omilomilo*—this doing away with the unborn.

Sometimes, there was a waiting until the child was born, then it was destroyed. This was called *'umi keiki* or child strangling.

A child sired by a *kauwa* (outcast) was put to death because a *kauwa* was despised; so was any child whose sire was regarded as worthless trash by the relatives of the mother.

In my husband's family there was an adopted daughter who was rescued from being put to death. An Ewa girl had two lovers, a Negro and a Hawaiian and her father swore that if the child to be born to her was a Hawaiian it would be spared, but if a Negro he would kill it. It was born Negro, and so the man made ready to fulfill his promise. Just at that time my husband's aunt arrived, and learning the man's intention she called his attention elsewhere. Then she quickly picked the baby up, wrapped it in the skirt of her *holoku* and fled. Thus it was that the child was saved from death.

A girl in Ka-'u was saved by my grandmother, who pretended that the baby she had just delivered was not the offspring of the man who was greatly despised by the grandparents. When the sire or mother was greatly despised, the child was gotten rid of, usually by strangling it; but none, so far as I have heard from my old folks, was ever destroyed because of laziness or pleasure seeking.

SACRAMENTAL FEAST FOR THE FIRST-BORN.

The *'Aha'aina Mawaewae*[11] feast was celebrated within 24 hours after the child was born, for the first-born (*hiapo*), for its safeguarding and welfare. *Mawaewae* can be translated " path clearing." If this ceremony which dedicated the child to the *'aumakua* (ancestral guardians) were not performed, the first-born, privileged and generally pampered by elders as he or she was, would be likely to grow up headstrong and unruly. So the feast not only " cleared the way ": it set the child's feet (*waewae*) in the way (*ma*) of the spiritual flow or channels (*'au*) of his responsible elders (*makua*).

Furthermore, this consecration feast was very important because it blessed not only the *hiapo*, but all the succession of younger children that would be born to the mother, who partook sacramentally of the special foods peculiar to this ritual.

This rite was strictly a domestic affair within the household. It really should be termed a psychic therapeutic sacrament rather than a " feast." It was an occasion of

---

[11] *Mawaewae* and *ukuhi* (weaning) was first described by Doctor Martha Beckwith in collaboration with Miss Laura Green in *The American Anthropologist*, N.S., Vol. 26, 1924, pp. 241-245. With respect to divergencies in the matter of the foods to be eaten by the mother and the wording of prayers, we have here an example of something typical of Polynesian ritual, namely, that it is the pattern of practice based upon theory of psychic relationship which is basic, not particular things or words. This is true both of the *mawaewae* and the *ukuhi*. Thus in weaning either two *lele* bananas, or two stones, or two blossoms might serve as proxies for the breasts.

worship rather than pleasure and festivity. When it was certain that the young mother had conceived in her first pregnancy, the father began raising a pig for *mawaewae*. In seven months or so this pig, which was well fed, would be a big hog.

As soon as the child was born, someone was sent to the beach to secure certain special sea foods. Especially important among these were *'ama'ama* (mullet) and/or *'aholehole* (*Dules sandvicensis*). Both of these can be caught near shore or even in streams and brackish pools. Mullet were raised in taro patches. These two fish were spoken of as " sea pigs " (*pua'a kai*), and as such, like the pig itself, were " bodies " (*kino*) of Камапџа'a, who is the hog-form of the *akua* Lono. In rituals in honour of Lono where a pig was required, either of these fish might be offered as a substitute if a pig was not available. For the *mawaewae* it was necessary also to have a taro leaf, which was one of a number of " plant forms " of Lono. [Presumably from the taro variety known as *Ipu o Lono,* Lono's gourd or cup, or some other variety sacred to Lono.]

For the *mawaewae* it did not suffice to have one or other form of Lono mentioned above: There must be offered and eaten an animal (the hog), sea (fish) and plant " form " or *kino* of Lono, all three.

In addition to these there must be also several other special sea foods. These were important because their names imply potency in " clearing the way " for the child. There must be shrimp, one name for which is *mahiki,* a word meaning to peel off like removing fish scales [or the skin of the shrimp]. There must be *kala* seaweed: *kala* means " to loosen," " set free." There must be *'a'ama* crab: *'a'ama* means to loose a hold or grip. These three foods helped to free the child from malicious influences, thus preventing bad behaviour and ill luck due to mischievous psychic effects. Another sea food that must be eaten was a chiton of the species called *kuapa'a* (*Acanthochiton viridis*), a bilaterally symmetrical mollusc with a shell consisting of eight transverse plates, found on the under surface of stones in shallow water to which it " holds fast," *pa'a.* This was the only occasion on which this shellfish was eaten: *pa'a* means to fix, hold fast, hence the implication that the *kuapa'a* would be instrumental in securing firmly through the mother and others who ate of it the goodness induced in the hearts of all present and especially of the child.

There may have been a special implication also in the offering of the *'ama'ama* or mullet, and the *'a'ama* crab, for the first born, in the fact that the word *'ama* means a first-fruits offering.

The food was cooked, never eaten raw. A cup of *'awa* was also prepared and when the hog was ready to serve, the *kahuna* cut off a piece from each of the four feet, the end of the tail, the top of the snout, the tips of the ears, a piece of the liver, spleen and lungs and placed them on a dish for the mother. Symbolically, she consumed the whole hog. A bundle of taro tops and the sea food described above, set aside for her, must all be eaten by the mother.

The remainder of the pork and other foods prepared for the occasion were eaten by the *'ohana* (relatives) and intimate family friends, who were gathered in the home on this notable occasion of the birth of the *hiapo*, or first-born.

It is evident from the foods that were eaten sacramentally in the *mawaewae* that this, the first ritual consecration of the mother of the *hiapo* or first-born and all subsequent children sealed the relationship to Lono, who was *akua* of rain, agriculture and peace. Kamapua'a ("Hog-offspring") was one of the myriad life-forms or "leaf-forms" (*kinolau*) of Lono. The *mawaewae* sacrament called for animal (the ears of the hog), vegetable (the hog-ear shaped taro leaf) and marine (*'aholehole*, a fish whose "snout" [*nuku*] is shaped like a hog's snout) "bodies" of Lono. Subsistence, livelihood, peace and plenty came first. Later, after he entered the *Mua* or Men's House, would come the training and consecration of the male *hiapo* in the warrior's craft, and his entry into the cult of Ku.[12]

---

[12] Mrs. Pukui's lineage and heritage is from the priesthood of Lono. Her grandmother, Na-'li'i-po'ai-moku by whom she was reared as a *punahele* (precious child), was the stepdaughter of Kanekuhia who was a priest trained in the temple of Lono at Kealakekua in Kona, in which Captain Cook was worshipped as Lono. Po'ai's father died when she was about a year old. Kanekuhia, her stepfather, had no children of his own. He reared her, and passed on to her much of the lore of the priesthood of Lono. We have no records from Ka-'u of the priesthood of Ku, the god of war. The rituals of Ku are described in some detail by David Malo, who was a native of the neighbouring district of Kona.—E.S.C.H.

Feast for Bearers of Gifts to the First-Born.

The *'aha'aina palala* was the first festivity in honour of the new first-born. It was not ritualistic in the sense that the *mawaewae* was: the *palala* expressed the *aloha* of all the relatives and friends, and in the case of an *ali'i*, of all the people, for the first-born newly arrived. This *aloha* was expressed in the form of gifts to the child, and in the composition of chants (*mele*) which were performed with dances (*hula*). The feast that was enjoyed by all who came to honour the *hiapo* was an expression of the family's response and pride in the occasion, making it a gay time.

In the olden days everyone brought whatever she or he had to offer: a pig, a dog, a *lei*, a song.

> After my baby was born, a woman from Lahaina, came to ask me for *kukui* nuts to make into medicine for her grandchild. She gasped when she saw me nursing the baby for she knew that this was a *hiapo*. Her husband was a native of Ka-'u and an *'ohana* of ours. She had nothing in her hands. She cried out, "*Auwe, o ka maka wale no keia*" (Alas! I brought only my face.") We assured her that we were glad to see her anyhow. She kissed my child on the head and offered a prayer. She felt better then, for she had given her gift, a *pule*.

The modern so-called "baby *lu'au*" (feast) for the newborn child is a perpetuation of the *palala* in a sense, but it retains little of the spirit of *aloha* in which good will, and not obligation, was the keynote. A calabash is put in front of the baby. Relatives are expected to drop money in it; and anyone, be he *'ohana* or stranger who drops in a dollar may enjoy the feast. The placing of the gourd before the baby expresses the old idea; but the money given cannot mean what a gift expresses.

In olden times, if it was the *hiapo* of the ruling chief of a district or island (*ali'i 'ai moku*, chief who "eats" the land) the folk came from everywhere bringing whatever they had to give: fisher folk brought the products of the sea, farmers brought vegetable food, weavers brought mats, tapa makers brought tapa.

Such was the quantity of gifts that would be presented to a beloved *hiapo* of a high chiefess, that storehouses had to be built to keep them safely for the child. From the legend of Puaka'ohelo, told in the district of Hilo, Hawaii, we quote this description of the *palala* of the chiefess Punahoa (*Ke Auoko'a*, May 5, 1870) :—

> . . . After Punahoa had given birth, the chiefs sent word to
> the people to come to the house to see the chiefess. Some time
> later, after the *kahuna* (priest) had finished his work and the
> baby had been cleansed and wrapped in baby tapa, the infant
> was brought to Punahoa to nurse at her breast. The people saw
> the features of the tiny stranger. She was lovely to look upon
> and the news that the chiefess had given birth was told abroad
> in Hilo. All came to offer their gifts for the [new born] chiefess.
> This was called a *palala*. When they came into the presence of
> Punahoa, they gave her many things of value which were laid
> away in the store house (*hale papa'a*). Some came with chants
> of praise for the little girl, and chanted them before the chiefess
> as they gestured this way and that [*hula dancing*]. The people
> came for days to the presence of the chiefess and this deed of
> theirs comforted her heart and made her rejoice.

At such times, with many people with their gifts, and
many chants and dances, the festivity and the rejoicing
would continue for days. But in the case of *'ohana* of good
birth it was just a happy feast of a day with gifts, *mele* and
hula, and plenty of good and choice things to eat, and much
gaiety.

Eulogistic Chants as Gifts.

There were two types of chants that were composed to
honour the *hiapo* of *ali'i*, *mele inoa* or chants praising the
name; and *mele ma'i* which honoured the private parts
(*ma'i*) of the new-born, which were worthy of blessing and
praise because this child would be the breeder from whose
loins or in whose womb would come a *hiapo* in the next
generation to perpetuate the noble lines. Throughout the
lifetime of the person to whom these compositions were
dedicated these *mele* would remain the sacred possession of
the person honoured: and after death, that chief or chiefess
would be remembered by them. So, these *mele* both blessed
for life and immortalized that *ali'i*, and in and through that
ali'i, added prestige to the occasion and to the *'ohana*. There
were master bards (*haku mele*) who were skilled in composition. Great care had to be taken in the choice of words,
because the words were believed to influence the character
and life of the child. Hence all words must be of good
import; and any with possible evil sounds or connotation
must be avoided. To the words and the rhythm of their
chanting a master of dancing (*kumu hula*) would devise
steps and gestures. The composition of these was not a
matter of mechanical fabrication, but rather of inspiration:
the *mele* and the *hula* were often given in a dream. Like a

name given through a dream, or a medical remedy given
through a dream, such a chant and dance would be held very
sacred. Hence the reluctance, sometimes, of Hawaiians
loyal to their ancient customs, to give away their *mele inoa*
and *mele maʻi*. Here are two examples:—

> ʻAole au i makemake ia Kona,
> O Ka-ʻu kaʻu.
> O ka wai o Kalae e kahe ana i ka po a ao.
> I ke kapa, i ka ʻupi kekahi wai
> Kulia i lohe ai he ʻaina wai ʻole
> I Mana, i Unulau ka wai kali
> I ka pona maka o ka iʻa ka wai aloha e,
> Aloha i ka wai malama a kane
> E hiʻi ana ke keiki i ke hokeo,
> E hano ana, e kani ʻouo ana,
> Ka leo o ka huewai i ka makani
> Me he hano puhi ala i ke aumoe,
> Ka hoene lua a ka ipu e o nei.
> E lono i kou pomaikaʻi, Eia!
> Mamuli o kou hope ʻole, ʻokoʻa ka hoʻi,
> A ma ka wa kamaliʻi nei, mihi malu,
> ʻU wale iho no.
> Aloha ʻino no ka hoʻi ke kau mamua.
> ʻUʻina ʻino nohoʻi ke kau i hala aku nei.

> I do not care for Kona,
> For Ka-ʻu is mine.
> The water from Kalae is carried all night long.
> (Wrung) from tapas and some from sponges.
> This land is heard of as having no water,
> Except for the water that is waited for at Mana and Unulau.
> The much prized water is found in the eye socket of the fish,
> The water prized and cared for by the man
> The child carries a gourd container in his arms.
> It whistles, whistles as the wind blows into it,
> The voice of the water gourd is produced by the wind
> Sounding like a nose flute at midnight,
> This long-drawn whistling of the gourd, we hear.
> Hearken, how fortunate you are!
> There is no going back, (our) ways are different.
> In childhood only does one regret in secret,
> Grieving alone.
> (Look) forward with love for the season ahead of us.
> Let pass the season that is gone.
>
> (From a name chant for Kupakeʻe.)

In both the *mele inoa* and the *mele maʻi* the language
was figurative and not necessarily descriptive.

> O Hea ka lauoho,
> O Lae-nui ka lae,
> O ʻIa ka pepeiao,
> O Makapioi ka maka,
> O Mene ka ihu,

O Waha-'ukele ka waha
O 'Auwae-lewa ka 'auwae
O 'A'i-nui ka 'a-'i
O Umauma-lahalaha ka umauma.
O Hakane ka 'opu
O Ipu-wai ka piko
O Halala ka ma'i.

He ma'i no ku'u kaikua'ana.

Hea is (the name of) his hair,
Broad-forehead is (the name of) his forehead,
'Ia is (the name of) his ear,
Tiny-eyes is (the name of) his eyes,
Flat-nose is (the name of) his nose,
Wet-mouth is (the name of)his chin,
Big-neck is (the name of) his neck,
Broad-chest is (the name of) his chest,
Filled-container is (the name of) his abdomen.
Water-holder is (the name of) his navel.
Halala is (the name of) his privates.

This is my chant for the privates of my cousin

In addition to the *mele inoa* and *mele ma'i*, there was one other type of chant composed to honour the *hiapo ali'i*. This was the *ko'ihonua* or genealogical chant, which recorded the *hiapo's* descent from the gods and his *ali'i* forbears. This, too, was a sacred private possession, a record of status for his lifetime, and a monument and memorial after death.

ANNIVERSARY FEASTS.

The Feast of the Fullness of the Year (*'Aha'aina Piha Makahiki*) was any kind of celebration of an anniversary, but the most important was that which marked the first anniversary of the birth of a first-born. The main feature of this occasion was the chanting and dancing of the *mele inoa* and *mele ma'i* composed in honour of the child (see *Palala*), and other chants lauding his land, the famous deeds of his ancestors, or of love and grief in the lives of the *'ohana*. Relatives from far and near gathered, brought provender, and gifts of all sorts—mats, rolls of *kapa*, gourds, calabashes filled with *poi*—which were presented to the composers and performers. The festivities, singing, dancing and feasting might continue a full week.

THE FONTANEL.

Hawaiians knew that premature ossification of the soft spot or fontanel at the crest of the baby's skull would prevent normal growth of the brain case.

The fontanel (*manawa*) was always examined in babyhood, and if, at the age of six or seven months, the fontanel had begun to decrease in size, crushed *popolo* leaves were packed on the spot to check it. This checking treatment was called *wawahi i ka manawa* (breaking the fontanel).

All through babyhood, *kukui* nut oil or crushed *popolo* leaves wrapped in cloth were rubbed on the abdomen, the rubbing began at the sides and worked toward the navel. This constant massaging about once or twice a day helped elimination.

It is interesting that the fontanel was referred to by the word *manawa*, which meant also feelings, affections, sympathy, and could also be used to refer to the spirit of a human being as a living entity, having a meaning slightly less definite than *'uhane* (spirit-form that leaves the body in sleep and at death, also referred to as *wai-lua*). *Manawa* is spirit as animating essence.

The *kahuna* of old were observant men, and deserved to be called, certainly, "natural scientists" in their knowledge of the natural history and the human species of their own land and race. This is proven by their systematic natural therapy, which Dr. Nils P. Larsen has said was more scientific in many ways, at the time of discovery, than that of their European "discoverers." It is probable that these priests and healers had observed that premature cloture of the fontanel was the precedent to serious pathological conditions, particularly affecting mentality and temperament; and that in consequence they had recourse to the practices described above as means to prevent premature ossification of the fontanels and sutures of the head. And further, that the obvious association of this with health led to the identification of that part of the skull as a point or centre peculiarly related to the animating soul or life principle.

INFANT'S DIET.

Gradually the baby was prepared for weaning by accustoming it by degrees to solid and liquid foods other than the breast milk of mother or wet nurse.

It was believed that a baby under four months old could be nourished by a small mound of raw, grated sweet potato on the fontanel.

A child four months old was given a little mashed sweet potato. If the potato was too hard, a little water was added. At six months, it was given fresh or day-old *poi*, but never sour *poi*. A little later the soft part of the *opihi* (limpet) and some broth were added to the diet. When the child was about a year old, mashed *kukui* nuts, '*a'ama* crab juice, and vegetables were fed to him.

'*Ilima* flowers were crushed and the juice squeezed into the baby's mouth whenever it needed a laxative. The slippery juice really acted as a lubricant.

A child over a year old was fed *poi* or mashed sweet potatoes, sometimes mixed with the juices of herbs. Herbs were included in the diet until the child was two years old, for they helped to build a strong body.

The juice of toasted sugar cane and the honey of banana flowers (*pilali mai'a*) were given to babies.

At two years, a child could eat anything his parents ate, except foods of strong, tart flavour. At five or six, all diet restrictions ended.

NURSING AND WEANING.

The *akua* Ku and his wife Hina were the gods appealed to in domestic life. Ku, the male, was identified with the right side of the body; Hina, the female, with the left. They were asked to help when delivery was delayed or painful. We meet them here again in connection with nursing and weaning. They were healers, they were prayed to by planters, and were also the fisherman's helpers.

When a mother's milk was not flowing as it should a length of sweet potato vine was plucked with the right hand with a prayer to Ku, then another was snapped off with the left hand and a prayer to Hina. These two lengths of vine, with the latex or white sap looking like milk oozing out of the broken ends, were tied together and worn around the neck for several days. Or two pieces of the vine would be put into a calabash of water from a spring. Facing the east at dawn, the woman took a vine in her right hand and smote her right breast, with a prayer to Ku for a copious flow of milk. Then, taking the other vine in her left hand and smiting her left breast with it, she said a similar prayer to Hina. Both the milky sap, and the water from a flowing spring in which the vines were floated in the calabash, were believed to help induce the flow of milk for the baby.

When it was thought that the baby ought to be weaned (*ukuhi*), Ku and Hina were asked to help in a little ceremony that would reveal whether the baby was ready to give up the breast or not. It is significant that the decision lay with the child. The person who was to perform the ceremony was seated facing mother and child, before whom two stones representing the mother's breasts were placed. A prayer to Ku and Hina requested that the desire for milk leave the baby. If the child reached for the stones and tossed them away, then the prayer had been granted and the child was nursed no more; but if the child did not toss the stones away, nursing must continue, and the little ritual would be tried again later. When the child threw away the stones, then the person performing the ceremony said to the child, " Do you, ————, wish the desire for milk to go away from you?" The mother, speaking for the child, replied, " Yes." " Nevermore to desire it?" " Never." That ended the rite—and the nursing.

The wild banana of the variety named *lele* was sometimes used instead of the stones, because of its name, which means "fly away." The two bananas were placed between the two persons, and the rest of the ceremony was the same.

Flowers were also used in this way. In this case, a calabash of water was placed between the two persons taking part in the ceremony, with two flowers floating around in it. The prayers, questions and answers were all the same. A recent instance of the use of this latter ceremony to wean a baby daughter, happened as follows: After the prayer, the child refused to put her hand in the water to take out the flowers. It was repeated several times but each time the child ignored the flowers. One night the grandmother dreamed that someone told her to put in flowers of different colours, one red and one white. This was done, and the ceremony was successful.

After weaning, a mother would, in rare instances, nurse a puppy at the breast, to be reared as a pet and protector for the child. Should the child die, the dog was strangled and buried with the body. If the dog died first, its fangs were removed and made into a charm for the child. It was believed that the spirit of the dog would guard the child and bite any evil spirit sent to harm him. (Dog-tooth ornaments which were worn as anklets by *hula* dancers had no such protective *mana*. *'A'ohe lohe o ka ha'i ilio*: " Other people's dogs do not heed your call.")

TEETHING.

Teething was aided in babyhood by letting the child bite the mother's finger. Later segments of sugar cane were

peeled with the teeth and chewed, and chunks of dried squid
were given the growing youngster to chew on to develop
good jaw muscles and strong teeth. Wood ash or charcoal
was rubbed on and between the teeth for cleansing, after
which the mouth was rinsed with fresh or sea water. A
diet with plenty of greens for the nursing mother was
believed to produce sound teeth in her baby. (*Poi* made of
taro, which is rich in organic and mineral salts, probably
was a large factor in producing the massive jaws and
beautiful dentition of the old Hawaiians).

INFANCY AND EARLY CHILDHOOD.

Responsibility for the child's diet and health, and for
its proper informal and formal training rested generally
with the grandparents, or, if and when a bright child was
apprenticed to an expert, with the teacher, into whose household the child was taken as a member of the family. Generally the tutor was a relative: if not, the apprentice became
for all practical purposes an adoptive member of the
teacher's family, and thereby the *'ohana* of the child and of
the teacher came into close and cordial relationship. However, there were no formalities to seal this bond, until the
pupil went through a ceremony like the *uniki* in the *hula,*
at "graduation," when the teacher consecrated the pupil,
who thereafter was one with the teacher in psychic relationship as definite and obligatory as blood relationship.

> The diet of greens and herbs for the mother continued
> through the nursing period and after weaning the child was
> given various herbs and herb concoctions (*'apu*) to build a strong,
> disease-resisting body.
> Children were usually reared by the grandparents. The
> oldest boy went to his paternal grandparents, the girl to the
> maternal. It was not that the parents lacked interest, but that
> the older grandparents who were unable to do much of the
> heavy work, tended the children while the strong young parents
> did the more labourious tasks. Being more experienced, the
> grandparents were the best teachers. " School " for the child,
> then, was at home with the grandparents.
> Unless a child showed an aptitude for an art in which his
> grandparents were not well versed, he continued to remain with
> them. Otherwise, an expert (*kumu* or *kahuna*) in that special
> craft or art was found, and the child became a member of his
> household. Gifts of food were brought from time to time, as
> long as the child remained there.
> Attachment between pupil and instructor grew stronger
> with the years, as between a parent and a child. The teacher
> was generally a relative.

There was always the intimate living together and community of work, play, and interests with other members of the family which established and strengthened the ties that united 'ohana. True Hawaiians normally acknowledge their relationship to each other even to the remote kin. Children growing up where family ties were regarded as important, loved and respected these ties.

In recent years, with modern ways and education, love of and respect for relationship other than within the immediate family circle has unfortunately waned very generally.

Unlike our modern children, who want to learn mostly by asking questions, the children of yesterday had to learn by observation and practise. Asking questions was bad manners, reproved with a single word, " Niele!" which implies that no one wants to answer questions.

Beauty-modelling.

It was thought by Hawaiians that the body of the baby could be modelled, if not to conform to, at least to approximate, certain standards of physical beauty.

Any bodily defects that could be corrected were treated in infancy, childhood, and adolescence. Infancy was the time to mould and perfect the bodies of favourite children. The ends of the fingers were gently rolled between the thumb and index finger to make them taper. If the nose was flat ('upepe) it was gently pressed to a sharper ridge. A tiptilted nose (ihu ku) was believed to be caused by the weight of the breast resting against it, so nursing mothers were careful to support the breast with the hand. Care was taken to hold the child's buttocks away from the lap of the mother lest it become kikala pai (flat seated). The buttocks of little boys were carefully moulded, as the wearing of the loin cloth hid only a small part of the body; a " flat seated" fellow was often teased by his play-fellows.

Ears that stood out were pressed back against the head, and care was taken that the child was never laid down with the ears folded forward. I never saw a Hawaiian in my childhood with ears that stuck out.

A flat head (po'o 'opaha) was avoided by not allowing the baby to rest always in the same position.

By pressing the outer corners of the eyes toward the nose, the eyes were made to grow larger.[13]

[13] Dr. Charles Snow, Professor of Anthropology at the University of Kentucky, has given us the following facts, gleaned from various sources, with respect to Hawaiian head moulding. A considerable number of skulls examined, excavated near Mokapu Point on Windward Oahu, show head deformation comparable to that characteristic of the skull of the Hawaiian King Liloa, examined by X-Ray through the woven envelope in which the skeleton is encased. This deformation consists of flattening of the occiput and depression of the upper forehead, producing a skull broadened in the rear and in profile shaped like a gourd. Not a few elder Hawaiians have been observed with heads approximating this form. Various informants have stated that the child's head in the first week was laid on a piece of coconut husk,

Treating Latent Organic Disorders.

The watchful concern of the old Hawaiians for the health of the baby as the primary consideration in guaranteeing a sound constitution for life was evident in the phase of therapy covered by the word *pa'ao'ao*. There were experts (*kahuna*) or diagnosticians (*haha*, palpation) who were experienced in detecting and prescribing for symptoms of latent functional feebleness or disease present in infants, manifested in habitual constipation, sluggish liver or kidneys, weak lungs. Another term was *'ea*, covering also a variety of symptoms: soft bones, bad breath, coated tongue, inability to gain weight. Treatment for these abnormalities was begun in infancy and continued until the patient was normal. Depending on the symptoms, a great variety of treatment was applied to the child, including special diets, herbal tonics, massage, manipulation of the limbs and members, sea and sun-bathing; and, for weakness (*lolo*), burying in firm sand or bathing in soft *poi* and allowing it to dry on the skin (to tone up and " stiffen " muscle and flesh). Many old timers have told of the beneficial effects, lasting the rest of their lives, of this careful and systematic old-fashioned native pediatrics.

General Physiotherapy.

Health and vitality (*ola*), comeliness and strength (*u'i*) were qualities of the whole body (*kino*) that were carefully fostered. A book could be written about the innumerable practices, physical and psychic, known in the old Hawaiian civilization, by means of which the parents strove to give perfection and soundness of form and life to each child, as a person that could be moulded, body and spirit, like a work

coconut shell, or gourd, with *pulu* (down from tree fern) or *tapa* for padding; or that two pieces of shell, or boards, were used behind and in front, bound in place, and removed once or twice a day so that the forehead could be massaged, with pressure to flatten and mold, and to restore circulation. The custom of moulding the head to produce a flat occiput, sloping forehead and rounded peaked crown was definitely a practice of the *ali'i* of Hawaii, whether done purely by manual manipulation as described by Mrs. Pukui or with coconut shell, gourd or board. *Po'o paki'iki'i* (broad head) described a head properly moulded into the ideal shape in infancy. *Po'o pu'u* (lumpy head) referred to a head with projecting occiput, indicating neglect. A high forehead was considered ugly.

of art, in accordance with a clear ideal of individual character. Suffice it to relate a few examples of the practice of the art of physical therapy, taken from actual experience.

> The body was gently massaged from infancy, to give the limbs strength.
>
> Between the creeping and walking stages, the sticky liquid (*kale 'ai*) remaining on the board after *poi* was pounded was rubbed over the child's body before it was bathed.
>
> When I was a baby, I fell off the bed and injured my spine. My grandmother gave me corrective treatment for several years. She buried me in sand up to my waist, then slipped her arms under my armpits as she stood behind me, and firmly pulled me up. She used to rub my back with warm *kukui* oil before I went to bed. *Pakolea*, the term used for such corrective treatment, means to change the way a thing grows.
>
> As fat was considered beautiful, mothers worried when their daughters were thin and gave them medicine to fatten them. The juice of young *'ohi'a* leaves (*liko 'ohi'a*) was one of the fattening medicines (*la'au kupele*). Taken in the morning before breakfast, it created a hearty appetite.

THE GENITALIA.

The old Hawaiian practices relating to the blessing and perfecting of the infant's genitalia were very important because procreation was a sacred process for these worshippers of Kane.

As was true in all phases of old Hawaiian civilization, coition had its psychic and its physical aspects: and each aspect received equally careful attention.

Since the first-born, be it boy or girl, was destined to be the breeder by means of whose genitalia (*ma'i*) the first-born in the succeeding generation would be conceived, perpetuating the noble lineage (*mo'okuauhau ali'i*), one of the most precious tokens of *aloha* from intimate *'ohana* was the Chant for the Breeding Parts (*Mele Ma'i*) which in figurative terms honoured the child's genitalia. Such *mele* were more than mere poems of praise: they blessed and endowed with investment of intoned words conveying *mana* of charm and potency.

> Every child of chiefly or priestly family had a special name given to his genitals. *Mele* were composed for them, but they were not necessarily descriptive of the genitals. In the olden days, every school chanted such *mele* without thought of immodesty or wrong of any sort.

The genitalia of the first-born male or female were also given particular physical care in early infancy. This care

94 THE POLYNESIAN FAMILY SYSTEM IN KA-'U

was therapeutic in the sense that it was intended to
guarantee health and efficient coition; and had also its
aesthetic aspects, since the sexual act was accepted without
shame in those days as being both creative and one of the
supreme pleasures; and beauty and pleasure in all ways and
forms were blessings with which loving relatives desired to
endow the first-born throughout life.

The purposes of health and effective coition were served
by subjecting the male child at the proper age to the operation of subincision (described below). To omit this, in the
case of the son of an *ali'i* or *kahuna,* was regarded as a
disgrace.

> To mold a girl, mother's milk was squirted into the vagina,
> and the labia pressed together. The *mons veneris* was rubbed
> with *kukui* nut oil and pressed with the palm to flatten it and
> make it less prominent. The molding continued until the labia
> did not separate.

What was true for the first-born was true for subsequent
children, to a lesser degree. For sometimes the first-born
died; and then the second would have to carry on the line;
or it might be a third or fourth, especially after infant
mortality became so prevalent from the earlier days of *haole*
invasion.

Subincision.

Kahe ule (slit penis) and the post-missionary term '*oki
poepoe* (cut round, i.e. circumcision) refer to the physical
operation on boys in childhood.

There was in the *moku* of Puna a stone named Pohaku-
kahe-ule (Stone-slit-penis). It was to certain celebrated
stones such as this that boys were taken for the operation of
subincision. Or the operation might be performed at home.
(We have no record of such a stone or special place in the
adjoining *moku* of Ka-'u.)

> In preparation for the event, the opening in the child's penis
> was blown into, daily, to loosen the skin so that when the time
> of subincision came the skin was quickly and easily slit. This
> treatment continued daily until the child urinated in an arch,
> wetting the blower, then it was done less often, perhaps three
> times a week.
>
> At the age of seven or eight the boy was ready, and a feast
> was held and relatives and friends came. Only *kahuna* trained
> in the art performed the operation.

The sharp knife used was made from bamboo obtained at Ho-mai-ka-'ohe in Hamakua, on windward Hawaii, a bamboo grove planted, according to tradition, by the god Kane when he came from Kahiki. The *kahuna* slit the foreskin, letting it contract of its own accord or gently pulling it back. He then slipped a clean morning-glory blossom over the penis, which protected the wound and helped it to heal.

According to David Malo (*Hawaiian Antiquities,* pp. 127-129), the following prayer was uttered by the *kahuna* before cutting the foreskin:—

> Bring the bamboo from Ho-mai-ka-'ohe.
> Here is the small-leafed bamboo of Kane.
> Cut now the foreskin.
> It is divided!

The *'Aha'aina 'Okipoepoe* (old term: *'Aha'aina Kahe*) marked the recovery of a boy after subincision. This was purely social. Any ritualism associated with this event in the boy's life was purely incidental, except that, from a ceremonial point of view, the sliver of bamboo with which the operation was performed was an item of prime symbolic significance. The purpose of subincision was to facilitate cohabitation and enhance the pleasure enjoyed. Tabus, precautions and prayers were simply prophylactic. There was no more significance in the occasion or the operation itself than in medication for illness or injury, or in the consecrating of a new tool. Nor was there anything in the Hawaiian life cycle that partook of the nature of " initiation," certainly neither the entry into the *Mua* (men's house), nor subincision. And adolescence was not celebrated either socially or ritually, possibly because casual intercourse was commonly experienced by Hawaiian boys before adolescence.

ENTERING THE MEN'S HOUSE.

The *Mua* was the men's eating and lounging house, and their sanctuary. At one end was an altar (*kuahu*) dedicated to the family *'aumakua* whose effigies stood there. Here the head of the household prayed and performed necessary rites sometimes without, sometimes with the aid of a *kahuna pule,* when came the time for the rites of the life cycle such as birth, cutting the foreskin, sickness and death. Here the

family rites during the monthly days of *kapu* were performed.[14] The common daily worship would seem to have
consisted in offering a bit of food (*hanai 'ai*) at the time of
eating.

When a boy child was four or five years old, there was
celebrated one of the most important sacraments of his
whole life cycle, namely his initation and dedication to Lono
the Provider, which marked his transference out of eating
and living " in common " (*noa*) with the women folk and
entering the company of men.

We have explained in the description of the *mawaewae*
that the hog was a body-form (*kinolau*) of Lono the Provider. The gourd was likewise a body-form of Lono. The
" Sacrament of the Gourd " (*Pule Ipu*) dedicated the boy to
Lono the Provider.

The father of the boy baked a pig and placed the head
on the *kuahu*. An ear of the pig was cut off and put in a
gourd referred to as " Lono's gourd," suspended from the
neck of a carving (*ki'i*) representing Lono. '*Awa* root,
bananas, coconut were laid there also. " . . . Here are the
hog, the coconut, the *awa*, god Ku, Lono, Kane, Kanaloa, and
ye ancestral guardians " (*'aumakua*). The *Pule Ipu*, as will
be seen, dramatizes the gourd vine, whose vigorous growth
and great fruit is a symbol of abundance: these words are
calculated to produce vigorous growth in the boy, to make
him big and strong, like the gourd.

His prayer finished, the father sucked the '*awa* root
which was said to be Lono's drinking of it. He then brewed
a bowl of '*awa* and drank it, eating with it the other foods
on the altar. This concluded the ritual and he declared the
occasion *noa*, free, saying:—

> Installed is the child, the '*awa* smitten against the brain.
> Free is the '*awa*; there is freedom to come to go; and *kapu*
> is entirely lifted. One is free to travel to the ends of the earth.

[14] In old Hawaiian worship, in each lunar month the days and
nights of the first two nights (*po*) of the new moon were sacred to Ku
(one meaning of whose name is " to rise "); the days just preceding
full moon were sacred to Lono, god of plenty, on land. The twenty-
third and twenty-fourth were sacred to Kanaloa, lord of the ocean.
The twenty-seventh and twenty-eighth nights were sacred to Kane.
The four deities mentioned were worshipped at their temples and at
the family shrines during these periods sacred to them respectively
and labour, fishing and planting were *kapu*.

To celebrate the event the father and men present then feasted on the pork and vegetables of which, presumably, the new husbandman of Lono—the child—consumed something as a token or symbol of his participation. (He did not taste pork at this time, however, for the eating of pork required a special consecration.) The child's entry into the *mua* or men's eating house and shrine was referred to as follows: *Ua ka i ka mua;* [he] is cast in the *mua*.

THE PULE IPU (Malo, pp. 120-121).

Ala mai, e Lono, i kou haina awa, haina awa nui nou, e Lono
He ula mai, e Kea, he pepeiao puaa, he pepeiao ilio, he pepeiao
    aina nui—nou, e Lono!
Halapa i ke mauli! Kukala ia hale-hau! mau, malewa i ka po;
    molia ia hai ka po.
O ku'u ka ipu; o ku'u hua i ka ipu; hua i kakala ka ipu kakala;
    he kalana ipu.
O hua i na mo'o Hi'i! I au i'a ko ia
Ahia la anoano a ke ahi-kanu, a kanu la, i pua i Hawaii?
A kanu la o ka ipu nei; a ulu; a lau; a pua; a hua la o ka ipu
    nei.
Hoonoho la o ka ipu nei. Kekela o ka ipu nei.
O uha'i o ka ipu nei. Kalai la o ka ipu nei.
O oki, o kua i o ka piha o ka ipu.
O ka ipu ka honua nui nei; o po'i o ka lani o Kuakini.
A hou i ka hakaokao; kakai i ke anuenue.
O uhao i ka lili; o uhao i ka hala; o uhao i ka la manolele i ona!
O ka ipu o ka lua mua-a-Iku, o ka ipu a makani koha, a kau ka
    hoku a'ia'i
Owahi! o kani mai, a hea o ka uka manu!
Ka lalau a ha'a ka manu; kalalau kulia i Wawau.
He malino a po, e Lono, i ka haunaele;
Na lili la i ka haunaele, na hala la i ka haunaele o mau kahuna
    o ke makala ulua
Ulua mai, o Lono, ulua kolea ino o Ma'a-ku-newa awa lilelile!
O makia, Lono, a hano, a hano wale no!
Kila i nei; muli o hala, muli ke kani o Waioha!

TRANSLATION.

Arise, O Lono, accept the offerings of *'awa* to you—an important
    offering, O Lono.
Grant abundance, O Kea. May there be an abundance of hog's
    and dog's ears—an abundance for you to eat, O Lono.
Accept this plea in the place of life! Proclaim it to the sacred
    shrines! [May the good] be lasting! Let it pass into the
    night—an offering acceptable to the gods!
Let down the gourd—the fruit of the gourd that it may bear
    from every branch—thus becoming a field of gourds.
Let it bear to the lineage of Hi'i[15]—gourds as bitter as the gall
    of fish.

[15] Hi'i—a shortened form of Hi'iaka.

8

How many seeds have been planted on the field cleared by fire
   to flourish in Hawaiʻi?
Planted is the gourd; it grows; it leafs; it blossoms; it bears
   fruit.
Let it be set so as to be well shaped—may this be an excellent
   container.
Pluck it off the vine; carve it out;
Cut it and empty it of its contents.
The great world is a gourd, its lid the heaven of Kuakini.[16]
Pierce the edges [of the container]; use a rainbow for a handle.
Take out of it all jealousies; all wrong doings; the wild
   tendencies.
[Which resembles] the gourd in the cavern of Mu-a-Iku—the
   container of gusty winds. Let it shine bright as a star.
Break forth with a resounding noise, let the bird of the mountain
   utter its call;
Grasp it as it crouches low; hold it high over Wawau.
The night has been peaceful, O Lono, from all disturbances,
The jealousies that lead to bickering; the bickerings of the
   priests who use the hook for the *ulua* fish.
Take possession, O Lono—drive away the bad plovers of Maʻaku-
   newa, with their shiny bodies.
Concentrate, O Lono, on goodness—only goodness!
Bind it here; put the faults away in the background, back of the
   babbling waters of Waioha.

(Translation by Mrs. Pukui.)

NAMING.

Naming is so significant in relation to the individual
within the kinship (*ʻohana*) that it deserves a whole treatise
in itself, but here we must confine ourselves to what will be
little more than a summary.

Some children were named for their ancestors (*inoa
kupuna*), some for events, some for or by chiefs, and some were
named by the gods. To name a child for a deceased relative was
to make the name live again (*ola hou*). An aged woman,
Ka-ʻahaʻaina-a-ka-Haku (The-Lord's-Supper) told us that she
was born on the day when the Lord's Supper was first
administered in Kona, Hawaiʻi, by the missionaries.

Keahi Luahine's son was named Renown Centennial for two
events. He was born when the Missionary Centennial celebration was held at Punahou in 1920, and the Prince of Wales
arrived here at that time on the ship Renown. His mother made
many of the *kahili* used in the pageant, so his Hawaiian name
(Ka-haku-hulu-aliʻi) means "Worker-of-royal-feathers."

When King Kalakaua was playing billiards in the amusement hall in Waiohinu, Ka-ʻu, my mother ran in with another
girl to call I-ka-ʻaka, the man who was playing with the king.
As soon as the king heard that I-ka-ʻaka was wanted at home

[16] Kuakini—*Kua* (back) and *kini* (multitude). Refers to the
multitude of gods.

because his wife was giving birth to a baby, he said, "Name her for my playing." And so the little girl was given the name of Ke-li'i-pahupahu-o-Kalakaua (Kalakaua-is-a-billiard-playing-chief).

Sometimes, in affection for a chief, a child was given the chief's name. After the death of a beloved chiefess, the name Keli'i-pa'ahana (The industrious-chiefess) was given to an ancestress of mine and handed down through generations to my mother and to a cousin.

The type of name given by the gods is called *inoa po* (night name). There are Hawaiians today who believe in *inoa po* but make no mention of it, lest they be laughed at and called superstitious. An *inoa po* is a name for a child, given in a dream to a member of the family. Refusal of the name will result in a crippled body and, if this warning goes unheeded, death for the child. The god who sends the name, or for whom the child is named, is believed to be a guardian over him. Such a name belongs to the individual to whom it is given and cannot be given to another. Some of these names do not contain the name of the god but the Hawaiians know to whom they belong; for example, such names as Earth-devourer, Mountain-dweller, Eater-of-'ohelo-berries, The-flame, Great-fire-pit all point to the Goddess Pele as their source.

A woman in Hilo dreamed of a red-headed woman who rose from a deep pool of water and asked that the child about to be born be named Noho-wai (Water-dweller). The dreamer was a member of a Christian church and had a fear of following old beliefs, so when her daughter was born she named her Clara for a favourite sister-in-law. In a few days the baby's neck began to swell on both sides. The doctor said that it was some glandular trouble, but in spite of the best medical care the swelling grew worse, until the baby's neck looked like that of a lizard. The aunt for whom the baby was named guessed that a water spirit was offended. She asked, "Have you ever heard from your grandfolk whether one of your ancestors was a water spirit (*mo'o*)?" "Yes, but I do not want to have anything to do with those old beliefs." "Has this baby been given a name in a dream?" "Yes, but I refuse to give the name to her." "What was the name?" "Noho-wai." Picking up the baby, the aunt said to it, "I will take back my name of Clara. Henceforth your name is Noho-wai." The swelling went down and in a short time was entirely gone.

Amu means to shear, *amuamu* to reproach, to revile, or to curse; and *kuamuamu* may be translated "uprisen curse or insult."

The conception and feeling behind the *inoa kuamuamu* is not easily understood except by Hawaiians. It is a memorial, (1) a living sign of *mo-ka-piko* or "the-blood-bond-broken" among blood kinsmen, or (2) a sign of contempt (*ho'owahawaha*) for anyone who has been rude enough to speak unkindly of a chief, a loved one or a favourite child. No matter if a feast of repentance were proffered to wipe out the curse uttered with the *mo-ka-piko*, the name of the child given in remembrance of the insult remained as a reminder of and a reproach for the shameful way in which the offender had behaved. Every time he or she heard it, there would be the memory, the reproach. This is the more common type.

Of another sort were those *kuamuamu* of deprecation. When a woman had given birth to several babies which died shortly after birth, a *kahuna* was consulted to find out whether the parents had sinned or whether a sorcerer had cursed the mother so that she might have no living offspring. If the latter were the case then the next baby to be born was given such a name as Kukae (excrement), Ka-pilau-nui (great stench) or something of like nature. The evil spirits who were in the habit of snatching away the life of the little ones found the name so repulsive that the new baby was left alone. The following are examples within current experience:—

> A boy in Ka-'u was named Kukae (Excreta) for this reason. When seven years of age, that is, old enough to be subincized, the name was set aside (*pale 'ia*) and he was then given the name of Ka'ihi-kapu. Another of the *'ohana*, a girl, was called Pelekunu (Filthy-moldy-odor); and still another, a boy, was called Pupuka (Ugly). These children had all, as babies, been thought to be bothered by evil spirits. The dangerous period was from birth to seven years of age, and after that a better name was given to the child.

Children with *inoa po*, or those named by the *'aumakua* were protected from such troubles, because each *'aumakua* stood guard over his own namesake. No *inoa kuamuamu* such as mentioned under type 2 could be given to children who had received *inoa po*. It is permissible, however, to give the first type of *inoa kuamuamu* to a person with an *inoa po*.

The following incidents from Ka-'u history illustrate the giving of *inoa kuamuamu*:—

> Lilikalani or Haililani, as he was sometimes called, was chief of Kama'oa, in Ka-'u. His constant companion was Mokila, my great-grand-father. Mokila was perfectly devoted to Haililani. One day he heard someone from another district remark, "I thought Haililani was a chief indeed but he has no servants to serve him." (*Kai no a he ali'i 'i'o o Haililani, he kanaka 'ole ka*). Mokila resented this remark, and when his first-born came he was named Ke-'li'i-kanaka-'ole-o-Haililani or Haililani-chief-without-servant. Haililani was a kindly chief, friendly and fair in all his dealings, but sickness, especially skin trouble made him unlovely to see. On one of their trips to a

neighbouring district, Mokila heard it said that Haililani was a disagreeable fellow. When Mokila's second son was born he was called Ke-'li'i-kahaka-o-Haililani or Haililani-the-disagreeable-chief.

Just before the birth of his third son, Mokila again heard a remark that roused his resentment. This time, it was that the chief was disloyal to his people. The baby was named Ke-'li'i-kipi-o-Haililani or Haililani-the-traitor-chief.

On another occasion Mokila heard it said that his *haku ali'i* was an *ali'i-pio* or a captive brought into the district to rule over the people of Ka-'u. This was not true, for Haililani belonged to the district. So he named his youngest child, a daughter, Te-'li'i-pio-o-Haililani or Haililani-the-captive-chief.

Next to the *inoa po*, the names given to link a child with his or her forbears were of the greatest importance in families of rank.

It was and is still customary also to give names of forbears (*inoa kupuna*), near or distant, for the sake both of identification and commemoration. Sometimes such a name will be given to a child born later when the child to whom it was first given has died. The naming of the *hiapo* or first-born with a name belonging to the genealogy (*kuauhau*) was so important that it required a family council. But today it is just a matter of different relatives " giving " a name informally; such a name " given " constitutes a bond, a token of *aloha*, an expression of gratification and mark of pride and esteem.

Showing Off Favourites.

Certain children were, because of their attractiveness and charm, " made favourites " (*pa'i punahele*). It was the grandparents who would lavish affection on these pets. They had the best of everything, choice foods, the best mats and *kapa*. Every few years the fostering elders would hold a veritable carnival for the display of their favourites. In Ka-'u these were always at Pu'u-ka-holua, a hill where chiefs raced their sleds (*holua*), and where also were held the *hula* contests in which trained dancers contested.

The *ho'o-kela-kela* was the carnival for the display of *punahele*. The people flocked to Pu'u-ka-holua from all sides. The persons who went to carry the *punahele* wore on the top of the head, like a *lei*, a hoop of plaited *lauhala* stuffed with *pulu* (down of tree fern), which fitted the head securely. On this hoop was carried a calabash of *poi*. The

hoop, with the *poi* bowl in the middle, had a rim wide enough
to hold small meat containers when the bearer sat perfectly
still. The bearer would sit motionless, while before him
the *punahele* was seated on a pile of fine mats. A relative
fed the child from this mobile canteen on the bearer's head.
Mele or "name songs" were chanted by the relatives in
praise of each contesting *punahele*, which were of all ages.
Those that received the loudest shouts of acclaim from the
onlookers were the winners, and after the ceremonial feeding and name chanting, a great feast was enjoyed by every
one, with general hilarity, and *hula* dancing. These were
family affairs. As all the contestants were *ʻohana* of the
locality, it mattered little to the feasters who had won:
they were there for a good time. Feasting would continue
several days.

We have never heard of this type of carnival anywhere
else except in Ka-ʻu.

Exhibition Feast.

The "Exhibition Feast" (*ʻAhaʻaina Hoʻike*) is a post-
missionary development of the Protestant Mission, a com-
petition for Sunday Schools in compositions and singing of
songs telling the stories from the Bible which have been
learned in Sunday School. But it was not just for young
folks: everyone from each church, from grey heads to
babies, was there, all singing together for the prize. The
singers from the same church all wore dresses and shirts of
the same colour, and each church had its colour. The song-
fest was followed by a feast.

Feast for Blessing Products of Craftsmanship.

When some skilful piece of work was completed, and the
thing made or done required the blessing of the spirit
guardians (*ʻaumakua*), there was a feast of blessing or
tending (*ʻAhaʻaina kahukahu*) which consecrated the product
of dedicated labour to its proper use. This was essential,
not for every product of craftsmanship, but for the *first*
thing made: a first mat, quilt, fish-net, bowl, etc. It was,
for a first-thing-made, equivalent to the *mawaewae* for the
first-born: it consecrated not only that first thing, but all
of the same type that would be made by that person. The

first-thing-made, and consecrated, was never given away: it must be put by and guarded carefully, for it was given to the *'aumakua* and held the *mana* for that work for the person who had made it. It remained the precious possession of its maker.

In the prayer used at this time, the *'aumakua* were asked to increase or multiply the thing blessed.

The prayer was composed to fit the occasion. It would be addressed to the *akua* or *'aumakua* identified with the material used in the work. For instance, a prayer consecrating a new gourd would be addressed to Lono. The prayer for *kapa* made of *wauke* (*Broussonettia papyrifera*) would mention Lauhuki and La'ahana, the first *kapa* makers, according to legend, who were the daughters of Maikoha from whose body sprang the first *wauke*; and who in dreams thereafter taught his daughters how to make and decorate the first *kapa*. Every such prayer would have in it the phrases:—

Ho mai ka ike nui, ka 'ike ike.
Grant knowledge of the great things, and of the little
    things.

Ka ike nui referred to the knowledge of the work as a whole, while by " little things " (*ka 'ike ike*) was meant all the exact little details affecting material and technique which the good craftsman must thoroughly comprehend.

The prized possessions of a person, which have been blessed by a *pule kahukahu*, were buried with that person at death unless specifically given by " command " (*kauoha*), i.e., willed by word of mouth, to a surviving relative.

FEAST FOR WORKERS.

The Feast of Countless Hands (*'Aha'aina Laulima*) celebrated any communal enterprise involving the labour of " many hands," but especially work connected with food raising, such as clearing land, making and repairing irrigation ditches and taro patches, or fishponds; or planting big patches of " dry " taro or sweet potato for *ali'i* (chiefs) and *maka'ainana* (the people) in the olden times. In preparation in advance for such a communal feasting, the people of the community would raise taro and sweet potato, pigs, chickens, fish (in ponds, and in the flooded taro patches).

FEASTS OF WELCOME.

As elsewhere in Polynesia, the return of a relative long absent was greeted with expressions of joy taking the form of wailing (*uwe helu*) like that for a departed spirit. Whether coming or going, the loved one was hailed with a wailing chant that gave vent to overflowing emotion, and expression to joy, grief, memory and affection.

The wailing was but the vocal expression of sentiment. The true welcome called for a family gathering, and a feast in honour of the returning relative. *Ho'okipa* means hospitality, and is derived from the word *kipa*, to turn in, lodge. The welcoming-feast, *'Aha'aina Ho'okipa*, re-established the returned relative in the *'ohana* and *'aina* or homeland, did honour to the person welcomed and created goodwill for all concerned. It was also an opportunity for joyous sociability, a " good time for all "—ever a welcome interlude in the humdrum of existence for gaiety-loving Hawaiians. The omission of these courtesies could be the cause of hurt feelings, resentment, even bitter enmity. It could be taken as a calculated insult. Especially in the case of relatives of distinction a true welcome was more than a token: it was a duty.

Wherever encountered, a long-absent relative was welcomed, embraced and wailed over. The wail was not a wordless cry like a baby's. In these wails of welcome, the relationship of the welcomed member to the person who wailed was mentioned, and perhaps the loved ones who had departed from this life, as well as portions of ancient poetry. One after the other as they came in, the welcoming relatives uttered this cry. A person has to hear it or see it to understand what it was like.

In 1935, I accompanied Dr. Handy to Hawai'i where my people came from. The Puna relatives, who were all under fifty years of age did not wail but some of those in Ka-'u, the aged ones did.

Near Kiolaka'a, above Waiohinu, was a beautiful food patch with no house anywhere near it. We wanted so much to see the owner, then one morning we found him there, old, stooped and leaning upon a heavy cane. He was like all old-timers, friendly and kind and most willing to have us walk in and question him on his food patch. There were tall sugar canes, bananas, neat rows of hilled sweet potatoes and many varieties of taros. After we were through questioning him he began questioning me as to my birthplace, my parents, etc. His interest grew when I told him that I was born in that very district, Ka-'u. He shook his head when I mentioned my mother. " And your grandparents were whom?" he continued. At the mention of my grandmother's name, he asked if she was the Nali'ipo'aimoku who lived at Waikapuna beach and when he was told that she was the same, he began immediately to wail aloud. He was her cousin. He had gone to Kona before my mother was born and naturally he would not know her. I wish there had been some way of recording that particular wail. Hills, beaches, legendary spots, rocks, ancient warriors, etc., all were mentioned in poetical terms. This wailing custom is dying fast and it will not be long when it is heard no more.

The feast to welcome a returned relative or honoured guest was a spontaneous affair. When news came to the other relatives that so-and-so had come and was at such-and-such a relative's house, they gathered there to welcome him. There was the wailing and then the feasting. Relatives usually came with food and no matter how many came, it was no burden to the householder. The feast was either large or small depending on the number of relatives one had and the prestige of the family.

FEASTS FOR HELPERS.

At any great feast, those who did all the work, the preparing and serving of the food, the decorating of the house and sheds, and who wrapped up in *ti* leaves the gifts of food to be taken home, got little to eat and would lose so much sleep that they were weary eyed (*makaluhi*). So it was the duty of the householder or host to provide them with a hog and other viands, which they would cook and enjoy after the guests had gone home.

BETROTHAL AND MARRIAGE.

Distinguished families betrothed (*hoʻopalau*) their *hiapo* during childhood, sometimes before birth. The betrothal was marked by an exchange of gifts between the two households in which the *ʻohana* participated, but there was no feast at this time. In one instance of *hoʻopalau* remembered on the Island of Hawaiʻi, the betrothal was sealed with a prayer and offering at Ka-lua-o-Pele (The pit of Pele, Halemaʻumaʻu). Later the betrothal was broken and subsequent troubles are believed to have been due to disregard of the *kapu* laid before Pele. To break the *hoʻopalau* was a serious offence. In another instance, breach of *hoʻopalau* resulted in chronic sickness from which the one responsible for the breach could never obtain release.

Customs relating to betrothal in Ka-ʻu and Puna, as related by some elders of these districts, may be summarized as follows:—

There was no set age for the *ho'opalau*, the participants ranging in years from unborn babes to young people of marriageable age. Age of maturity was recognized as about twenty years. There were several ways of selecting a wife. The first one, *mai ka po mai* (according to instructions " out of night ") was said to be the best. A close relative of a boy might have a dream indicating where and to whom to go to find a mate for the boy. At the same time a dream was given to the girl's near relative telling him whom to expect and why. This often led one to another locality or island for the bride-to-be. It was understood that such a mating *mai ka po mai* was only for those who came from the same family stock or were children of the same *'aumakua*. When the relative of the boy came to the home of the girl he was treated with every courtesy, for to fail to receive him properly was an offense to the *'aumakua* who sent him. After talking the matter over and the betrothal having been agreed upon, the date of the wedding was set if the couple were of *'aumakua* who wished this union. Then the *ho'opalau* became binding. To break a *ho'opalua* was inexcusable and the one who did so paid the penalty in suffering. The relatives of both sides made fine mats, tapas and whatever else was needed for the new household. The relatives of the boy gathered the material together for the new house and the relatives of the girl assisted in building it. Neither side wished it said that their child came from an *'ohana puhikole* (destitute *'ohana*) and so they saw to it that their son or daughter was well provided for when the *la ho'ao* or wedding day came.

If the period of *ho'opalau* lasted a long time, the young man sent gifts every now and then to his wife-to-be, perhaps a pig, a catch of fish, chickens, a feather *lei* or a fat dog. When the young man showed himself mindful of his future wife it was welcomed as evidence that he would be a good provider. When the house had been made ready, and furnished by the *'ohana* on both sides (see below), the young couple were taken into it. The *kahuna* prayed that the union be fruitful. In his prayer occurs the phrase: " *E uhi ia olua i ke kapa ho'okahi*" or " *You both shall (forever) share the same kapa*," meaning, that they were to share all things between them. Perhaps elsewhere, as described by David Malo (*Hawaiian Antiquities*, Chapter XVIII) a *kapa* was actually draped over the pair, but it was not so among the Puna-Ka-'u people. If the young wedded pair were chiefs, the people came with their *ho'okupu* (gifts)—food, mats, tapas, canoes, everything that they had to give. The marriage house (*hale ho'ao*) was *kapu*, only for the bride and groom, where they could have privacy and be by themselves if they chose. The *'ohana* had their feast out of doors or in sheds (*halau*) built for the purpose, where they ate and enjoyed themselves.

Another way to make a *ho'opalau* was by studying the genealogy of the family and selecting a youth and maiden of equal rank. After the selection was made the parents and grandparents talked it over and the *ho'opalau* was agreed upon. *Ho'opalau*, however arranged, was characteristic of families of rank, with whom a favourable union from the point of view of genealogy was of importance.

Amongst commoners there were no formalities. When a lad

saw a maiden that he wanted for wife, he spoke of it to his parents or grandparents. Then his people went to see the girl's people. If it was agreeable to the elders, and if the girl agreed, the young man simply came to her home to live with her, becoming one of the household. Hawaiians preferred girl children because the girl remained with her people while a boy went to his wife's parents' household. An old saying puts it: *He malama makua hunowai ke keikikane.* " A boy supports his parents-in-law."

Sometimes a girl's parents would take the initiative in making a proposal to the parents of a good looking, industrious boy. This might be at the girl's behest, or on their own initiative. No girl would " propose " to a young man herself—she would be too shy. But she had her ways of attracting him. Neither girl nor boy was forced to marry contrary to heart's desire, except perhaps in certain rare instances when compulsion was necessary.

Their words and expressions relating to mating and marriage are capable of telling in brief more about the habits and points of view of Hawaiians past and present, for persons who at all comprehend Polynesian mentality, than many pages of " learned " dissertation. Below are some of the more common of these words. To those who do not comprehend that even modern Hawaiians are, like their ancestors and all Polynesians, people to whom natural functions are "natural," hence nothing to be ashamed of, and who may be shocked by some of the terms or implied *mores*, it may be necessary to say that it is not just to judge these people by standards of morality other than their own. The collapse of standards due to the sudden abolition of the *kapu* in 1819 preceded the first teaching of Christian principles. Yet responsible Hawaiians, both before and since Christianization, have had and still have a code of right and wrong of their own as definite and as honestly adhered to as that of any other civilized people. In fact, the suffering to be expected from neglect or wilful disobedience to this code affecting sexual relations and responsibility to *'ohana* was more drastic and immediate than anything in Christian ethics or modern common law. The *'aumakua* (family guardians) did not postpone to an indefinite and vague " future life " punishments for broken *kapu* or shameless behaviour, neglect or irresponsibility. Present behaviour determined the future state, but it also induced immediate effects, good or bad. " Sin " (*hewa, hala*) will be discussed in our next chapter.

The following are post-discovery terms.

In old Hawai'i there was no such thing as an illegitimate child. After the coming of the missionaries and the introduction of the Christian marriage, such terms as these became generally used:—

Wahine mare. A wife whom one has married.
Kane mare. A husband whom one has married.
Wahine manu-ahi. A mistress; a woman who is not legally a wife.
Wahine kapae. (A woman set to one side.) A mistress.

The word *manu-ahi* (fire-bird) was originally the name of a Hawaiian who used to work in a store in Honolulu. He would often give a little extra as a gift to a customer; so, many went to buy *manu-ahi*. Soon *manu-ahi* became synonymous with free: something freely given.

Thus a *kane manu-ahi* or *wahine manu-ahi* became a mate free of the ties of marriage, and a *keiki manu-ahi* (illegitimate child) was the result of a free union.

Noho kapae (living to one side) is another way of saying, an affair without wedlock.
Keiki kameha'i (mystery child) is one term for an illegitimate child, and the *keiki po'o-'ole* (headless child) is another—because he has no sire or "head of the family." (How my mother hated this term, and often said that every baby has a head, including those born out of wedlock!)
Inoa 'ole (no name) is also used to indicate an illegitimate baby.

The following are all old terms relating to mating and marriage.

Noi wahine is the old word for a proposal. *Ua hele mai lakou e noi wahine.* (They came to ask for a wife.) Today, it is *noi mare*, or marriage request.

Ua 'ae ia ka noi means "The proposal is accepted," and *Ua ho'ole ia ka noi* means that it is rejected.

As a *ho'opalau* or betrothal was very binding in the olden days, I have never heard of any term or expression meaning a broken engagement. To break an engagement today is to *uhaki* or *ho'opau i ka ho'opalau* (break or end the engagement).

Nohu pu—"Just to live together," as man and wife.

Ho'omau keiki—A mating of a high chief and chiefess for the purpose of obtaining a child of high rank.

The marriage between young *ali'i* who were brother and sister (or with half-brother or half-sister), which was permitted only at the level of the highest *ali'i* for reasons of genealogical status and what is termed today "line breeding" in biology, was referred to as *pi'o* (arching) and a child born of such a union was a *ni'aupi'o* (coconut frond arched back upon itself).

Marriage within the family circle was called a *ho'i* or returning. "*Ho'i i ka makuahine a puka o mea.*" (He returned to his aunt and so and so was born).

Very close intermarriage among the people in general was not encouraged, such as the marriage of brother and sister, nephew and aunt, niece and uncle. Should such occur in a family, they were made fun of and referred to as *'ohana kiko moa*, or "relatives that mate and hatch like chickens."

Marriage between cousins was approved of and there were instances in which betrothals were made in early childhood. They were equals in generation and in their position in life and so the older folk would say, "*I pa'i aku no o kahi i kahi, o laua no ia.*" (Should one slap the other, it wouldn't matter, for they belong to each other).

For a stepfather to mate with his wife's daughter was considered a disgrace. The people would say, "*Ka! mai kahi huna no o ka makua a kahi huna o ke keiki!*" (Ugh! from the privates of the mother to the privates of her child!)

In some legends (not of our locality) and in rare instances I have heard of elsewhere, a woman might adopt a boy, rear him and later take him for a mate. I have heard the comment of my people on such a practice. "*Ho'opailua! O ka malama no i kahi huna o ke keiki a ki'i iho no.*" (Disgusting! After caring for his privates [in childhood] she takes him for her mate!)

Should a man take his wife's younger sister or cousin for a mate with his wife's approval, no one worried about it, because, "*O lakou no ia.*" (They all belong to each other). Should this be done without the approval of the wife, and the sister had deliberately set a snare to take the husband away, then such an act was called *po'alo maka*, a scooping out of the eyeballs of the wife. If a good friend, having shared the hospitality of a person, eating of his bounty and sleeping in his house, should then try to take the mate of his host, that act was also called *po'alo maka*.

Polygamy and polyandry were not frowned upon if the first mate had no objection, and very often it was the wife or the husband who would suggest it. A wife might say to her husband, "I love my cousin so much that I do not want her to go away, so you take her for your wife," and to the cousin she might say, "*Eia no ka kaua kane*, or "Let him be our husband." The children of one were the children of the other.

With many of the families, who were admitted to the royal court because of blood relationship, the virginity of the daughters was strictly guarded and when a girl became of marriageable age and was spoken for as a wife, she was taken to the chief who would remove her virginity. *Na ke ali'i e moe mua.* (For the chief to sleep with for the first time.) After that she was free to be married. Should an offspring result in this union with the chief, the husband would be proud of and make much of that child because the baby was the offspring of his *Ali'i*.

Sometimes it was a dying wife or husband who would select a successor. The wife might say to her husband, "When I am gone, take my sister (or cousin) so-and-so to be your wife, that our children may have a *makua* (mother) in our family. An outsider may mistreat them." Then to her sister she would say, "Here is our husband. Take care of our children." With a request like this, the husband and sister would become wife and husband for the sake of the children. Without such a request, the taking of a new mate soon after the death of the old drew forth the comment, "*Auwe! 'a'ohe i nalo ka 'ula'ula o ka lepo, o ka loa'a no ia o ka wahine hou!*" (Oh! the redness of the [broken] earth had not had time to be covered with grass, before a new wife is taken!) It denoted a lack of affection for the wife who had just passed away.

In the days in which there were no divorce courts, a miserably unhappy marriage could be broken very easily by going elsewhere and refusing to live together again as wife and husband. In time she would find another husband and he another wife and a friendly relation was generally maintained. Marriages were for the most part permanent, and the affection of *kane* and *wahine* for each other was very deep.

Sex knowledge was not kept from children, and though they were not ignorant of sex there was no unseemly behaviour on the part of the young folks going about together. They went swimming together with nothing on their bodies, but used the hands as a shield when coming out of the water. It was impressed into their minds that it was not good to indulge in sexual practises when too young and a boy who did so was called a *keiki pu'e* (a rapacious child) and avoided by the other boys and girls. When a girl or boy felt matured, he or she withdrew from their young playmates and associated more with the older people. This was a sign that he was beginning to feel his responsibility, and thinking of marriage. He was closely observed by the neighbours and if industrious and well behaved, they knew that he would be a good husband, but if he was lazy, none cared to have him as an addition to the family. This was also true of girls.

Among the chiefs, a boy was not only trained in warfare and government but when he was grown physically, a matured chiefess was chosen to train him in sexual practices. This was part of his education. Should a child result, he or she was reared by the mother. Thus it was that Kamehameha claimed Ka'oleioku as "the son of my beardless youth," at the dedication of the *heiau* of Pu'ukohola. This was the son born to him by Kane-i-ka-polei, one of the wives of his uncle Kalaniopu'u.

The people of Ka-'u married mostly within their own district and discouraged marriages to those of the outside district or islands. If there was a marriage with one outside of the district, that person was encouraged to remain as one of them. Generations marrying within their group welded the families into one, hence the saying, *Mai ka uka a ke kai, mai kahi pae a kahi pae o Ka-'u, he ho'okahi no 'ohana.* (From hills to the sea, from one end to the other, Ka-'u is one family).

The intermarriages of relatives which bound them to each other and to the homeland, produced this saying, *Ka-'u lepo 'ula'ula.* (Ka-'u of the red earth). That is, the blood of Ka-'u is thickened by intermarriage.

Palama. When the house of a chiefess or chief was enclosed with a fence of *lama (Maba Sandwichensis)* wood, no one was allowed to enter except a chosen few. To enter such an enclosure was punishable by death. The *lama* wood is very hard, and made an impenetrable fence.

High chiefs often placed their favourite wives and children under the restrictions of the *palama.*

Pulama. The *palama* is not to be confused with *pulama*, to cherish and care for. To *pulama* a wife (or a child) is to treat with loving care, seeing that she is happy, not allowing her to wear herself out with hard work and so on.

ANCIENT MARRIAGE CHANT.

'E'ele mimo ka lani
'Uwe'uwehe ke ao ho'okiki'i
Kiki'i ke ao 'opua lani e
'Ola'olapa ka uwila
Ho'oku'i, nei, nakolokolo ka hekili
Ke wawa kupina'i nei i Ku-haili-moe
O Haiha'ilauahea
O na wahine i ka puoko o ke ahi
O 'imi'imi, o nalowale a loa'a
Loa'a ho'i ka hoa e.
Pupu'u aku o ke anu o ka Ho'oilo
Ke 'iloli nei ka lani
Loa'a ka hale kipa maha o Hako'ilani
Na ke aloha i kono e hui 'olua e.
O ka hakamoa keia, ke halakau nei ka lani
O haka, o haka, i ka lani
O nei, o nakolo, o 'u'ina,
O nakolo i luna, o nehe i lalo
He nehe na ka 'ili'ili kaka'a o 'Ikuwa
A wawa 'ia no he hale kanaka
Nawai e wawa ke hale alaneo,
Pili olua e—
Moku ka pawa o ke ao
Ke moakaka nei ka hikina
Ua hiki ho'i,
Ua kapu i ka po
A ho'oma'ama'ama i ke ao
Ho'ao e! ua noa!
Lele wale aku la ka pule a ke kahuna,
Ua ao ho'i—amama ua noa.
Lele uli! lele wai!
Lele wale ka pule.

The sky is covered with darkness,
The tilting clouds begin to part,
The leaning bud-shaped clouds in the sky.
The lightning flashes here and there,
The thunder reverberates, rumbles and roars,
Sending echoes repeatedly to Ku-haili-moe,
To Ha'iha'i-lau-ahea,
To the women in the rising flames.
There was a seeking of the lost, now it is found—
A mate is found,
One to share the chills of winter.
The sky is changing,
For Hakoi-lani, the house of welcome where rest is found.
Love has made a plea
That you two become united.
Here is a perch, a heavenly resting place,
A perch, a perch in heaven.

There is a trembling, a rumbling, a crackling
A rattling above, a rattling below,
A rustling of the rolling pebbles of Ikuwa.
There are sounds of voices in an inhabited house,
But what voices are heard in any empty one?
You two are now one,
The darkness has begun to depart,
The east is beginning to brighten
For day is here at last!
The night has been made *kapu*
Until the light of day arrives.
You are wedded!   Free [to each other],
The prayer of the priest has taken flight.
Day is here!
Amama, the *kapu* is freed!
It has flown to the darkness! flown to the waters!
The prayer has gone its way.

A NEW HOME.

The various houses that made up the Hawaiian home-
stead (*kauhale*) were described in Chapter I. The basic
functional units were the Common House or *Hale Noa*
and the *Mua.* The *hale noa* served the whole family as
sleeping and living room. The *mua* was *kapu* to women, for
there the men slept when consecrated for war, fishing, canoe
building, or other work that required segregation from
contacts with women and little children that might be con-
taminating, as offensive to *'aumakua* and *akua.* Here was
the shrine of the guardian spirits also, the *kuahu* (comparable to the Maori *mua* and *tuahu*). All other structures
were for special use, and were little more than sheds: for
the men's oven (*imu*), for the women's oven, for *kapa* beating, housing canoe and fishing gear, storage, or for segregation of women while menstruating.

When we speak of the new home, we refer to a new *hale
noa,* which was the central living unit, built with a care, for
comfort in all seasons.

The building or refurbishing of the terrace faced with
stone (*paepae*), cutting and erecting of timbers for the
frame, and thatching were done by the men of the immediate
family. There existed in Hawaii no professional carpenters, or
guilds, like those of the wood workers in the southern islands.

Relatives might be counted on to furnish the new home
for the young people. They came from far and wide, bringing them gifts: mats, tapas, bowls, calabashes. In anticipation of the event, the head of the household had raised or

acquired hogs, dogs, chickens. Relatives went out for fish, and brought taro, sweet potato and greens. A ground oven was filled with foods for the men; and another for the women, omitting the pork and dog.

Before the ovens were opened, the *piko* (umbilicus) of the house must be cut by trimming the thatch hanging over the doorway with an appropriate prayer, and offerings to *akua* and *'aumakua*.

A red *kumu* or red *weke*, and a white *'ama'ama* or *'aholehole* fish were placed under the threshold.

The householder then chopped back the rough thatch over the arched lintel with his adze, cutting down against a block of wood held beneath the thatch, making a smooth, recessed arch.

For this operation, here is a prayer that he recited as he did the cutting.

PULE HO'OLA'A HALE (HOUSE DEDICATION PRAYER).

E 'oki i ka piko o ka hale
He hale ku i ka 'ele-ua, i ka 'ele ao
He hale noho ho'i no ke kanaka.
E Lono e, eia ka hale la,
Ua ku i Mauli-ola.
E ola i ka noho hale,
E ola i ke kanaka kipa mai
Eola i ka haku-'aina
E ola i na 'li'i
Oia ke ola o kauhale e Mauli-ola,
Ola a kolo-pupu, a haumaka 'iole
A papa lauhala, a ka i koko
A kau i ka puaneane.
Oia ke ola au e ke akua—[Amama ua noa].

E Ku, e Kane, e Lono
Ku'ua mai i ke ola,
I na pomaika'i,
A ea ka lani, ka honua
Ea ia Kane-i-ka-wai-ola
E ola mai kahi pae a kahi pae,
E ola mai luna a lalo,
Mai kaupoku a ke kahua—
E ola—a ola loa no.

Cut the umbilical cord of the house
A house that resists the rains and stormy elements.
A house for man to dwell in.
O Lono, behold the house,
A house in the presence of the giver of life
Grant life to those who dwell therein,
Grant life to the visitors that come,
Grant life to the landlord.

Grant life to the chiefs,
Let that be the life from the life-giver,
Life until one creeps and is weak-eyed with age
Until one sprawls like a withered hala leaf,
Until one reaches the very extremity of life.
Let this be the life granted to us by the gods.

O Ku, O Kane, O Lono,
Let down the gift of life,
And all the blessings with it.
Till the heavens and earth be heaped,
Let them be raised up by Kane of the living waters.
May there be life from one boundary to the other
From above to below
From roof to foundation.
May there be life—everlasting life.

When the new doorway stood clear and trim, with its fresh lintels showing and threshold in place, the mats and other interior furnishings were carried in and put in place. Then the new abode was beautified with fresh greenery and flowers of whatever kinds were available: in particular sweet-scented fern, *maile* vine, *'ilima,* pandanus seed *lei,* blossoms of *lehua* and the shiny foliage of *'ie'ie* from the uplands. These were an essential part of every ritual, bringing the life of the *wao akua* (hinterland of the gods) into the home, and making it delightful for gods and guardian spirits, as for the people there. The people were all wearing leis of flowers, or *maile* vine interwoven with fragrant fern.

Banana and *'awa* were laid on the *paepae.* Then the ovens were opened and the food spread out on the *paepae* and in nearby sheds, and all set to with a will to enjoy the feast. Nothing must be left uneaten: every particle of food must be wrapped and taken away with them by the visiting kin and kith.

The householders in the new house immediately made full return for the courtesies received, by giving to departing relatives and friends all that had been brought to it as gifts by those coming to the feast, everything except what was essential for furnishing and a few prized items that might be kept without offence. So the feast was a sharing of dedicated foods; and the giving and taking of presents was actually a general exchange in which the prestige and pleasure of giving and receiving was enjoyed by all concerned. It was a gay time, one to be remembered with *aloha.*

Family gatherings like this often lasted several days. Even then every departing guest must be given a bundle of food to take home. This was called the *ho'ina* (return). A feast without a *ho'ina* was a poor one indeed.

While the merry-makers were eating there was much banter, joking, relating of anecdotes, matching wits. No unpleasant or malicious talk was wanted, for the *poi* bowls were visible evidence of the presence of Kane as Haloa, the taro; and other *akua* and *'aumakua* in Nature were right there in the greenery all about. The feasting and jollification roused some to rise here and there to dance a *hula*, as someone chanted a *mele*. The old people would be moved to chant *mele* and *oli* belonging to the family or the land, or relating some event, or perhaps honouring a beloved *ali'i*. At family festivities in the old days the " entertainment " was spontaneous, not rehearsed, except for formal festivities of *ali'i*, or during the Makahiki harvest festival in honour of Lono.

SICKNESS AND DEATH.

The next chapter describes in some detail the psychic phase of *'ohana* relationship. Since for Hawaiians the ultimate cause of all illness, and even of accident, was psychic; and in view of the fact that death and everything associated with it, even the physical handling of the body and the bones, was primarily psychic in purpose and significance, we have deemed it logical to reserve the description and interpretation of sickness and death for the next chapter. From the Hawaiian point of view the major " life cycle " for the *'ohana*, was that extending from the birth of a first-born to the birth of a first-born in the next generation. This was the full life cycle: for the individual, the span from birth to marriage with offspring. In a very true sense, sickness was, in infancy an intimation, in older years a beginning, of another cycle which might well be termed the " death cycle," in which the *'uhane* or spirit is poised to enter its discarnate phase of existence.

VI.

THE PSYCHIC PHASE OF RELATIONSHIP

Before entering upon our description of the psychic phases of experience and theory of the Ka-'u family relationship system, it seems advisable to make certain points clear to our readers, who will range from those interested in Polynesian lore as such, for its own intrinsic interest, to ethnologists, ethnographers and other professional scientists versed in the conceptions and terminologies of cultural and sociological anthropology.

We are not unacquainted with the terminologies and concepts of current anthropology, psychology and psychiatry. But we do not conceive it to be our role in this description of the Hawaiian Ka-'u 'ohana system as such, to incorporate in this description either terms or interpretive comments which are foreign to the native Hawaiian philosophy and theory of nature and man.

Our sole and only concern is to relate truly in terms clear and comprehensible to layman and professionals alike, what Ka-'u people experienced, did and thought. We leave it to each reader to interpret and analyze in terms of whatever set of concepts he may adhere to, or that interests him—be it religious or non-religious, spiritualistic, psychological, cultural, sociological, comparative or historical.

To ask what either author "believes" is idle. Here follow descriptions of some of the things experienced, done and thought by natives in Ka-'u on the island of Hawai'i. For the sake of objectivity we always seek in study to keep our own personal beliefs out of the way, in so far as possible. It is not sensible, of course, for any human being, as a cultured creature whose thinking is pervaded by his own subjectivity, to pretend to be wholly objective in recording what others experience, think, feel and do.

The social anthropologist focuses his interest upon sociological phases of relationship. The psychological anthropologist measures factors affecting relationship in accordance with the concepts of one or another "school":

psychoanalytic, analytic psychological, psychiatric, etc. No one of these "schools" has intimate direct bearing upon what we are concerned with here, namely, telling about Hawaiian psychic experiences and "ideas" as the subjective element in consciousness of a folk living and moving within or as a part of nature and family and community in Ka-ʻu, Hawaiʻi.

A Hawaiian's oneness with the living aspect of native phenomena, that is, with spirits and gods and other persons as souls, is not correctly described by the word rapport, and certainly not by such words as sympathy, empathy; abnormal, supernormal or neurotic; mystical or magical. It is not "extra-sensory," for it is partly of-the-senses and not-of-the-senses. It is just a part of natural consciousness for the normal Hawaiian—a "second sense," if you will, like the Keltic "second sight"—but it is not "sight" only, or particularly, but covers every phase of sensory and mental consciousness. *Psychic,* in its original Greek meaning as referring to that which related to the soul, is the word that we prefer to use.

EXPERIENCE.

One notable fact is that the *"beliefs" of our people in Ka-ʻu arise out of sensory-emotional-mental experiences.* They were conceptualized in terms of traditional heritage of interpretation and rationalization. But the commonly held foreign notion that these "beliefs" represent nothing more than an intellectual accumulation of traditional "superstitions" will be seen to be devoid of truth, in the light of the examples quoted below. These examples in every instance illustrate the fact that the " belief " originates in some concrete and tangible complex or psychological sequence involving sensation - emotion - observation - interpretation-rationalization. In a word, these are not " beliefs " merely: they are records and interpretation of experiences.

LARGER MEANING OF RELATIONSHIP.

To comprehend the psyche of our old Hawaiians it is necessary to enlarge the implications of the word "relationship" beyond the limitations of the "interpersonal" or social. The subjective relationships that dominate the Poly-

nesian psyche are with all nature, in its totality, and all its
parts separately apprehended and sensed as personal. The
Sky-that-is-Bright-and-Wide (Wakea), the level Earth
(Papa), were primordial Father and Mother.

Thunder is Kane-hekili (Male-in-the-form-of-gentle
rain),[17] and Ka-poha-'ka'a (Kane-pohaku-ka'a) (Male
[=sky]-the rock-roller),[18] who is the same as Ka-'uila-nui-
makeha (Male [=sky] lightning-flash-great-streaking).[19]

The rain laden clouds over The Breast (Ka-'u) of
Earth (Papa) are Lono Makua, one of whose forms is
Kamapua'a (see section on Kino-lau). Pele is vulcanism in
all its forms, while her sisters are rainbows seen at sea,
rosy glow of dawn on clouds and mountains (Hi'iaka), the
green cloak of jungle of the upland forest (Wahine-'oma'o).
More particular are tree and other plant and bird bodies:
The four *maile* sisters (Maile-ha'i-wale, Brittle-*maile*, Maile-
pakaha, Many-branched *maile*, Maile-kaluhea, Large leaved-
fragrant-*maile*, and Maile-lau-li'i, Small-leaved-*maile*);
sweet potato and *kukae-pua'a*, a native crab grass, and
various other forms which are "myriad body-forms" (see
kino-lau) of Kama-pua'a; Ohi'a-lehua-a-Laka (Laka's
[Maori Rata] *'ohi'a lehua*)[20] and the hawk, Io, were forms

[17] The downpours, which come in late January, February and
March predominantly and with greatest frequency and violence,
develop in the following sequences of meteorological phenomena:
lowering dark cumulus over sea and uplands, with atmospheric still-
ness inducing an increasing sense of ominous oppression; "dry"
thunder, sharp and threatening if near, like distant cannon if far
away: followed very soon by slow, gentle precipitation, which increases
rapidly to a downpour; with continuing heavy thunder, then, in the
cloud and rain shrouded uplands, resounding and thudding, slowly
passing along the ridges or round the mountain's flank and often
then out to sea, where it resounds in dull thuds, and may return in
a direction opposite to that along the ridge, a phenomenon produced
by the miniature cyclonic action of winds, and by convection.

[18] Lightning not infrequently strikes a rain drenched tree or
prominent rock or foreland, or a cliff face, causing stones to come
rolling and crashing down cliffs and into ravines. That is
Ka-poha-'ka'a.

[19] Ka-'uila-nui-makeha was much dreaded, for hunters and gath-
erers of foods and medicine in the uplands, as well as people on the
plain (*kula*) knew well the sudden searing death, or blindness or
paralysis or burns resulting from lightning stroke. His *kapu* required
one to lie face down, never breast and face up, when he was about;
and to keep all water containers covered.

[20] This Laka, male, a form of Ku, is not the same as the female
Laka, *akua* of the hula, who was the same as Kapo, Pele's elder sister.

of Ku; the owl, Pueo, on the other hand, was a "body" of one of the Kane of the Pele clan—these were two very sacred 'aumakua to which particular lineages had affinity, due to genealogical relationship. All the lizards (mo'o) are "bodies" of the legendary giant Mo'o Kiha-wahine, who is ancestress likewise to certain lineages.

The list could be multiplied at great length; if completed, would be encyclopoedic, comprising in fact all forms and phenomena of sky, earth and sea that were to Hawaiians noteworthy. The acute faculties of this native folk noted with exactitude the generic characteristics of all species of terrestrial and marine life, and the subtlest variations of natural phenomena such as winds, light and colour, ruffling of water and variation in surf, and the currents of water and air.

None of these observations, expressing a sense of significant relationship, were idle. One of the most notable things about the psychic (or subjective) relationship of our Ka-'u folk to external things is the fact that whatever is noted and distinguished as significant, psychically, has some real, specific and definite role in the business of living. It may be utilitarian, or aesthetic, or psychic. Breezes, colours, ruffling surfs, are noted and named because related to fishing and voyaging and because they enter into the symbolism of mele (chant), hula (dance), and naming. Every botanical, zoological or inorganic form that is known to have been named (and personalized), was some thing in some way used. Almost certainly there was an infinite variety of living things in forest and sea, of meteorological or marine phenomena, which were unnamed (because unnoteworthy), since they were of no use or interest. Living was experience fraught with exact and definite significance. One had relationship only with what was tangibly a part of one's living[21] The old Hawaiians had no " pure science," and did not indulge in "art for art's sake."

[21] I well remember the hilarity of Marquesan friends in the valley of Pua-ma'u, Hivaoa over the (to them) fatuous interest of the botanist of our expedition in 1921, who was collecting nameless (" useless ") " weeds " and asking their names. Useless weeds naturally had no names. The lack of interest of the modern scientific horticulturalist in native domesticated plants and their cultivation is of the same order! And likewise, we might add the disregard of most modern fisheries experts, for the native fishermen's knowledge of marine life; and of the habits of fish and factors of environment affecting them.—E.S.C.H.

RELATIONSHIP THROUGH ANCESTRAL SPIRITS.

Sometimes an 'aumakua would reveal through a medium, or in a dream, a desired relationship which was referred to as *pili mai ka po mai,* or a spirit relationship coming from the night. When such a revelation was received it became as binding as a blood tie and involved the same rights and obligations.

A woman in Puna was once in great distress over the failing health of her youngest child. In a dream she was told by a man to go to Ola'a to her cousin Kahalaomapuana and there she would receive help. She knew of no such person and asked, "Where is her house?" He answered, "Go on until you come to a house where a plover circles and screams. There your cousin lives." She awoke and went, in obedience to the instruction.

In the meantime, the other woman dreamt that she was told to arise and prepare for her cousin's arrival. She did as she was told and waited. Suddenly a plover circled the outside of her house and screamed. It was not the season for plovers and so she exclaimed, "So! it is you!" (One of her 'aumakua had the form of a plover.) Just then she saw a stranger on horseback pause at her gate and hurried out to the gate saying, "I guess you are the guest that I am expecting!" "Are you Kahalaomapuana?" asked the visitor. The other woman was surprised at this, for the name was never used except by her nearest relatives, but she replied, "Yes, I am she. Come in."

All the help needed by the Puna woman was given her. Thus began a close relationship, established by a Puna 'aumakua who was related to both. Whenever the Puna woman went to Ola'a, she always took fish or whatever she could get at the sea and when she went home she took with her the gifts that her relative *mai ka po mai* had grown or made.

SPIRITS AS MATES.

Occasionally, Hawaiians believed, an 'aumakua or a *kupua* came during the night and had marital relationship with a human being. This is referred to as *kane* or *wahine o ka po* (night-time husband or wife).

Such relationship sometimes proved to be dangerous to

the health and life of the person. Perhaps a man would become desperately in love with his *wahine o ka po* and would seek to sleep all the time so as to dream of her. He lost his appetite for food and as a result, sickened and died. Perhaps it was his *wahine o ka po* who would be so enamoured that she would coax his spirit to remain away from his body. In a case like this, if a *kahuna* was consulted he sought to drive away the spirit by incantations and by placing the love-sick person upon a layer of *'ape leaves*. The irritation-producing substance in the *'ape* was believed to keep the spirit away. Also the flower sheath of the banana (*pola mai'a*) was laid between the legs half way above the knees. These were Ka-'u methods.

There was a woman from Ka-'u said to have had a *kane a ka po* who was a *mo'o* water spirit. She had gone to visit relatives in Honolulu, and there she fell in love with a handsome person who came to her only at night. She did not know where he came from, but thought he was a human being like herself. It was not until she grew listless, lost her appetite and longed continuously for the night to come that her secret was discovered. Her right side, which came in contact with his body during the night, was said to have become slimy and pale like a fish's. The uncle with whom she was visiting undertook to exorcize the night visitor with incantations. Finally the woman was restored to health again, and returned to her native land.

The *kane* or *wahine o ka po* was not always to be feared. A man in Hilo was said to be unable to have children of his own. Whenever his wife dreamt of a man coming to her from the sea, who was the perfect image of her husband, she became pregnant. All of these children were said to be the offspring of her husband's brother, who was a shark *'aumakua*. He was her *kane o ka po*; and his brother, her husband, was called the *kane i ka 'ili* (the husband for the skin). It is said that there was no jealousy between the two brothers, and no harm ever came to their common wife.

Sometimes the child born of a *kane o ka po* was mischievous and destructive when a command given by its supernatural father was broken. A child belonging to human parents on both sides was regarded as not half as hard to rear as a child who was sired by an *'aumakua*.

Should the *'aumakua* be vexed at something the mother or
other relatives had done, he would cause the child to be
unusually naughty, and punishing it only tended to make
matters worse. Should this happen, the *ho'oponopono* was
resorted to and the cause of the trouble studied. Then an
offering was made with prayer for forgiveness.

Sometimes the child was born in the animal form of
its sire. In this case it either took itself away or was carried
by a relative to the stream, the sea or wherever it properly
belonged. It in turn became one of the family *'aumakua.*

The *kane* or *wahine o ka po* was often very helpful,
guiding and protecting his or her human companion, just as
any *'aumakua* would.

ANIMAL AFFINITIES.

It is noteworthy that most fantasies of the mind and
the heart that adorned and enriched the consciousness of
the people of Ka-'u, were wrought out of actual relationship
with intimately known creatures, not out of old wives' tales
about fictitious phantoms. The brothers, sisters, cousins and
uncles and aunts in the forest and in the sea were not ful-
minating dragons, or gargantuan monsters of the deep.
They were the owls and the hawks who actually soared
above and lived in the *wao* (the forest jungle) and on the
kula, or slopes. They were the sharks and the eels that met
the fishermen, as he hunted in the depths of bays and open
sea, or that approached his wife or his daughter along the
beaches and rocky shores as they garnered seaweeds and
'opihi and small-fry in rock pools.

NATURAL PHENOMENA AND GENERA AS MULTIPLE-FORMS OF ANCESTRAL BEINGS.

The comprehension of the relationship of persons and
families in these islands to natural phenomena and to
various genera of plants and animals, requires an understanding of the old Hawaiian theory of Natural
History. This theory was based upon the observation of the resemblances, in form, in colour, in some
notable detail of marking, or of habit, between natural
phenomena, plant and animal forms. On the basis of these

observed resemblances, the old Hawaiians developed a systematic theory which considered forms (*kino,* body) having notable resemblances of particular sorts to be multiple-
forms (*kino-lau*) of one or another of the ancestral nature
gods which mythology and tradition purported to be either
(a) primordial, i.e., born of the union of Sky with Mother
Earth, in these islands; or (b) proto-historic or historic
migrants from abroad, or (c) native Hawaiians who, long
ago became elevated to the rank of gods of high rank and
power. For example, the edible tree-ferns which cover the
uplands are "bodies" of Haumea, who is Papa, Mother
Earth herself. The sharks, on the other hand, are "bodies"
of one of the brothers of Pele, goddess of vulcanism, who
was an immigrant from abroad. Lizards seen to-day are
related to a deified chiefess of the island of Maui who was a
worshipper of the ancient goddess who was ancestress of all
lizards, whose *kino-lau* all lizards are.   Caterpillars are
cousins of sea-cucumbers and baby eels, all descended, as his
"multiple-forms," from a nature god who rose from the
bottom of the sea in an age long past.

The rationale of these old Hawaiian theories of nature
will be plain, in the notes that follow, for anyone who can
understand the logic-by-analogy of old Polynesian thinking.
The significance of the theory of *kino-lau* in relation to the
'ohana, as family and community, lies in the fact that these
concepts form the basis of *kapu* affecting individuals and
groups; while equally they serve psychologically as common denominators of descent, relationship, status and duty
for the kindred affected.

> Pele, sometimes called *akua malihini* (foreign deity) be-
> cause she came to Hawai'i from abroad (Kahiki) after these
> islands were peopled by the descendants of Wakea and Papa,
> had but two forms, fire and human, the latter in all of the
> stages from childhood to decrepit old age. She is seen on occasion
> as a child, a beautiful young woman or an ugly old hag, depend-
> ing on which she chooses to appear as.   When I was a child I
> saw a ball of fire (*popo-ahi*), smaller than the full moon, appear
> from the vicinity of the volcano crater Kilauea, on the side of
> Mauna Loa and move slowly toward the top of Mauna Loa,
> and I remember hearing oldsters say quietly (as it was *kapu*
> to point or exclaim), "The old woman of the Pit is going to
> her other home," referring to Moku'aweoweo, the crater at the
> summit. The various human forms she assumed, as well as her
> fire forms, were her *kino-lau.*

Her favourite brother, Ka-moho-ali'i, was so dearly loved and highly respected by her that she never permitted the smoke of the Kilauea crater to blow over the cliff above the east side of the pit, which was dedicated to him, and called *"Ka pali kapu o Ka-moho-ali'i"* (Sacred cliff of Ka-moho-ali'i). His *kino-lau* was the body of the shark, for he was the lord of all sharks; but also he would appear as a dark-skinned man, whose loin cloth, or *malo*, was usually red. That was the reason why the native people of my homeland, and in other localities too, object to the wearing of red on their beaches. It was a sacred colour and to wear it brought no luck at fishing. Boy babies who were born "circumcized" were said to be under his special guardianship.

Very recently, my daughter who bears the name Pele, mentioned to an elderly Hawaiian friend that she was fortunate in having her son born "circumcized." The woman immediately exclaimed, "That comes from your mother's side of the family!" As the old lady said no more, my mystified daughter came to ask me what connection my side of the family had with her baby's being born "circumcized." I explained that it is the Hawaiian belief that *'ohana* of our Pele clan, who are kin to Ka-moho-ali'i, may be born "circumcized," and if so, are under the protection of the lord of the sharks.

I have heard of other boys, all over the islands, who were so born, and of one instance in which a boy was born "uncircumcized" but was "circumcized" in a dream. His mother, being old-fashioned Hawaiian, had refused to have the doctor do it for him, choosing rather to wait until he was older so that he might have it done with a proper ceremony and a feast. When the baby was three weeks old, she dreamt of a dark-skinned man in a red *malo*, who came up out of the sea, walked into her house and removed the baby's diaper. On waking from her strange dream she went to look at her son and found him peacefully sleeping, but "circumcized!"

Another brother of the goddess Pele, Ka-uila-nui-makeha-i-ka-lani, also had a dual form, that of a man and of lightning.

The migration of Pele and her brothers and sisters had been preceded by that of her sister, Kapo, with a following of other sisters. This migration, like the later one, also came by way of Ni'ihau, Kauai, Oahu, Moloka'i and settled on Maui, but on every island where she paused, Kapo estabilshed a school for the *hula*, ritual dance-drama. Her nature was dual. As Kapo-'ula-Kina'u (Kapo-red-spotted) she was the Kapo invoked by *kahuna* when sending evil back upon a witch. This Kapo was a goddess whose temper was violent and vengeful. But when worshipped by dancers and chanters, this same person was the gentle Laka, the spirit of the wild wood. Yet when the *kapu* of seclusion was disregarded by a student or teacher during the period of devotion to *hula* training in the *halau*, the loving Laka quickly changed into vengeful Kapo and smote the culprit. So was the *hula* respected in the olden times; it was beneficent when rules were kept, yet deadly when they were not. The *hala-pepe* (*Dracaena aurea*), a plant used on the *hula* altar, was one of Kapo's *kino-lau*, as Laka; and the tree *'ohe* (*Tetra plasandra* Hawaiiensis) was another. The tree was associated with sorcery, of which art Kapo also became the patroness, due to her ferocious side.

Lizards are derived from quite another source. The *mo'o* or lizard migration came under the leadership of Mo'o-i-nanea (lizard-that-enjoys-itself), who was their chiefess. There were male and female *mo'o*, and some were benevolent and some were malignant. They first landed on the island of Oahu. I have never heard of a plant form that was a *mo'o-kino-lau*, but the *'o'opu* or guppy fish, the brindled dog (*'ilio mo'o*), the skinks and geckos (the two lizards native to Hawaii) were all *kino-lau* of the *mo'o*, who were water dwellers. They were fond of the colour yellow. Their homes were in ponds and streams and it is said that their presence was recognisable by the yellowing of the trees and shrubbery surrounding the ponds; in the accumulation of yellowish foam on the surface of the water; and in the peculiar yellow-green hue of the water itself. (This is an illustration of the way in which a colour is associated with species of *kino-lau* that are "bodies" of a native deity.)

A chiefess of Maui named Kiha-wahine was a member of the Pi'ilani family. She is said to have died in infancy; and thereafter was deified by means of worship (prayer and offerings) thus becoming a very powerful *mo'o* goddess, whom Kamehameha I included amongst those he worshipped. There were two other things that were *kapu* to Kiha-wahine besides the lizards, brindled dogs and *'o'opu* fish: yellow chickens and mullet. (The mullet was also one form assumed by Kamapua'a when Pele pursued him.) Members of the Kiha-wahine clan were not allowed to eat them. A family whose forbears lived on Lana'i and Maui to whom Kiha-wahine was sacred, came to Ka-'u when I was a child. Under no circumstances would they eat mullet, chicken or *'o'opu* fish, and they would not harm a lizard if they could help it. Spiders, too, are said to be akin to the *mo'o*. And so are human beings on whose skin are patches suggestive of lizard's skin.

The *mo'o* clan, if they may be called that, were not always friendly to those of the Pele family and many a battle was fought between the two. In the legend of Pele and Hi'iaka, the latter's journey to Kaua'i and back was beset with battles against interfering and unfriendly *mo'o*, who did all they could to cause her distress and annoyance.

Stories are told of *mo'o* who became wives or husbands of human beings, concealing their true nature, which later would be revealed by a gradual change in the skins of their human mates. The skin became like that of fish, with a coating of slime (*walewale*) when wet, a condition derived from the person's supernatural water-dwelling mate.

Kumuhea, whose animal form was the caterpillar that eats sweet potato leaves, is said to have risen originally from the bottom of the deep ocean. He drifted first to Moloka'i, where he remained a short while and then to our land of Ka-'u, on the island of Hawai'i, and there he made his home, up on a hill called Pu'u-enuhe (Caterpillar-hill). He married a woman of Ka-'u, took his wife home and fed her on his favourite food, sweet potato leaves. A continued diet of this almost killed her. Fearing lest she die and Kumuhea continue to acquire more wives to share the same fate, the woman's father prayed to the god Ku, who was the father of Kumuhea, whereupon Ku took away from Kumuhea his power to assume human form. Thereafter Kumuhea might take a spirit form if he chose, *resembling* that of a man (*kino-aka*, *aka*=shadow), but no more could he wed a human wife, living with her as a human being. Thereby he became the caterpillar-god; and in the sea he had another *kino-lau*, the *loli* or sea-cucumber. Eels were also believed to be related to, or children of, the sea-cucumber, because tiny eels were found inside of them when cut open. Those of us who are related to the caterpillar-god Kumuhea, refuse to harm caterpillars and never eat either the sea-cucumber or the eel. Kumuhea was sometimes referred to as a *kupua 'ino*, a malignant nature god, because he could be destructive when angered, devouring the plants in the sweet potato fields even down to the tubers. Anyone related to Kumuhea who broke this *kapu* forbidding the eating of one of his forms usually perished and no amount of begging for forgiveness would make Kumuhea relent. I myself have seen one of my *'ohana* swell, and die in agony, in consequence of eating *loli*.

DREAMING.

Dreaming and related experiences which are common amongst Hawaiians are dominant factors in personal and family life for Hawaiians. This was even more true in the pre-Christian era. A dream is an individual experience; but for every person in a Hawaiian household the dreams of any member of the family may be significant for two reasons. (1) By thinking Hawaiians, dreams are taken seriously. They are interesting, hence they are noticed and told and remembered. Consequently they affect the whole family, even though the dream be related primarily to some particular person; and more so when the dream reveals something of importance to the whole *'ohana*. (2) They are seriously regarded and carefully studied by elders skilled in interpreting their meaning because they represent the most direct and continuous means of communication and contact between those living in this world of light (*ao malama*) and the ancestral guardians (*'aumakua*) and gods (*akua*) whose existence is in the Unseen (*Po*).

To-day as heretofore, dreams foretell good and bad fortune, sickness, ways to heal illness or correct faults committed in relationship or in disregard of duty to *'ohana* and *'aumakua*; sacred names are given in dreams,[22] and a song or *hula* may be learned in sleep.

Hawaiians logically infer, from their experience of night dreams (*moe 'uhane*) and waking visions (*akaku*) which subsequent experience and events prove to have been prophetic, the existence of a shadowy spirit world and drama that foretells or is synchronous with, or that duplicates, events and forms seen in "the world of light." *Akaku* (derived from *aka*, meaning reflection, shadow) describes those clear flashes of imagery that seem so tangible, so real, across the threshold of sleep, generally just as waking consciousness dawns, particularly in the dim early hours of morning. They may come at the moment of dozing. Or *akaku* may be a sudden total shift of vision, displacing or overlaying physical sight, in full daylight when all the faculties are alert. *Hihi'o* is another word that refers to such visions, whether in sleep or waking consciousness: *hihi'o* is the act of visioning, whereas *akaku* is the vision seen.

> Dreams are the doings of the *'uhane* or soul after the body has fallen asleep. All the things that the *'uhane* sees and remembers after the awakening of the body is the dream. Some dreams are merely pastimes or trickery (*he ho'ohala manawa wale no*) of the *'uhane*; some are riddles that one must think over and analyse (*he nanenane a nau ia e no'ono'o a e wehewehe*), and some are dreams that are self evident, literally that "come up straight" (*pi'i pololei*). The understanding of dreams is important amongst Hawaiians, because in dreams one receives revelation from the *akua* "out of the night" (*mai ka po mai*). Some interpretations concerning the meaning of dreams are understood throughout all the Hawaiian islands, while others belong only to certain family groups.
>
> To dream of canoes means the unfulfilment of a thing planned on, or death. This is true for all Hawaiians. Here is an example: In 1933, the older sister (*kaikua'ana*) in one branch of our family was very sick in Keaukaha, at Hilo, Hawai'i. The younger sister (*kaikaina*) was also sick in Kalepolepo, at Hilo. Neither could go to see the other and when the older sister died

[22] See Section on Naming in The Life Cycle, Chapter V.

the relatives were afraid to tell the younger lest she grieve and
grow worse. When the body of the older sister was being taken
to Puna for burial, the other had a dream. She saw a canoe
being paddled out of Hilo harbour with the prow turned toward
Puna. On the canoe lay her sister. When she awoke with a start
her tears flowed for she knew that her *kaikua'ana* was gone.
When she asked her relatives in the house they replied that she
was all right. The next day she had another dream, in which she
saw her *kaikua'ana* come in and sit beside her, saying, " Little
sister, our relatives are afraid to tell you lest you come and see
me and we both go on the same trail." She awoke and heard
the voice of the man who married her sister's granddaughter,
and called to him, "How is grandma?" He answered, "Fine."
She replied, "Don't hide the truth from me, for I have had two
dreams telling me that my sister is dead." Then her relatives
admitted to her for the first time that the old lady was dead
and had been taken to Puna to be buried beside her husband.

To dream of water is a good sign, that is if the water is
clear and clean. To dream of going into a mud puddle is a sign
that one is going to take part in some wrong act. If it is clean
water it is a sign of a blessing to come. Here is an illustration
of this kind of dream. A certain woman was filled with sadness
because she was unemployed, as was her husband, and there
seemed no way out of their numerous troubles. One night she
had a dream and saw a woman in a white *holoku* standing by
the side of a well whose top was neatly encircled with stones.
The woman was dipping up the water with a long handled
dipper and pouring its contents into two buckets standing there
beside her. When the buckets were filled full she put her dipper
in one of them and turned around to look at the dreamer. She
said, "You over there, tell your husband that in February my
work will be finished and that I am coming for him." The
dreamer awoke and thought, "This is December, and what is
the reason for my waiting for two months?" But when February
had actually come, the husband found work. He sailed to California, remained three months and thus this family was relieved
of many of their troubles.

Much help has come through dreams in days of trouble.
There was a woman in Honolulu who received words of comfort
when deep in trouble. She was very ill, and her doctor decided
to operate on her. In her home were many little children and
a mother who was convalescing. She was told by a certain
man who called himself a wise *kahuna* that she would never
recover or regain her health, but that she would die. That same
night she had a dream. She saw herself in a strange house.
Beside this house was a spring on whose bank grew some bullrushes. She saw a white horse approach, pawing with his fore
legs before the threshold of the door. A voice was heard from
among the bullrushes saying, "You shall not die! You shall
not die!" The spirit of this woman came out to see who it was

that was speaking, but saw no one, yet she heard it again speaking very distinctly, "You shall not die!" When she awoke she said to her mother, " Mama, when *kua'ana* (elder cousin) comes to see me, let her have the baby to take care of till I return. I will be all well again." This was done. Her dream came true, for she recovered.

The dream of someone nude is a sign that sickness is coming. This is a belief in all parts of the island group. Here is a short dream of this sort. A girl dreamt of carrying her older sister's baby and of going to the home of a certain Chinese friend. There was no clothing on the baby except a sun-bonnet. When they arrived at the friend's house, the friend clothed the baby in some clothing belonging to her granddaughter. When the dreamer awoke she told of her dream. Only a few days after that, the baby took sick with bronchitis and fever. The mother of the baby also had a similar dream. She saw herself walking unclothed from the bathroom to her bedroom. A few days later she fell sick.

Another well known omen is to dream of tooth pulling. If the tooth comes out, a relative is going to die; if it is on the right side, it will be a man, if on the left, a woman. If in the upper jaw, it means a close relative, and in the lower jaw, a distant relative.

To dream of injury to the navel is a sign (*hoailona*) of trouble that is coming to a near relative (*i'o pono'i*). The Hawaiian saying, *E ka ana no i ka piko* (it is going to strike at the navel) means that trouble is coming to a very near relative or to the dreamer.

To dream of seeing excrement signifies that food is coming. To some people, dreaming of a person who has died means that one will receive a gift of food, but among our own relatives it means that someone wishes to see the dreamer. To dream of oneself or some one else climbing up to a high place denotes a blessing for the person that is seen climbing. To dream that some one is exposing his private parts is a sign of disappointment, of contempt (for the dreamer). He will not succeed in the work that he is planning on. If a person dreams that a calabash, drinking gourd or a bowl filled with water breaks and spills the water, it signifies the death of some one. To dream of leaping off a cliff and not being seen again is a sign of death to the person seen to leap.

Many of the remedies used for sickness from olden times down to the present day, have been given in dreams. Here is an example: A certain woman had a big open sore on the sole of her foot. When medicines were applied it grew much worse. This woman went with her husband to stay at Kapu'euhi, Ola'a, Hawai'i, with some of their intimate friends, to ask if they knew what to do for that foot. The friends did not know but asked them to stay a while. One night the husband had a dream. He saw a woman who said to him, " Tell the family in the house the medicine to heal your wife. Send a pre-adolescent child to gather tender *palapala'a* fern fronds, a whole hand full; crush fine with the fingers and apply as a poultice five successive times." When the dream was related, one was chosen to gather the medicine, a girl ten years old. When it was applied, it did not take long for new flesh to grow and the foot was entirely healed.

Here is another example. A woman was too sick to do any work, her throat was very sore and so was her head. She had a dream—she saw a certain woman who said, "Seek a *popolo* (*Solanum nigrum*) plant that stands alone. Wash it clean and boil it in a gallon of water, strain and when cold drink whenever you want to. Drink no other liquid but this and you will find relief." The woman awoke and told the dream to her mother, who did as she was shown in the night. That evening one of their friends telephoned and said, "I had a dream. I saw that you were sick and a certain woman came and told me to tell you to drink water in which *popolo* was boiled." Thus two dreams were given for that same trouble.

Speaking of dreams—time and time again I have had bits of *mele* in dreams but not a complete one. There were a few lines of a *mele* called "*Lono-hali'i.*" I chanted it when my uncle was here on a vacation and he got up and called out, "Kawena, your grandmother used to chant that. Where did you learn it?" Maybe some day I'll have it in completion. Then one night I received a complete *mele*. Keahi had asked us (her pupils) to get our paddles ready as she was going to teach us a canoe *hula*, but she never did. Later when I visited her on Kauai she told me to watch her and see how much of this *hula* I could catch. Well, I caught on to some but not all. Then when I got home I had a dream of an old woman who was dressed completely in white. She stood by the wet cave called "Ka-wai-o-Kanaloa" and told me of her canoe that went within the cave many years ago, and then said, "I want you to ride it too. Some people look down at mud, but I want you to look up at the sun. You see, I have put my white hat on your head. You may not feel it, but it is there." I looked up and sure enough, there was a white hat with the rim covered with small, fine writings. Then she smiled and taught me this *mele*:

> Ku'u wa'a e, holo ku'u wa'a,
> Holo ku'u wa'a palolo i ka 'ino o Puna e,
> O Puna ka 'aina noho o ka wahine,
> Wahine i ka 'iu 'o na mauna.
> Nona ka wa'a i 'ike ia,
> I ho'okele kapu ia e ke kaikunane,
> Ua 'ike a.

> My canoe—my canoe sails on,
> It sails and weathers the storms of Puna.
> Puna is the land where the Woman dwells,

The Woman who dwells on the summit of mountains.
Her canoe is very well known,
It was steered with *kapu* by her brother.
This is so.

I woke up at the end of it.

The *"ua 'ike a"* of·*mele* is like the *amama ua noa* of the *pule*; it is like the period at the end of a sentence, and a *mele* is not complete without it.

I repeated it (the *mele*) to Keahi and she was so startled that she burst into tears. This is the story she told me.

One of her *tutu*, a very large man, always used this *mele-pule*. When her brother went out to catch turtles at Wanini, he used to stand to one side of the door of the house and chant this until the boys returned. It was an old, old *mele* for Pele and was used for the canoe-rowing *hula*. Keahi never taught me a *hula hoe*, but I know one now of my own, *"mai ka Po mai"* (out of the Unseen). If any one that understood *kapu* things were to ask me, " Kawena, do you know the *hula hoe*?" my answer would be, " *Ae, ua 'ike no* " (Aye, indeed I do!).

I feel confident that some day I will learn the old *"Lono-hali'i"* *hula* of old Ka-'u. Things do not come all in a day and one must wait and listen and bide one's time, and the doors will open one by one.

From the one survivor of my generation still living in Ka-'u, George Kawaha, comes this story: "I loved my father, Luhi Kawaha. I have been told hundreds of times that my natural father was a *haole* but it made no difference in my love for Luhi nor his for me. Of all of their children, I, the oldest, was the closest to him.

"When he became very ill I knew the best place for him would be the hospital. He agreed to it and I placed him in the Pahala Hospital, the nearest, and he seemed to improve. In the early afternoon I went into the house to lie down and rest and before I knew it I was asleep.

"I felt some one shake me and my father's voice say, 'Son, is that all you have to do? Wake up and be about.' I opened my eyes and although I saw nothing I felt his presence. As soon as I stood up, the telephone rang. I answered and heard a nurse at the Pahala Hospital say, 'George, your father just died about five minutes ago.'

"In life he always turned to me first—and in death."

More specialized and less universal than dreaming, but of great significance in the family life of old Hawai'i, was spirit possession, or mediumship — an intensification, through chosen "mediums" of the relationship between the living *'ohana* and the *'aumakua,* or those who have gone before.

SPIRITS SPEAKING THROUGH MEDIUMS.

Spirits (*'uhane*) of various types—gods (*akua*), ancestral guardians (*'aumakua*), disembodied souls endowed with *mana* by worship (*'unihipili*), and individual nature-spirits (*kupua*)—could "possess" or enter into a human being and control the body and its faculties.

Noho, meaning "to sit" or "to dwell," is applied to the temporary dwelling-with or sitting-upon a chosen person who is the medium (*haka*) for a particular spirit, which may be an *'uhane* (disembodied human soul), an *'aumakua* (ancestral guardian) or an *akua* (god). The characterization of the person, when the spirit is in possession of the medium's body and faculties as *haka,* implies the conception that the spirit *perches upon* the medium rather than entering by way of the mouth into the stomach (as in the Marquesas, for example), for the word *haka* means literally a bird's perch, or a rack to hang things on. Nevertheless, the spirit is heard speaking through the mouth of its *haka,* and who it is that is speaking can be recognized sometimes by quality of voice. In Hawaiian the *haka* is, in fact, referred to as the " speaking-mouth " (*waha-'olelo*) of the spirit.

The *haka* was chosen by the spirit, or spirits, to serve as "speaking-mouth." The spirit, be it *'uhane, 'aumakua,* or *akua,* was, in family seances, always one to whose lineage the *haka* belonged: that is to say, the spirit was a relative. It is said that in the old days there was no lineage, or *'ohana,* which did not have someone who served as a channel of communication. We know of no Hawaiian today who is a true *haka.* We are, however, fortunate in having very full notes describing this phase of Hawaiian psychism from an old lady of Ka-'u derivation who had served as *haka* for her *'ohana* for many years before she died.

Some *akua* imposed strict *kapu* of one sort or another, others did not. The *kapu* would forbid the eating of particular foods. The *haka* referred to above ate only vegetable foods, and even vegetables like the varieties of taro and banana whose sap was red, suggestive of blood, were forbidden. The *kino-lau* of the *akua* were of course *kapu.* The person who helped the *haka* (*kanaka lawelawe*) was subject to the same rules. These were positive also in the matter of colours, suitable offerings, etc. White is Pele's colour, pink is Hi'iaka's, red is Kapo's. And it was necessary for the *haka* to avoid behaviour that would be offensive to an *akua;* cursing, malicious talk, adultery, stealing. The *haka* would find herself deserted if the *akua* was angered.

The spirit would refer to the *haka* as *iwi* (bone)—i.e., a solid or substantial thing (*he mea pa'a*) upon which to sit or into which to enter. Where the *haka* lived and slept was *kapu.* No menstruating person might come there. A woman could become a *haka* only after menopause. There must be no filth, no treading about. The *haka's* clothing was sacred, and must be kept clean and free from contact with pollution.

A helper (*kanaka lawelawe*) was charged with the duty of setting the mat on which the *haka* sat, preparing the cup of *'awa,* knowing the proper clothing for robing the *haka* when the *akua* was to come. This attendant was also the one who prayed (*kanaka pule*), inviting the spirit, and the one who transmitted the message or carried out the commands. These weighty duties must be performed by a man, a pre-adolescent girl, or a woman past menopause.

In more recent times the place for the work (*papa hana*) would be a table and a spread of trade cloth, and glass tumblers, for liquor. The tumblers, after the seance, were thrown into the sea or buried, and the cloth or mats were folded or rolled and put away in a high, clean place. But the true old Hawaiian setting was a *kapa* mat, especially plaited. There was always the *'awa* bowl (*kanoa 'awa*). On the mat was laid the mantle of bark cloth (*uhi kapa*), its colour depending on the *akua's* preference. In the middle of the *kapa* were laid *la-'i* (ti-leaf)—one, two crossed at right angles, or three, perhaps, with points to centre and stems out; or four braided flat like a mat. On this was set the bowl of *'awa.* Then all was sprinkled with salt water with *olena* (tumeric) in it, for purification.

When the *akua* would come upon the *haka* he (or she) would fall into a deep sleep, like a person under ether. He knew nothing, heard nothing. Just before falling into this state a *haka* was conscious of some kind of weight upon the shoulders before being entirely "covered" (unconscious). Some *haka* have a sort of quivering at the time of covering. But while the *'uhane* was in possession, there was a change of facial expression. If the *akua* were one youthful in body, then the *haka* looked youthful, even though the *haka* be old. If the *haka* were young and the *akua* coming had the body of an old woman or of an old man, the *haka* would exhibit the feebleness and shakiness of the aged spirit.

There are several kinds of "possession" (*noho*), in which gods (*akua*) or guardian spirits (*'aumakua*) speak to the family through the *haka*. An *'unihipili* (the disembodied spirit of a person who has died, which has been endowed with psychic potency or *mana*, by means of food offerings and prayer, *ho'omanamana*) may "sit" upon a relative who is a *haka* for the purpose of explaining the cause of some trouble that is afflicting the house. Such an *'unihipili* would be a beneficent *'unihipili*. These *'unihipili* were beneficent or malevolent, depending upon the good or evil motives and purposes and practices of its *kahu*, or keeper (the person who has endowed it with *mana*).

There is another type of possession that is personal rather than familial. But it might be a family problem, if, for instance, the adhering spirit excited the jealousy of a parent or spouse. This is the *noho ho'ohihi* (covetous, or adhering (possession). Some disembodied human soul (*'uhane*) or a nature spirit (*kupua*) embodied in rock, tree, or the like, may take a fancy to a person and enter into that person, who will then behave strangely, without being seriously ill. If a *kahuna* who knows about such matters is consulted, he will induce the *kupua* to speak through the person "possessed" in order to find out what it covets. If it is companionship, then the person "possessed" knows that he has a friend who will help him when in need, and all is well.[23]

---

[23] In the *Fornander Collection of Hawaiian Antiquities and Folklore*, Third Series, Memoir, Vol. 6, No. 1, Part 1 (Bernice P. Bishop Museum, Honolulu, Hawaii, 1919-1920), pp. 112-114, edited by Thomas G. Thrum, there is an inexplicit reference to spirit possession, termed there *ho'onohonoho akua*, induced by a *kahuna makani* (wind [spirit invisible like wind] -expert), or spirit dispatcher, a practitioner skilled in diagnosing the cause of sickness, detecting theft, and the like. *Ho'onoho* is the true term for induced spirit-possession; while the reduplicated *ho'onohonoho* signifies "pretended possession," a word commonly applied by missionaries with disparaging implications. (M.K.P.) It is mentioned in David Malo's *Hawaiian Antiquities* (Bernice P. Bishop Museum, 1903, Dr. N. B. Emerson, Editor), pp. 135-141 and 155 *et seq.*, in relation to witchcraft. The Fornander and Malo references are clearly sources descriptive of pre-discovery practice in Hawai'i (E.S.C.H.).

In "Hawaiian Customs and Beliefs Relating to Sickness and Death" by Laura C. Green and Martha Warren Beckwith (Am. Anthropologist, N.S., vol. 28, 1926, pp. 176-208) there is a brief account of mediumship in historic times (pp. 204-208).

There are other types of mediumship besides the simple *noho* or "dwelling." *Noho* is the "covering" entirely of the thought of the medium by the *'uhane,* as described. *Ho'oulu* is a definite lighting upon a *haka* for the purpose of "causing to grow" (in knowledge). *Ulu-kau,* on the other hand, is the unexplained growth of knowledge in a person without visible "possession," until he has acquired prophetic powers and the gift of interpretation. Another type is *kihei-pua* (the "mantle of flowers"), which is, precisely, the strengthening of the physical body by the *akua* for purposes of guidance.

This latter involves not merely guidance in the sense of revelation. It is the animation of the body of a person without "covering" the mind. If a feeble old woman receives the gift of *kihei-pua* she becomes as lively as a young girl. If there was work to be done that she was unskilled in, or even unused to seeing done, she became skilful in that work, through this good gift of animation from an *akua* who loved his *'ohana.* Although aged and feeble to behold, yet there was strength in the limbs to farm, to fish, to dance, to travel far. Young people might weary, but the old man or woman kept on. If the *'uhane kihei-pua* is with one who is sick he can get up out of bed to do some special needful task as though there were no sickness in his body. Only when the *'uhane* has left him does he feel his body to be weak again. The sickness is never made worse by this moving about.

> Because of this gift of *kihei-pua* many strange things have been seen. For example, there was an old woman whose son-in-law had died. Then her daughter also died, leaving their small children to the old woman's care. The youngest was an infant in arms. The grandmother was saddened because there was no milk for him, and any nursing mother lived far away. She prayed for her breasts to yield milk for her grandchild: and it was seen that her breasts did flow and it was she herself who nursed the baby until he grew big. The *kahuna* of that community recognized an *'uhane kihei-pua* that dwelt with and helped that old woman.

EVIL WORK OF MEDIUMS.

There is a mischievous type of possession known as *noho ho'ouluulu.* The *ho'oulu* mentioned above means to cause to grow; *ho'ouluulu* means to irritate, to provoke, to incite. The latter form of possession was recognized as evil, and might be fostered by a designing *kahuna* for his own purposes.

> This kind of *noho* is practised as follows: A *kahuna* who desires the control of some person as a *haka* may see that a certain *'uhane* is attached to a man or woman. The *kahuna* then proceeds to irritate that man or woman and incite him or her to fury. That person's angry behaviour then irritates the *'uhane* into similar fury and he "steps upon" (*hehi*) the person to whom he had been attached in friendship. When this happens the *kahuna* then soothes and flatters the spirit until all anger ceases, after which time the spirit will regularly "sit upon" the possessed person, making of him or her a regular *haka*. So, by the *kahuna's* irritation and flattery, both *'uhane* and new-made *haka* will be subject to his control, for the accomplishment of any sort of evil thing. This type of *haka* makes a nuisance of himself, and thus all mediumship comes into ill repute. A *haka* "stepped on" in this evil way aches in body when the *'uhane* leaves him. His back has to be massaged and he moans over the pain in his legs.

> Another kind of evil possession is by mischievous earth spirits (*'uhane kolohe*, or *'uhane 'ino*) which ascend through the feet of the *haka*. These are not *'uhane ali'i* (noble spirits), which always "cover" the head and shoulders and whose possession is a sacred (*kapu*) work.

SPIRIT "SENDING."

Another kind of *noho* is the *ho'oaunauna* (sending), coming from the "filth-eating *kahuna*" (*kahuna 'ai kukae*). The *'uhane* is sent by its keeper (*kahu*) to enter the body of someone who is to be the victim of malicious torture. This kind of *'uhane* will hide itself, refusing to reveal its identity. If asked, "What do you want?", it will not reply. It will not reveal itself until seen by one with knowledge of such things; and until given something to eat and given drink (*'awa* or liquor—brandy or whisky) and asked to have compassion and reveal what it is up to. Thus it can be induced to reveal its name, the name of its keeper or keepers, and the reason for its coming. When this revelation is made, the person troubled can be cured. But if the mischievous spirit stubbornly hides everything there is no hope except with the aid of a *kahuna* possessing real skill in "peeling off" (*mahiki*). Sometimes these troublesome *'uhane* sit (upon a victim) in a swarm, and as soon as one is "peeled off" another sits in its place, and when that is "peeled off," still another sits. One who has a mature forehead (*lae o'o*) can peel them off all at once.

AN EXAMPLE OF BENEFICENT MEDIUMSHIP.

(The names used are not those of the actual persons described. Mediumship has always been considered reprehensible in Christian Hawai'i, consequently Hawaiians have been loath to discuss or to admit its existence.)

Pu'uwahine was a woman of Ka-'u who at one time many years ago, was living on Oahu. She was a gifted and genuine *haka*. Her younger sister, Pa'a, a good chanter and *hula* dancer, was her "prayer" (*kanaka pule*).

Kaiona, a *kupuna akua* (ancestor-god of Pu'u (the *haka*) was a youthful *akua wahine* (female). She was the principal *akua ki'ai* (protector) of the Wai'anae mountains (just as Malei was of Makapu'u). When she would sit upon Pu'u, she would ask Pa'a (the *kanaka pule*) to sing for her entertainment the *mele inoa hula a Kaiona* (name-dance-chant of Kaiona) which she (Kaiona) taught Pa'a, speaking through Pu'u in trance. Here is the *mele*:

Ua nani ke kula o Kaiona
I ka ho'olai a na *'iwa*.
Kahiko i ka pua ko'olau,
He 'ohu kapu no ka wahine.
I kui'ia mai e Li'a
Ka wahine noho i ka ulu mano.
No Kaiona noho i ka la'i,
O ka ua naulu i ke kula
Hea aku makou 'o mai 'oe,
E Kaiona noho i ka la'i.

Translation.

Beautiful is Kaiona's plain,
Over which the *'iwa* bird poises.
She [Kaiona] is bedecked with the *ko'olau* [blossom]
The adornment that is sacred to her.
It was strung into a wreath by Li'a,
By the woman who dwells in dense forests.
To be worn by Kaiona the peaceful
Whose windblown rains water the plains.
We call to you, answer us,
O Kaiona who dwells in peace.

This chant, given through the collaboration of the two sisters, became a treasured heirloom in the family.

When *'uhane ali'i* (as distinct from *'uhane 'ino*) were coming to dwell upon a *haka* it was customary for them to give the household a visible sign of their coming, and these signs made it plain which *akua* it would be.

If thunder peals right over the house and the foundation rocks that is Kane-hekili, who comes.[24] It was *kapu* to whisper, for that made him very cross. It was *kapu* to exclaim when any of the sights were seen or to point at them with the finger. To look, to understand, and to keep the mouth shut, those were the great things taught to the *'ohana* by the *akua*. When lightning flashes and the light darts into the house, the family observes whether it is red; if so, it is a Ka-uila-nui-makeha-i-ka-lani (Kane-lightning-streaking-in-the-sky, a brother of Pele);[25] but if it is yellowish light, it was Hi'iaka-i-ka-poli-o-Pele (-of-the-bosom-of-Pele). There are many signs. If Lono, the sign he sends is a sudden heavy downpour, which quickly clears. If it is Hi'iaka-i-ka-poli-o-Pele who comes, no one must pass back and forth behind the back, because her back is *kapu*. Because the *kapu* belongs to her back, the back of her *haka* is also *kapu*, so no one must ever step across, or step on it (in physiotherapy, or *lomilomi*). Nor must anything unclean come in contact with it. The white dress and the pink were those that I have seen worn by her *haka* (Hi'iaka's). Little lumps of salt were another requirement, for her *haka* or in her *hula*, never to be omitted upon her *papa hana*. It is said that when she came from Kahiki she brought her salt with her. Because of the dropping of some of the lumps of salt at Moanalua, Oahu, there grew the salt of Aliapa'akai, and this made that large lake salty.

If it is Pele coming, she also has a *kapu* back, and it is so hot that it is impossible to go back and forth behind the *haka*—thus making it perfectly clear that the *akua noho* is the *Ali'i Wahine* of Kilauea. If an *akua noho* claims to be Pele and the back of the *haka* is not hot, then those in the house may question indeed. From times way back this hotness of the back has been the sign. Pele likes *lu'au* (young taro greens) when she comes but not *lu'au* already cooked. Wrap the green *lu'au* in *la'i* (*ti* leaf). When the *akua wahine* sits on the *haka*, the body of the *haka* lies face down, and the package of *lu'au* is placed upon the back of the *haka* until the heat of her back has cooked it. When it is cooked, she (the *haka*) eats it all.

When it is Ku who comes, he makes his own *'awa* (*Piper methisticum*) grow before the eyes of the people who are looking on; and when grown he gives it to the *kanaka pule* to prepare and put in the *'apu* (cup for *'awa*). So it was with bananas that serve as *pupu* (food savory) to be eaten after the *'awa* is drunk, the stalk grows right up there before the eyes of the people looking on, and bears and is eaten right away: but it did not have much flavour in comparison with those that grew outdoors in the sunshine and rain.

---

[24] He was black on one side, natural brown on the other. Kahekili the famous Paramount Chief of Maui of Kamehameha's time, who was named for Kane-hekili, was tattooed solid black on one side.

[25] On the back he was like stone from head to feet; in front he was like a human being.

If it is Kapo-'ula-o-Kina'u (Kapo-of-the-red-streak) the *papa hana* would be covered with red, and so it was with respect to the colour of the dress of her *haka*. So, indeed, it is with Kane-i-kaulana-'ula (-in-the-floating-red [cloud]), red is the colour for the *papa hana*. Similarly for Ka-moho-ali'i (Lord-of-Sharks) red also is called for, but not the same shade, one is a black red (*ula maku'e*), the other is a clear red (*'ula*). *Ka-moho-ali'i* is a pleasant *akua*, although he was very *kapu*, having a playful manner of speaking and of joking with the helper and with others in the house, thus setting aside their fear of him. This kind of *noho* is a good *noho*, for the *akua* chooses his *haka* and comes of his own accord.

PRAYER.

In our description of the life cycle several examples of long prayers have been given—a prayer for a boy-child when he was consecrated to Lono on entering the *Mua,* or men's house; and a prayer dedicating the new home built for a young couple recently married.

The chant (*mele*) to Kaiona, which we have given above, is really an invocation, although it is termed a *mele* rather than a *pule*. This is true of the following chant, which was used in the family of Mrs. Pukui for many years, by her grandmother with whom she spent her childhood, and by the priest of Lono, Kanekuhia, who was her grandmother's foster-father.

Noho ana Laka i ka ulu wehiwehi
Ka ohi'a ku i luna o Mauna loa,
E 'aloha mai ia'u e Kaulana'ula,
Eia la ka 'ula leo.
He kanaenae 'aloha na'u ia 'oe,
E Kaulana'ula,
Ho'i mai kaua.
Eia ka 'ai la, 'awa lau,
He pu'awa hiwa, he ko kea,
He iholena, he aheahea,
E hea ana 'au ia 'oe e 'ai kaua
Elieli kapu, elieli noa,
Noa ke ku, noa ka hele,
Noa kanawai o ke akua.

Translation
Laka dwells in a beautiful grove,
As an *ohi'a* tree that stands on Maunaloa,
Have compassion on me, O Kane-i-Kaulanaula,
Here is an offering, just the voice,
A prayer of love from me to thee, O Kaulanaula,

Come home to me.
Here is the food, the leafed 'awa,
A root of the dark 'awa, a kea sugar cane,
Some iholena bananas, some aheahea,
I am calling to you to partake of food with me,
The kapu of the prayer was profound; it is freed.
Freed that I may stand, freed that I may walk,
Freed by the law of the gods.

On occasions of crisis or festivity, when the presence
of akua or 'aumakua was desired because their help was
needed, or required for reasons of ceremonial and ritual,
the following was the *pule kahea* (calling prayer) that was
used by her relatives:

Eia ka 'ai, e ke akua,
He 'ai lani wale no.
'Inu a ke kama iki
I ka 'awa lau lena o Ke-ahi-a-laka
Halawai aku la me Pele,
Ke 'ako la i ka lehua,
Ke kui la i kai o Hopoe e,
He 'awa no na kane o ka lani,
He 'awa no na wahine o ka lani,
He 'awa no na kane o ka Lua,
He 'awa no na wahine o ka Lua,
Pela aku, pela mai.
E mu ka waha,
E holoi i ka lima,
'Eli'eli kapu, 'eli'eli noa,
Noa ke ku, noa ka hele,
Noa kanawai o ke akua.

Translation

Here is food, oh gods,
Only a morsel of heavenly food,
A gift from me, thy little child,
Of the yellow-skinned 'awa of Ke-ahi-a-laka.
(My prayer) has gone to meet Pele,
Who is gathering lehua blossoms,
Who is stringing them into wreaths by the sea of Hopoe,
Here is 'awa for the men of heaven,
Here is 'awa for the women of heaven,
Here is 'awa for the men of the Pit,
Here is 'awa for the women of the Pit,
Hither and yon,
Come, rinse out your mouths and wash your hands,
This (rite) is sacred and profound, let the kapu be released,
Freed that we may stand, that we may walk about,
Freed by the decree of the gods.

The following is the house prayer that was always said morning and evening by her maternal grandmother, Po-'ai-wahine, in the home named Haleola (House of Life) in which Mrs. Pukui spent her childhood as foster-child.

E 'ou mau kia'i mai ka po mai
E nana ia mai ka hale o kakou
Mai luna a lalo
Mai kahi kihi a kahi kihi
Mai ka hikina a ke komohana
Mai ka uka a he kai
Mai loko a waho
Kia'a 'ia, malama 'ia
E pale aku i na ho'opilikia ana i ko kakou nohona
Amama. Ua noa.

Translation
O my guardians, from remote antiquity,
Watch over our home
From top to bottom;
From one corner to the other;
From east to west;
From (the side facing) the upland to the (side facing the) sea;
From the inside to the outside.
Watch over and protect it;
Ward off all that may trouble our life here.
Amama—(the prayer) is freed.

The effectiveness or *mana* of a *pule* lay partly in the words and names used. The words of a prayer, like those of a *mele* or dance-chant, had to be good words in their connotations, and not words whose composition or sounds might be offensive to *akua* or *'aumakua*. And the proper names, be they personal or place names, must also be good in their connotations and pleasing to the beings listening to the prayer. The gods and guardians were relatives, more sacred and powerful than any living person. If a member of an *ali'i* family were chanting or dancing for the beloved (and, because of his *mana*, revered with awe) senior *ali'i*, the words and the steps and gestures must be good and pleasing. Furthermore, the recital must be correct and unfaltering. A slip (*hala*, fault, error) of the tongue would naturally be displeasing to the *akua* or *'aumakua* listening to a *pule*, for it was disrespectful, and inaccurate. It would anger the god or guardian, as a forgetful or careless

chanter or dancer would anger an *ali'i,* or faulty workman-
ship would be contemptuously discarded by a master canoe
builder (*kahuna kalai wa'a*). Hence it was that the composition and reciting of prayers was a form of craftsmanship, exactly as was canoe or image adzing.

Equally important in praying is the breath (*ha*). The
mana of the prayer was in the words and names, but it was
the breath that carried the words and names.

> I have seen Tutu Pa'ele, a dear old neighbour in Ka-'u, do as
> follows when I was a child. He used to pray over a glass of
> water in which there was a pinch of salt and turmeric and
> then, "*Ha,*" expelled his breath over it after the amen, to impart
> a *mana* to the water.
>
> A person about to die passed his knowledge to his successor
> by expectorating (*ku-ha*) or by expelling his breath (*ha*) into
> his mouth. With this, the *mana* he had in whatever he was an
> expert in, passed on to the person to whom he had given it. If
> he was a skilled medical *kahuna,* the recipient would become
> one in later years. So it was that knowledge passed directly
> from one person to a particular one and not to other members
> of the family in general. If the person to whom the sacred
> legacy was given was a small child, the *'aumakua* who guided
> and helped the giver would guide the receiver until his skill
> was equal to that of the one from whom he received it by means
> of the *ha.* The *mana,* imparted by the *ha* kept the art alive,
> and the *'aumakua* of one, through dreams (*moe 'uhane*), visions
> (*akaku*) or *'ula leo* (speaking directly to) led him until he, too,
> was an expert. An adult successor did not take as long to become
> an expert as a child would, if his understanding was already
> greatly advanced.

SICKNESS.

Sickness was completely a family matter, both in its
causes and cure. To the Hawaiians there were many causes
for sickness. An apparently "natural" sickness was called
ma'i kino (body sickness) ; the sickness caused by the displeasure of an *'aumakua* was a *ho'opa'ipa'i 'aumakua;* the
one caused by the *'ohumu* (the disgruntlement of a relative)
was a *ma'i 'ohumu 'ia;* by the *'anai* (spoken curse) was a
mai 'anai 'ia and so on down through every type of sorcery.

The sickness due to an apparently natural cause did
not cause concern to the medical *kahuna* in the least. He
knew his herbs and how to use them to good effect, but the
ho'opa'ipa'i 'aumakua did disturb him greatly. The

'aumakua must be appeased by prayers and offerings. What the offerings were depended on the *'aumakua*. The water spirits called *mo'o* had a fondness for dogs; Pele and her sister Hi'iaka for taro greens and salt; some of the gods liked pork, and others chicken. A lingering sickness that did not yield readily to medical treatment was considered to be due to the displeasure of a family *'aumakua*, or to sorcery.

Before anything else was done, the *ho'oponopono* (to make right) ceremony was resorted to. There must be a spiritual cleansing; a forgiving of one another in the family; a confession of sin and so on, so that there would be no obstruction of the *kahuna's* work from within. He might then devote himself to the work of appeasing the offended *'aumakua*, or return the evil influence (*ho'iho'i*) to its source.

Attention was duly paid to dreams, for in them the *'aumakua* often gave directions, what to do and how to treat the patient. This was called *na ho'ike a ka po*, or revelations from the night.

Mrs. Pukui's grandfather, a noted *kahuna* of Waikapuna in Ka-'u, also regarded the phases of the moon. He would wait until the *'Ole* nights were passed before doing anything of importance, as *'ole* meant *no* or *not*, therefore not at all auspicious. He continued his pleas to the *'aumakua* for mercy, but did not perform any rites or ceremonies during that period. *Hoaka* was a good night, as the name meant casting a shadow, and the gods could be persuaded to come and "reveal their presence by casting their shadows" on the *kahuna*. *Mahealani* was not so propitious a night except when the *kahuna* desired to know where (*mahea*) a certain thing was hidden. *Hilo* meant a very faint light, therefore the night of *Hilo* was not desirable. The *Kaloa* nights, which were in reality *Kanaloa* nights, were very good and so were the *Ku* nights, and the night of *Kane* and of *Lono*. *Muku* means "cut off short," therefore the night of that name was inauspicious.

In effecting a cure the *ho'omalu*, or period of quiet, was necessary. There must be no quarrelling, no pleasure seeking, no idle gossip. All members of the family concentrated their thought on one thing, the recovery of the patient. Not only was quietness in the home and family required, but also the avoidance of quarrelling and fighting with those outside. Should one disobey, the work of the *kahuna* would be *haki* (broken) and the *ho'omalu* had to be done all over again until the patient was on the road to recovery.

This same *kahuna* also forbade the eating of the *lipe'epe'e* seaweed and the squid (*he'e*) when he was seeking a sign from the gods, as the word *pe'e* meant to hide away and *he'e* to flee, hence the gods would hide the information sought after and cause it to flee.

> The *ho'omalu* was not uncommon. Should any one call from outside, or enter the house while a ceremony was going on, the *kahuna* paid particular attention to his appearance, what he had in hand, his relationship to the patient and so on. If the intruder was an uncle who had brought a *lei* he had strung, then the *kahuna* knew that one of the patient's uncles was offended with him over a *lei*. Whoever it was, he was led to come in so that the *kahuna* might know who was approaching and why. If the person who appeared was a woman acquaintance, then it was known that the trouble was due to a female acquaintance of the family.
>
> When on Kauai in 1936, one of my relatives was holding a *ho'oponopono* over a sick child. Not knowing about it, I went to call on them and when they saw me, the aunt exclaimed, "*A kupuna* (forebear)! The child's sickness is due to an offended *kupuna!*" Then turning to me she asked, "Did we have the right to name this child, 'Ke-li'i-kipi-o-Haililani?'" (an ancestral name). I assured them that they had every right in the world to it. I left them still wondering which female *kupuna* was at the bottom of the trouble, for I did not know.
>
> The kind of prayer used in such trouble was the *pule kala* or freeing prayer, a few of which still exist in my family, handed down from the grandfather. Just what rites and ceremonies were used depended often on the revelations given in dreams. Here is an example:
>
> A woman lived not very far from a house where the inmates delighted in singing insulting songs and using offensive speech. She was a quiet person and could never "talk back" in the same manner, and finally she became nervous and sick. One night she dreamed of a little man who perched on a *kukui* bough very much like an oversized owl. He told her to take three dried *kukui* nuts and three stones and bury them at the corner of the lot nearest these unpleasant neighbours. Next morning she obeyed, though not knowing what it was all about. That afternoon, angry voices were heard in the other house. The quarrel soon developed into a fight, both fistic and verbal. Half of the family, the most offensive, packed up and moved away. They never returned again. Freed from this annoyance, the sick woman recovered from her nervousness.

The *wai huikala* or water of purification was always required in a *kala* (freeing) ceremony. It consisted of sea water, and if that was unobtainable, of fresh water with a little salt dropped into it. A pinch of *'olena* (turmeric) root might be added if there was any at hand. This liquid was sprinkled (*pikai*) all over the house. (An ordinary sprinkling with fresh water was called *pipi*, but a ceremonial sprinkling with salt was *pikai*). This was to give the house a cleansing from spiritual defilement and no evil spirit belonging to others would remain in a house so sprinkled.[26]

Wherever purification was needed, whether for the *kala* ceremony, for the erection of a *hula* altar, the dedication of house or canoe, the *wai huikala* was always required. After one had been to a funeral or had any contact with a corpse, he was sprinkled with the *wai huikala* before entering the house. Even to-day this is occasionally practiced.

In most cases sicknesses in which the *kahuna* tried to free the patient from disturbing influences with the *kala* prayers, required a *pani*. The *pani* was the thing to do or eat at the end of the treatment. Very often it consisted of the *kapu kai* (ceremonial sea-bathing), and the eating of the *kala* seaweed or *kala* fish, or any other thing with the word *kala* (freeing) in its name. *Pani* means to close.

The treatment of sickness was generally, of course, a strictly domestic affair; but in the case of a ruling chief the whole community was affected. Equally, when it affected the *hiapo* (first born) or *haku* (master) of an *'ohana* it may be assumed that it affected not only the household but the whole kinship group. Under some circumstances treatment involved payments, offerings and feasting. These occasions were like the feasts marking fortuitous happy events such as the return of a distinguished *'ohana* after long absence or the visit of distinguished friends, strangers or *ali'i*, in that the whole family connection joined in helping and contributing.

---

[26] I have heard of the use of the *'awi'aki* grass for this purpose, a grass with a sharp, pointed blade that grows in the sand, but my own people did not use it. The sharp points were supposed to stab into the evil spirits—just as bamboo cut into them like knives.—M.K.P.

DEATH AND THE LEAP INTO THE SPIRIT WORLD.

Every island (*moku*) had its especial point overlooking the sea which was the leaping place (*leina*, to leap) for spirits on their trek to the *ao 'aumakua* after death. The spirit left the body not with the breath, but out of the corners of the eyes (*eua 'uhane*), whence tears flow. If on the way to the *leina* an *'aumakua* of the person meets the *'uhane* and sends it back, then the body revives. Otherwise the *'aumakua* will lead it safely to and over the *leina*. Once beyond that hurdle, the soul is safe with the *'aumakua* in the Unseen (*Po*). Lost souls are those that literally have gotten lost while feebly searching for the *leina* because they have no *'aumakua* who cares enough to show the way, and for whom none feel grief, there are no prayers of loving *'ohana*.

For people of Ka-'u the *Leina* is at Ka Lae, or "South Point," which is the extremity of the southern coast of Hawai'i. Ka Lae was the domain of the High Chiefs of Ka-'u, famed for its underground water, its *heiau*, and for the rich fishing grounds that lay to the southward where eastward and westward currents conjoin. It is self-evident that any man who had earned the enmity of the *ali'i* would think with anxiety of the inevitable day (or night) when his *'uhane* must leave his body and find its way past the chief's home and temple to take its last leap.

CONTROLLED SPIRITS.

Instead of sending the *'uhane* on its way into the realm of the unseen, there were means by which it was sometimes held and converted into a controlled spirit living in the unseen but tied to a place or object and to a keeper (*kahu*). Little has been written about this phase of old Hawaiian religion, but it goes to the very heart of the old theory and practice. An understanding of it is essential for it is the simplest and most direct form of ritual worship, and is one key to the understanding of the more elaborate ritual of *akua* and *'aumakua*, some of whom doubtless came to be what and who they were, in the ancient ritual and legends and myths, out of beginnings as simple as those described below. This is one of the phases of family life which exhibits in miniature the prototype of elaborated cults of witchcraft, handcraft, fishing, planting, war, and phases of the *kapu* ceremonies associated with the *ali'i*, such as the consecration of *kahili* as a royal symbol or of the sacred remains of a high chief whose power would be that of an *akua*.

The *'unihipili* is the spirit of a dead person who was kept because of love and affection. The bones, finger nails, hair or some such relic, were kept in a gourd calabash, wooden calabash, or in a bundle or in a box or trunk. Sometimes the relics were kept in the dwelling houses of their keepers; but sometimes they were put in a separate house built for the spirit. Sometimes the body or relics were hidden away, while the spirit was constantly called upon (*hea*) by worshipping (*ho'omana*) and feeding. Such an *'unihipili* might return and "sit on" a *haka*, thereby helping its keeper (*kahu*) by showing what remedy to use for healing and how to prepare it. Such an *'unihipili* was evil only when the *kahu* who fed it was evil. If the *kahu* was a "filth eating" sorcerer (*'ai hamu*) so the *'unihipili* became, in consequence of being sent here and there on deeds of evil. But if the *kahu* was good, the *'unihipili* was also good.

In Ka-'u a certain spirit was kept and made *'unihipili* and there are a number of old people still living who knew her and the way she was made into an *'unihipili* after her death. Her mother's name was Loki, and Ka-pua was the name of the person whose spirit became an *'unihipili*. She was part White.

The mother had sworn an oath saying that she did not want her daughter to commit fornication with any man until after she married, but the thing that she did not want done was done and the daughter herself paid the penalty. When the mother found out, it was too late to do anything.

Ka-pua was buried in her mother's yard and on her grave stood a small one room house. The floor was covered with Chinese matting and in the room was a bed with all its furnishings, such as blankets, white bed spread, pillow cases, sheets and mosquito netting. In one corner of the room stood a big bureau and in it were laid ready made dresses and materials that were not made up. On the other side of the room was a table on which were placed such foods as fruits, candy, pork and *poi*, as well as chicken, wild duck and such delicacies.

Many were the tales told by those who knew about the doings of this *'unihipili*. Before her death she took a great fancy to a horse owned by an uncle, and asked him to trade horses with her. The uncle refused for he hated to part with the horse and so she asked him to sell it to her for cash. He would not hear of it. When he heard that she was very ill, he came to see her. She said, "Listen to me, my uncle, your horse is going to be mine. When I die you will be without a horse." The uncle did not believe what she said.

When the uncle heard that Ka-pua was dead, he came on

the horse to see and to mourn for his niece. As soon as he came directly in front of the house the horse stumbled and died on the spot. Ka-pua was buried that day and on that same day the horse was buried.

Some months later two aunts in Waiohinu saw her spirit coming along on the horse. She left the horse at the gate and came up to the porch where they were sewing on a quilt. One of them spoke to her, "Listen to me, Ka-pua, do not go from place to place or from one relative's house to another's. It is true that relatives are loved but perhaps some of them may meet with trouble and you will be blamed because you pass to and fro before the doors of their houses. Abide in your own place and when trouble comes to us your relatives, we can not point to you and find much to say against you." She was never more seen again at Waiohinu.

It was the spirit of this girl who on another occasion brought a stranger, an old man, and took him to her mother's house. Once when this old man got very drunk, Ka-pua's mother became angry and sent him away from her house. The old man crept, without Loki's knowledge, under Ka-pua's house, and there he slept for two nights. Ka-pua's spirit was vexed; and her mother was startled when suddenly she saw her daughter come in, and when she started to pull at her hair. She did not know why the spirit of her daughter was angry until that night. Then she saw Ka-pua in a dream, and her daughter said, "Why did you send my servant away? What if he did get drunk, he was bothering no one as he lives all by himself. He is under my house, asleep on my grave. Go and get him to go back to his room." The mother awoke and went down to Ka-pua's house. Sure enough, there she found that old man curled up under Ka-pua's grave house. She called him to come out from there and took him back to her dwelling house.

The mother was a beautiful woman who was well supplied with ornaments to deck herself with, such as rings, old fashioned necklaces and those made of gold, all kinds of bracelets, brooches and so on. When Ka-pua died, her mother, knowing herself to be childless, buried her ornaments on Ka-pua's coffin. That night she saw her daughter's spirit in a dream. Ka-pua said, "Mama, why were you so foolish as to bury your lovely ornaments. Go and get a man to dig at once till he finds your box and bring it home. I want to see my mother wearing her pretty ornaments for she is a beautiful person." The command was carried out that very day.

It is said that when the mother became elderly she behaved queerly and said things that were not right to say and for this reason Ka-pua also did improper things. It may have been so but I do not know for I left my birthplace in my childhood. Because of these things that were not good, some of our relatives went to consult those who knew how to exorcise (*'oki*) this girl from themselves.

This work termed "*oki*" (cutting) was work in which certain people of Hawai'i *nei* were skilled. If one had a dream that was not good he prayed to cut its evil influences from him when he awoke in the morning. He prayed that all unpleasant results be removed and all good be made fast to him. It was possible, if it was the kind that could be so treated, but if it was not, nothing would help change it.

So it was done with spirits, if the *kahuna* blamed the trouble upon a certain spirit, that spirit could be cut away (disowned). It was cut off and separated from one by prayers. But sometimes, if the *kahuna* was unscrupulous, he would not tell the truth but would accuse a good spirit-relative who was close to someone in the family so that he would cut him off; thereby the way was open for that *kahuna* to control that spirit. It was not well to cut until one was positive that it was that certain *'aumakua* or *'unihipili* who brought on the trouble. If it was indeed bad then it was well to cut it off, but if the *kahuna* was one who was seeking mischief, better let things be.

The thing that was taught to our branch of the family was to leave *'unihipili* worship alone and to let all spirits go to the place prepared for them and if any other relative kept an *'unihipili*, not to bother to go through a cutting ceremony or say unkind things till we had sufficient proof that it was really the cause of our troubles.

This is what my ancestors did in the olden days, they took the bodies of their dead to their *'aumakua* so that the spirits would dwell there with them. Before taking the body from the house, the hair or other personal things belonging to his survivors were put with it, with this little prayer:—

E (inoa) e, eia ka lauoho o mea ke ho'omoe 'ia nei me 'oe. O kou ho'omana'o ia nona, mai ho'i mai 'oe e hoaka, e halo, e muki, e lapu, e ho'omaka'uka'u e ho'opilikia. Ina he kauoha na ke akua ia 'oe e ho'i mai e nana i ka pilikia o hope nei, ho'i mai a ho'i hou aku no i ke alo o kou akua. He ala huli hope 'ole kou, na makou no e 'imi aku i ke ala i ko makou manawa.

Translation

O (name), here is so-an-so's hair that we are laying away with you. This is your keepsake from him. Do not return to show yourself nor to peer in doorways, to make sibilant noises, to haunt, to frighten or to make trouble. If the god (with whom you are to dwell) wishes you to come back to help us in our time of need, come and then return to the presence of your god. You are on the trail on which there is no return, so let us seek the path ourselves when our time shall have come.

Sometimes it was the *'unihipili* that did the mischief for which the *akua* was blamed. It is explained thus: It may be that at the birth of a child he was named in a dream Ku-hai-moana. When this man Ku-hai-moana died, his wife through love of him kept him and made him an *'unihipili*. When this woman was about to die, she told her relatives, " Take care of Ku-hai-moana, the *'unihipili*." But as time rolled on Ku-hai-moana the *'unihipili* became confused with Kua-ha-moana the shark *akua*. When the *'unihipili* did the mischief, the *akua* was blamed, for their names were alike. So confusion came in at times and the *akua* was said to be evil, an eater of filth, a destroyer of men, and so forth.

The story of Ka-pua is an example that occurred not so long ago of the conversion of a beloved departed soul into a controlled, *mana*-endowed spirit (*'unihipili*) by means of gifts which attracted and held the *'uhane*; and of causing it to have power (*ho'omana*) by a routine of prayer (*pule*).

The ancient Hawaiian procedure was identical with this in principle. But in olden times the primary offering was *'awa*, which was the gift most desired by *akua* and *'aumakua*; and which was the narcotic used by mediums as an aid to inducing the desired state of trance when the god or guardian spirit was summoned by prayer to " sit upon " the *haka*. There was this difference, too: that in the old days the *ho'omana* was more effective because the *kapu* of the various *akua* and *'aumakua* were fully understood and rigorously respected, and the prayers were recited by an expert pray-er (*kahuna pule*), whose lifelong training in praying, and whose close relationship to his *akua* and *'aumakua*, gave him *mana* of a sort and to a degree, under the Hawaiian system of worship, that ceased to exist in later days when the old *kapu* and *pule* were only partially remembered and understood.

There were several ways of creating an *'unihipili*. One was by keeping a portion of the body in the home and calling upon the departed morning and evening to come and partake of *'awa*. This method was called *kahukahu*.

The *kaku'ai* method was more elaborate. After the death of a person, his body was prepared with the proper sacrifices and taken to the dwelling place of his *akua* or *'aumakua*. Those who claimed Pele as their *akua* and wished to take their dead to her, took the bones of the deceased, wrapped in red and black *tapa*, to the priests of Pele. At the pit the *kahuna* chanted a long prayer, threw in prepared *'awa* and a cooked pig, and then last of all the bundle of *kapa* containing the bones. If the deceased was accepted by Pele, the bundle made a circuit of the pit without being burned and then burst into flames and vanished. A flame appeared on the surface later which was taken to be the spirit of the person just accepted by Pele.

Those who were related to the *mo'o* (reptiles), or water spirits, took their dead, wrapped in yellow *tapa* to a stream with an offering of a reddish brown or brindled dog. There prayers were chanted till the *mo'o* appeared, large and small, and the body was lowered into the water to become a *mo'o*.

The relatives of Kane-hekili, the thunder god, offered their dead, wrapped in black *tapa* and laid this bundle with offerings before the dwelling house. A priest of Kane-hekili completely dressed in black called upon him until the sky darkened and thunder pealed. Then a bolt of lightning darted downward, and the body vanished. It was said that in the bolt of lightning were seen many hump-backed beings, "*Na kuapu'u o Mai'akuapu'u*" (The hunchbacked-ones-of-Mai'akuapu'u") who ran swiftly about gathering up the offerings and the body of their departed relative.

A body presented to sharks to be changed into a form such as theirs, was wrapped in *tapa*, with a design chosen by the family, and the marking of the *tapa* became the markings of the shark body. This enabled the family to recognize their relative now become their shark *'unihipili*. Thus new guardians were created.

PHYSICAL REMAINS AND LIFE OF THE SPIRIT.

Few *'uhane* became *'unihipili*. Some who had neither loving relatives to care for the corpse, nor the guardianship of family *'aumakua* who help souls find their way to the world of spirits, became lost souls (*kuewa*) wandering about the vicinity that they were familiar with, unfed and hungry, chasing butterflies or spiders for food, or stealing it when they might. For this reason Hawaiians in Ka-'u in the old days never ate after dark, for fear of molestation by one of these *kuewa*. These were the *lapu* (ghosts) that might leap upon a person in a lonely place at night.

Normally, in post-Christian times, the corpse (*kupapa'u*) was laid out in the dwelling, with feet towards the door. In pre-Christian times a shed was built for it, away from the house, in which it awaited ultimate disposition. If destined for burial, the body was drawn up into the position of a foetus before birth, knees to chest, arms folded, and with face down over the knees. But, since it was with the bones (*iwi*) that the *'uhane* remained identified, and therefore the bones that must be kept safe from molestation, the usual practice was not burial. Instead, a relative tended the corpse, removing the decaying flesh and organs by hand, to clean completely (*ho'okele*) the bones. This

was a labour of love, for a devoted relative. The fleshly
refuse (*pela*) was thrown into the sea.

Through a purloined bone, an enemy or a *kahuna*, even
a mere fisherman, could enslave the *'uhane* and make
it serve him, as the *kahu* of an *'unihipili* used a spirit of
that type to help in his work, good or evil. (For example, a
fishhook made of a high chief's shinbone would have great
mana.) Hence the necessity of disposing of the bones
secretly, in a safe hiding place.

The cleaned bones were made into a light compact
bundle tied with sennit cords, and borne to the place of
concealment. It was easily carried on the back by the *kahu*
(guardian), who went alone in the night so that no one
but he would know where they were placed.

Sometimes the bundle of bones was buried under the
dwelling house; for *ali'i* it was a cave that was known only
to his *kahu*. But generally the bones were taken to a place
identified with the *'aumakua* of the family, because the
'uhane is with its *'aumakua*.

> It was usually the daughter's or granddaughter's duty to
> attend to the body of a woman; and the wife's, son's or grand-
> son's, of a man.
>
> The body of the dead was washed by the nearest of kin,
> the wife, mother or the children, especially the eldest, and
> then clothed in a fresh garment. A pad was placed between
> the legs before putting on the loin cloth or skirt, to absorb
> any discharge. Salt was placed in thin *kapa* (later, thin cloth)
> and placed over the navel. This was believed to slow down
> decomposition. Other relatives brought in banana stalks
> trimmed flat on two sides. These were laid on the floor side
> by side, then a second layer was put on these, then a mat was
> placed on top. On this bier the body was laid. The banana
> stalks kept the body cool. They were changed several times
> a day.
>
> It was the duty of a very near relative to hide the body
> away in the family burial cave. The hiding away was always
> done in secret. Then for years, the wife, husband or children
> went to the cave to keep the place where the corpse was laid
> neat and tidy. The various belongings he loved in life were put
> in the cave with him. Even food was placed near the dead
> soon after the burial, in order that the spirit might have food
> on its long journey to the spirit world, or if the body should
> be restored to life, there would be something to eat before he
> sought his way out.
>
> As my family belonged to the lineage of Pele, the bodies of
> our dead were laid away in a cave until after decomposition

was all over. Then the bones were carried with the appropriate
gifts to Kilauea fire pit, where lived the Prophet of Pele (*Kaula
Pele*). The *Kaula* went with the relatives to the rim of the Pit
(*Ka Lua*) and with prayers the gifts (*mohai*) of pork and *'awa*
were tossed to the Woman of the Pit (*Ka-Wahine-a-ka-Lua*).
The bundle of bones were then thrown in with the words, "Here
is your offspring, O Pele, please accept him." The *'uhane* was
then believed "to live with Pele for all time." If the dead was
not acceptable to Pele, that is if she would not recognize the
kinship, the bundle was thrown back to the feet of the priest.
It was then carried back to the cave. There had never been a
time when the bones of our own relatives were ever thrown
back. This justified our belief that a kinship existed between
our *'ohana* and the dreaded fire goddess.

The *ao 'uhane*, or realm of spirits, was not some place
like Heaven and Hell, above or below the earth. For any
family, its *ao 'uhane* was the *ao akua* and *ao 'aumakua*, i.e.,
the place, element or realm in which the ancestral *akua* and
'aumakua of the *'ohana* lived. If related to Kamoho-
ali'i, Lord of the sharks, the *ao 'aumakua* was the ocean. So
was it for people of Kanaloa, whose *kinolau* were the squid
and octopus. The bones of these people went into the sea.
For a family descended from the *Mo'o* (reptiles), such as
that of Kiha-wahine on Maui, the bundle of bones was wrapped in yellow *tapa* and let down into a freshwater pool. The
remains of members of the Pele clan in Ka-'u were thrown
into the crater of Kilauea Volcano, which was Pele's home,
as described above.

THE DEATH FEAST.

The death feast (*aha'aina makena*), or feast of lamentation, was the gathering of relatives and friends, or in the
case of a high chief, of all his people, to mourn the passing
of the spirit (*'uhane*). It was not in the nature of a festival, for this was the time of grief: the feasting was merely
a matter of feeding the assembled people. All who came
brought food, and the mourners did the work of preparing
it. No one stayed away, unless it be a very old person, someone too ill to travel, or a woman about to give birth or with
a baby too young to be carried. Anyone not seen mourning
and crying to the dead would be suspected of harbouring
hate and perhaps of having caused the sickness or accident
that brought death.

As the corpse lay with feet in the direction from which the mourners would enter (toward the front door), the close relatives sat behind the body, the next of kin by the head. As a relative was seen approaching, one of the family within would call out with a cry of grief, and in response the relative coming would begin the wailing call to the dead that was termed *uwe helu*. Here is an example:

> Auwe ku'u hoa hanau, ku'u hoa pili o na la kamali'i; ku'u hoa ohumuhumu, hoa 'alo 'inea. E ha'alele mai ana ka 'oe ia'u! Aloha na kai lawa'ia a kaua i noho ai. E Ka-wai-uhu e, ua pau kou 'ike hou ana i kona mau maka; e Pa'ula e, ua hala aku la ku'u hoa i ke ala polikua a Kane.

> #### Translation.
> O my cousin, my companion of childhood days; companion with whom I shared my troubles; companion who shared my woes. Ah—you have deserted me! Beloved are the fishing places to which we have gone; the sandy stretches where we sat. O Ka-wai-uhu, you shall never more see his face; O Pa'ula, my companion has gone on the hidden pathway of Kane.

The cries from the family within, and from the mourner approaching from without, were an expression of genuine emotion. In between, the relatives would lapse into normal conversation. Then another mourner would approach, and again there was the cry of welcome from within and the responding cry from without, which was called the *kaukau*. Foreigners who thought it was all mere acting, did not understand that the feeling in the wailing cries was very real. It was one expression of grief.

> Loud wailing was called *ku-make-na*.
> Once at my grandmother's funeral, I have seen that form of mourning termed *pa'iauma*. Three very old women, all near relatives of hers, sat in a row and as they wailed they clasped their hands behind their necks; beat their chests with their fists and flung their hands up in the air in a gesture of despair, swaying all the while to their wailing. Their faces wore an expression of deep anguish.

Kanikau is a general word for all forms of mourning. The outcry described above was termed *kumakena* (*ku-make ana*). *Uwe helu* was a "recounting cry" in which the mourner recalls old associations, family connections and anything else that comes to mind. For example:—

"Oh, my beloved, now that you are gone, there will
be no one to help me bring our cows from the pasture.
Alas, I am alone, alone to do the many things we liked
to do, alone to rear our fatherless children, etc."

An *uwe helu* might also be addressed to a departing
friend, or by a mother as an expression of her grief over
an ungrateful child or the loss of a prized possession, or
upon the return of a relative who has been away long and
far.

Lamentations for a loved one sometimes were poetic
compositions which were treasured by the *'ohana* in after
years, as were the name chants (*mele*) of close kin. This
is the lamentation composed by Mrs. Pukui's mother after
the death of her first child in infancy.

He kanikau, he aloha kei a
Nou no e Miss Mary Binning,
Ku'u kaikamahine i ka makani kuehu lepo o Na'alehu,
Aloha kahi a kaua e noho ai,
'Auwe ku'u kaikamahine ho'i e,
Ku'u kaikamahine i ka pali o Lauhu,
E hu'e pau mai ana ko aloha i ku'u waimaka,
'Auwe ku'u kaikamahine, ku'u aloha la e—
Ku'u kaikamahine i ka wai hu'i o Ka-puna,
Aloha ia wahi a kaua e hele ai
Ku'u kaikamahine i ka ua nihi pali o Ha'ao,
Aloha ia wahi a kaua e pili ai,
Pi'i aku kaua o ke ala loa
O ke alanui malihini makamaka 'ole
'Auwe ku'a aloha ku'u minamina e
Ua hele i ke ala ho'i 'ole mai
'Auwe ku'u lei, ku'u milimili la e
Ku'u hoa pili o ua 'aina nei,
Eia au ke noho a'e nei,
Me ka ukana nui he aloha
'Auwe ku'u lei momi la e
Ku'u kaikamahine i ka wela o Wai-ka-puna
Aloha ia wahi a kaua e hele ai,
Ku'u kaikamahine i ke 'ala o na pua,
'Auwe ku'u lei kula e, aloha no, a . . .

—HAKU 'IA E PA'AHANA.

This is a dirge, an expression of affection,
For you, O Miss Mary Binning,
My daughter in the dust-scattering wind of Na'alehu,
In the home we shared together,
Oh —— my daughter!

My daughter at the cliff of Lau-hu;
Love for you makes my tears flow unchecked,
Oh my daughter at the cold spring of Ka-puna,
A beloved place to which we went,
My daughter in the rain that passes the hill of Ha'ao,
A place we were fond of going together,
We used to go up the long trail,
A little known trail, unattended by a friend.
Oh my darling—how sad I am at losing you.
You have gone on a road on which there is no returning,
Oh my darling—my pet.
My constant companion in the homeland,
Here I remain
With this great load, a yearning for you,
Oh my darling, precious as a necklace of pearls,
My daughter in the warm sun of Waikapuna,
Beloved is that place where we used to go.
My daughter among the fragrant flowers,
Oh my necklace, my golden chain, farewell—alas——!

by PA'AHANA.

Another expression of love for the departed, which persists to this day, was the singing of songs that the person had loved, the chanting of *mele* (eulogistic "name songs") that had been composed in honour of the person at birth, and the dancing of the several *hula* which dramatized these *mele*. This was a phase of Hawaiian custom entirely misunderstood by foreigners, especially early missionaries. To them it appeared an expression of "unseemly levity," whereas it was truly a token of *aloha*, for the *'uhane* would naturally be made happy by hearing and seeing those things that were loved throughout life.

Such was the mourning at the time of the "feast of death" for any beloved relative. In addition some would express their feelings in more violent ways. *Na'au'auwa* described violent grief in which the mourner grimaced, would roll about on the ground, pick up possessions of the dead one and wail over them, fling himself across the body or coffin. The word means grief from "deep within the very bowels."

A high *ali'i* who was beloved would be mourned with even more violent demonstrations, termed *manewanewa*, such as knocking out front teeth and gashing the head and scarring the body. A man might trim the hair on his scalp in a peculiar fashion. In the old days people would abandon themselves in an orgy of passion *en masse,* and do such things as dashing about with the *malo* (loin cloth) or *pa'u* (skirt) about the neck instead of the loins. At such times, it is said, there was general promiscuous indulgence of sexual passion: a climax and venting of pent up feelings that was doubtless salutary for the people, and believed to be gratifying to the dead *ali'i* as an expression of the ultimate sentiment of passionate love.

The Memorial Feast.

Exactly one year after the day of death of any person —man, woman, child, even a newborn baby—there was a memorial feast. "We had it in our family for every single one who died" (M.K.P.). This feast was called the *Aha'aina Waimaka,* because it was for all those *'ohana* who on the day of death and departure of the *'uhane* had come to shed their tears (*wai-maka*) out of respect and love for their relative. For the whole extended *'ohana* this was one of the three greatest occasions, the others being the feasts of rejoicing for the first-born and the marriage festival. Each of these occasions brought all branches and members together when the *aha'aina* was for a great or loved one, or for the *Haku* (Master) or *Hiapo* (First-born). For any person it at least brought together all the close and faithful relatives.

It was absolutely obligatory for every person who had come to weep for the dead at the *Aha'aina Makena,* to come now for this feast of rejoicing on behalf of the living and the dead. The *Aha'aina Waimaka* was a time of rejoicing because it marked "for the dead a relief from the burdens and woes of life; for the living, from the burdens of mourning." In the old days, war alone might interfere with this feast and the preparation for it. The *Ali'i* and his *Konohiki* (Supervisors) would respect it. Any work that the family or any person or group had under way would be suspended.

It was obligatory for all to come who had mourned the dead: but it was forbidden for any one to come who had wilfully remained away at the time of weeping, for such a one would be suspected of having had a hand in bringing about the sickness or accident, and consequent death, by means of witchcraft or a curse. Even if that were not the case, he would not be welcomed, either by the living or the *'uhane* for he had not shown due respect or love. He would

be ashamed to come to the *Aha'aina Waimaka* if he had not
come to the *Aha'aina Makena.*

What was called the *Ho'okupu* (causing to sprout) was
commenced immediately after the *Aha'aina Makena* by the
immediate family. This consisted particularly of the raising
and fattening of hogs and chickens for the feasting a year
hence, and also the planting of taro, sweet potatoes,
bananas. As their contribution to the *ho'okupu* all the visiting households and branches of the *'ohana* brought generously of what they had—fish, taro, coconuts, bananas, sugar
cane, salt, *'inamona* (candlenut-oil sauce), *limu* (seaweed),
shellfish. This was a time for bringing food only, not gifts.
The gifts that were tokens of love had been laid with the
kupapa'u (corpse) at the time of death and putting away
of the body.

Now was a time for rejoicing (*'oli-'oli*). This word,
'oli, with a short, accented *'o,* meaning to rejoice, is quite
distinct from *oli,* spoken with a long *o,* which was the
Hawaiian word for religious chanting.

In the case of the beloved ruling chief (*Ali'i-'Ai-Moku*
or *Ali'i Nui*) of a *Moku* (island or major tribal section
carved out by conquest as his domain—*moku* means to
"cut"), the *ho'okupu* for the *Aha'aina Waimaka* of this
Hiapo (first-born) involved raising food on a vast scale by
his own relatives, and contributions from all the *'ohana* or
dispersed family groups and individuals that made up the
people of his *Moku,* even those who were living in other
Moku. (For an unloved *ali'i,* one who had been stingy, selfish, brutal, one for whom there was only contempt in their
hearts, the people apart from close relatives neither
mourned nor joined in the *ho'okupu*). In families related
to the *ali'i* and in other families also, the *ho'okupu* and
the festivities attending the *Aha'aina Waimaka* for a departed kinsman were in proportion to the family's rank,
prominence, popularity, wealth.

In Ka-'u when the *ho'okupu* was for the *Ali'i Nui,* the
Aha'aina would be at his place of residence. This place, for
Kalaniopu'u, the chief of Ka-'u who raised Kamehameha,
was just west of Ka Lae ("South Point") at Wai-o-Ahukini,
because Kalaniopu'u was a great lover of fishing. Other
Ka-'u *Ali'i Nui* had their court in Waiohinu, which was
a peaceful and verdant place.

For the *Aha'aina* of the *ali'i* a great open shed (*lanai*) would be built for the work of preparing the food, and for shelter. All was festive, all the folk of the *Moku* were there and others who had come to mourn. The feasting and rejoicing were the main thing for the people. But for the *Ali'i* and his relatives, equally as important was the chanting and the dancing which were a part of this *aha'aina*. The Court Chanter (*Mea Oli*) sang traditional *Oli* belonging to the *Ali'i's* ancestral line, others about his homeland (*'aina*) and his people (*poe ma-ka-'aina-na*). During the chanting of an *Oli* before the *Ali'i*, all the people must remain silent, and seated. The *Hiapo* (First-born) listened in silence, and at the end of each *Oli*, looked toward the Chanter and responded, *"E o"* (pronounced E-yo-oo, with a rising inflection). "I am here." He responded likewise with these same words to each *mele* that was chanted before him. These were *Mele Ku'auhau*, reciting the genealogy of his line; the *Mele Hanau* or birth chants (such as the *Kumulipo* of Alapa'i Wahine) ; the *Mele Ma'i* (Chants for the Genitalia), and *Mele Inoa* (Name Chants) which had been composed at his birth and during his lifetime in praise of the deceased *Ali'i*. The *hula* that had been composed to accompany the recital of the *Mele Inoa* in honour of the deceased were danced now before the *Hiapo*, for his pleasure and for his people, and for the *'uhane* as well. During the chanting and dancing of *mele* all was gaiety, the people moving about, talking, laughing, joking. So it went on while they feasted and made merry. But no new *mele* or *hula* were composed for the *Hiapo* at this time: his had been composed before and at the time of his birth; and he would be honoured with others during his reign as *Ali'i Nui*, now commencing.

For the *ali'i*, these festivals continued day after day. For others, how long they lasted would depend upon how long the food lasted, how many *'ohana* were there, how gay and happy the people were.

In the chapter on the Life Cycle we pointed out that death marked the ending of the earth cycle and the commencement of existence in the Unseen with the *'aumakua* and *akua*. At the *Aha'aina Waimaka*, the *'ohana* celebrated this climax for the *'uhane* of each one who had "passed on."

VII.

TRADITIONAL MANNERS AND CUSTOMS, AND THE SOCIAL ORDER

In this chapter are summarized briefly various Hawaiian attitudes and practices characteristic of the old Polynesian civilization in Ka-'u, which have not hitherto been described, in such a way as to give a lively sense of relationship and the home; of status and obligations; of *kapu*, manners and etiquette. It has seemed to us that a simple and effective means of conveying a sense of these intricacies as actualities in the doings of a lively people would be by interspersing the descriptive matter and our comments with sayings and expressions relating to the topics under discussion. Te Rangi Hiroa (Dr. Peter H. Buck) once described how, in his early days as a Public Health Officer visiting Maori communities, it often was necessary to explain to the assembled elders of a tribe the reasons for some regulation or medical measure that he had to enforce. His careful exposition of the dry facts of the situation without recourse to a chant or an anecdote or a story to flavour and enliven his discourse, would be interrupted by some friendly old fellow calling out: *Te vai! Te vai!* ("Water! Water!") This final paper on the Ka-'u family system we endeavour to flavour with sayings, expressions and some anecdotes.

FAMILY CHARACTERISTICS.

Hawaiians, like all Polynesians, were keen observers of physical, temperamental and mental characteristics. There are a great number of terms and numerous sayings descriptive of physical form and appearance of the body, face, eyes and other features. These refer to individual characteristics rather than to relationship, so we do not include them here. The two sayings that follow show that Hawaiians were observant of the inheritance of traits both physical and psychological.

Ku no i ke keʻa.	He has the ways of his sire.
E like me ke kekeʻe o ka lala laʻau, pela no kona aka.	According to the crookedness of the branch, so is the crookedness of its shadow.

Like parent, like child.

MARRIAGE AND MATING.

There were figurative ways of expressing the readiness of a youth to mate and to assume the responsibility for making the fire and preparing the food, which was the man's function in the household.

Aia a wini kakala, a ʻula ka lepe o ka moa, alaila kau i ka haka.	When the spur is sharp and the comb red, then shall the cock rest on a perch.

When a boy becomes a man, then shall he take a wife.

Kokoke e ʻa ke ahi o ka ʻaulima.	Almost ready to make fire with a fire-stick held in the hand.

Said of a boy: almost old enough to mate.

Nui e moʻa ʻai ka pulehu.	Old enough to broil food.

Old enough to have a wife.

This was the period of courtship for youth and maid. Whereas for the first-born of *aliʻi* families the marriage was pre-arranged, for the younger lines of *aliʻi* and for commoners (as likewise for the ranking *aliʻi* in the love matches which took place in addition to the arranged marriage) freedom of choice and spontaneous, casual, or passionate attachment were the sanctioned prelude to unions which became permanent. These permanent unions were monogamous amongst the people in the lower ranges of the economic scale and polygamous among the wealthy. Though there was freedom of choice in most cases, nevertheless the young folk were given plentiful advice concerning the practical characteristics most desirable in a husband or wife, of which the following is a good example; but one may doubt that the practical was always a prime consideration with ardent youth!

Nana no a ka 'ulu i paki kepau.   Look for the breadfruit that is gummy on the skin.

Advice to a girl to look for a prosperous husband.

Love making and courtship were a subtle art in which love songs with hidden meaning, the nose-flute and musical bow were used to carry to the ear of the maiden wooed the delicate innuendoes of sentiment and passion. The maid and her lover both had their own subtle language of glance and gesture.

Ho'oipoipo.   To make love.

Refers to the courtship and love-making between lovers, or a song or chant for a sweetheart.

Ho'oha'i.   To strut, to preen.

A flirtatious coyness. It is perhaps a furtive glance, a coquettish smile, etc.

The notion, for which uncomprehending whites in the early days were responsible, that Hawaiians in their old culture-setting were promiscuous is a false one, for promiscuity was indulged in only by the dissolute and was held in contempt by the majority. The saying quoted immediately below, expresses this contempt for the promiscuous; while that which follows is a slap at a woman whose favours are available to any man—in other words, the harlot.

He nohona huikau, noho aku noho mai.   A life of confusion, living this way and that.

Referring to promiscuous people sharing each other's mates.

He 'uha leo 'ole.   A thigh over which no word is spoken.

Said of a woman who never refuses to have sexual intercourse with any man who asks her.

Young people were taught the wisdom and practical importance of pleasant " in-law " relations, as the next two sayings indicate.

Ho'ohoihoi makua hunowai.   A pleasing of a parent-in-law.

Said of one who begins with a great deal of enthusiasm which soon fades into a lack of interest.

E aʻo i ka hana o pa i ka leo Learn to work lest you be
o ka makua hunowai.   struck by the voice of the
             parent-in-law.

Advice to a son or daughter before marriage.

Respect for the parent-in-law, for the sake of a peaceful
and kindly existence, was stressed; but equally an attitude
of unkindness toward any relative by marriage was decried,
such as that expressed in the following saying, which was
regarded as extremely rude.

He pili papakole.   A backside relationship.

Relative of a relative-in-law and not by blood. A disrespectful term used only in anger.

MAN AND WIFE.

Compact and explicit is the following saying which describes the faithfulness, in crises, of man and wife. In
travelling, the danger on lonely trails, along shore, or on the
rough slopes or in the forested uplands, was the pouncing
of the marauder or murderer from behind. Even greater, at
night along lonely paths, was the dread of malevolent nature
spirits or ghosts that leapt upon the back and strangled the
victim. And we must picture also those times known not
infrequently when a family was in flight before raiders,
overland or by sea, during the wars which were common in
this land where fighting for conquest or for vengeance was
the preoccupation of chieftains and of their warriors trained
in the arts of war. At such times the man, as protector of
wife and children, came close behind his loved ones.

Ka pili kua; ka pili alo. Close to the back; close to
           the front.

A husband is referred to as *pili kua*, standing back of his
 mate as her protector. She is the *pili alo*, the protected
 one.

Another saying is this of a woman whose husband was
gentle:—

He kane ʻeha ʻole o ka ʻili. A husband that doesn't
           [even] hurt the skin.

Said by an appreciative wife of a husband who never beats
 her.

As with all Polynesians, passionate attachment often became jealous, and from this violence could result. The following somewhat equivocal saying is the expression of a wife whose husband was perhaps too easy-going:—

He kane maika'i; na'u ka hana.   A good husband; the doings are mine.

A husband who never bothers, leaving me free to do as I please.

The lazy and negligent man was unfortunately not uncommon, and his laziness was recognized as leading to an unthrifty household and uncared-for children, as in this saying:—

Hiamoe-wale ke kane, Nana-wale ka wahine.   Sleepy-head is the husband and Gaze-about is the wife.

When the husband sleeps too much, the wife just looks about her and does nothing.

But even negligence seems to have had a limit, for a complaining wife was reminded that even the worst husbands could be expected to make some provision for their families:—

'Aohe kane hanai nalo.   No husband feeds his wife flies.

Every husband has some virtues, some more, some less, but none has ever been found that gives his wife nothing but flies to eat.

CHILDREN.

To a mother her child is a lovely thing.

Ka 'opu'u pua i mohala.   A flower bud that unfolded.
A baby.

Ka lei ha'ule 'ole, he keiki.   A *lei* that is never cast aside is one's child.

The carrying of the beloved child—the mother's arms around the child and the child's arms around the mother's neck—evokes the simile of the flower garland, the *lei*.

He hi'i alo.   One borne in the arms.
A child dearly beloved.

| He hiʻialo, ua milimili ia i ke alo, ua haʻawe ia i ke kua, ua lei ʻia i ka ʻa-ʻi. | A beloved one, fondled in the arms, borne on the back, whose arms have gone about the neck as a *lei*. |

Said of a beloved, favourite child.

Especially treasured was the only child, which seems to have been of sufficiently frequent occurrence to have been coined into these sayings: *He hua kahi.* A single egg. An only child. *Hoʻokahi no hua a ka aʻo....* An *aʻo* bird lays but a single egg. A mother who has borne an only child.

Perhaps the first expression of what the Hawaiians termed *aloha* was between mother and child.

Hoʻoheno.   To fondle.

Caresses such as patting the hand, kissing the ear, and so on. As an adjective it is applied to a demonstrative child.

Hoʻoalohaloha or **hoʻaloha-**   To increase in affection.
loha.

An intense demonstration of affection, perhaps of child for parent. (Not applicable to lovers, for in that case it is *hoʻoipoipo*). Also making oneself loved by doing lovable deeds. When an undemonstrative child suddenly becomes demonstrative, some believed it a sign of impending separation.

ʻAʻa.   An ejaculation.

A demonstration of joy at the sight of a person who is loved. When a child extends his arms eagerly, makes an audible sound of joy or other demonstrations at the sight of a home-coming parent, that is *ʻaʻa.* When any person is so glad to see the other that he can hardly contain himself, this is *ʻaʻa.*

Hoʻopunini.   To charm, to lure.

Commonly applied to children or pets. It refers to a child who clings to a person, refusing to go to someone else who tries to take him, holding fast to the person he wants to stay with; or when left on the floor, the child stays close. A dog going round and round his master, wagging his tail, barking, creating a great fuss and refusing to leave: that, too, is *ho'opunini*. When fish circle in one spot, never leaving it for long, this term is also applicable. *Ho'opunini ka 'ia i ka punawai*—The fish gather and remain at the spring.

The following is a very wise observation, applied to the rearing of children, showing an appreciation of the life-giving power of the sun's rays for healthy golden brown little bodies.

O ka moa i hanai ia i ka la,   A cock raised in the sun-
ua 'oi i ka moa i hanai ia i   light is stronger than one
ka malu.   raised in the shade.

If you want a strong son, raise him with plenty of sunlight.

Equally, there was scorn for the parent who neglected the health of a child, as expressed in the following.

Hupe kole.   Red, runny nose.

Often used to small children who do not bother to wipe their noses. *"Kamali'i hupe kole"*—"Runny nosed kids!" is a common expression.

When a tot showed a tendency to hide away, the mother became fearful.

Pe'epe'e.   Literally "hide-hide."

If, for no apparent reason a child sought to hide it might imply impending illness or separation. In the old days, Hawaiian children would not run and pretend to hide from an approaching friend, much less "boo" at him, as they have learned to do nowadays.

The following saying shows that the well and happy child is one who is cared for:

He keiki mea makua   A child who has a parent
(or mea kupuna).   (or grandparent).

Said of a child whose parents, uncles, aunts or grand-
parents show affection by making beautiful things for his use or composing songs and chants in his honour. It is said in respect and admiration, for, to Hawaiians, it was a great thing to show love for their children.

A good mother, foster-mother or grandparent who raised a child must see to it that each child had as a dowry its own bed coverlet—in the old days a handsome sheet of *kapa,* in post-missionary days a hand-quilted coverlet of some favoured design.

He keiki no he kapa, he keiki no he kapa. For each child, a bed covering.

For parents not to make a *kapa* for each child (in later times a quilt) bespoke laziness.

The importance of the example set by the parents was well recognized.

Ka hana a ka makua, o ka hana no ia a keiki. What parents do, children will do.

The best examples for a child are his parents.

Ka ʻike a ka makua, he hei na ke keiki. The knowledge of the parent is unconsciously absorbed by the child.

There are a number of sayings that characterize the state of infancy and childhood and the relation of the child to elders.

Mai ka wa huli iluna ke alo. From the time the face is turned up.

From infancy.

Ua pau ka ʻino. The filth is ended.

In olden days diapers were unknown and the nursing mother was soiled by the baby. This saying refers to a child old enough to go to the toilet.

Na la e lana ana ke koko. In the days when the blood circulates freely.

The days of youth.

Aia i ka mole kamaliʻi. Still rooted in childhood.

Said of one who remains physically or mentally a child.

FOSTERING.

Anyone who knows Hawaiian family life even today has seen many instances in which an adopted child has become as intimately one with the feeding parent (*hanai*) as a child born to the parent. This is well expressed in the following saying:—

He ʻoha pili wale.　　　A young taro that attaches itself to an older corm.

Said of one who attaches himself to another in order to receive care.

It is a mistake, however, to think that the desire to adopt children was always motivated by pure altruism:—

Hanai kanaka, hiki ke hoʻo-unauna.　　Feed human beings for they can be sent on errands.

An adopted child, well cared for, will be a help later on.

And there is a saying that expresses disgust with an adopted child that proves itself an ingrate:—

Poho i ka malama i ko haʻi keakea.　　A waste of time to rear the result of someone else's semen.

Used by foster parents angered by ingratitude and neglect of adopted children not related to them by blood.

AFFECTION.

The leaven of love makes the joy of gathering together and sharing.

Ono kahi ao luʻau me ke aloha pu.　　Delicious are taro greens when love is there.

The simplest fare is delicious when shared with loved ones.

Holo iʻa ka papa, kau ʻia e ka manu.　　When the shoals are full of fish, birds gather over them.

Where there is food, people gather.

Blood relationship makes for affinity, and this affinity is the cement that makes the members of the *ʻohana* adhere one to another.

E kolo ana no ke ewe i ke ewe.   The rootlets will creep toward the rootlets.

Kinfolk seek the society of other kinfolk and love them because of their common ancestors.

Pipili no ka pilali i ke kumu kukui.   The sap sticks to the *kukui* tree.

Said of one who remains close to a loved one—as a child, perhaps, to his parent or grandparent.

The constancy of devotion between *'ohana* from infancy to old age is coined compactly into the following sayings:—

Aia i hi'ikua, i hi'ialo.   Is borne on the back; is borne in the arms.

1. Said of a beloved child carried about on the back and in the arms.
2. When one is gone to a far place where he cannot be seen by those who love him, he is said to be in *hi'ikua* (borne at the back) and when one is where he can be seen daily, he is in *hi'ialo* (borne in the presence).

Ola na iwi.   The bones live.

An expression meaning that there is comfort, contentment and happiness for one. When a child is good, thoughtful and loving, the oldsters of his family say of themselves, " *Ola na iwi.*" A complimentary saying to a friend who finds contentment with his loved ones or is blessed greatly.

Devotion and companionly friendship and hospitality were and are typical of the Hawaiian people, both within and outside the bounds of blood relationship and homeland and race.

In Hawaiian lore, as well as in contemporary life, countless instances of devoted and faithful companionship are to be found. Here are a few sayings which convey a sense of the quality of such affection in friendship.

Ku'u hoa 'ohumuhumu.   The companion I voice my complaints to.

An expression of affection for a sympathetic, understanding and helpful relative or friend to whom one goes with all one's problems.

Hoa pupu'u o ka po anu.   A companion to crouch with
                               on a cold night.

A sweetheart, a wife or husband.

Anu ko'u ka hale, ua hala ka   Cold and damp is the house
makamaka.   when the friend (or kins-
                                    man) is gone.

Since the earliest days of discovery and white contact,
and unchanging even in these times when the Hawaiian
people see themselves overwhelmed and outnumbered by
other races from West and East, the spirit of *aloha* in the
form of hospitality has been and is so spontaneous that it
seems innate in the breed.

He makamaka, ke pa la   That is a friend, for he calls
kahea.   out an invitation.

This pleasant invitation quoted by Dr. N. B. Emerson
is characteristic (*Malo*, p. 203) :—

E kipa maloko e hanai 'ai,   Come in and have food,
A hewa a'e ka waha.   And loosen the tongue.
A eia ka uku, ka leo.   And the pay—your voice.

He ukana na ka wai.   A burden for the water.

A kindly reassurance to a friend who has, perhaps, accidentally tracked in mud, or spilled something. "'A'ohe
pilikia." " Never mind, it is only a burden for the water
to carry away."

Mu ka waha heahea 'ole.   Silent is the mouth of the
                               inhospitable one.

To call a welcome (*heahea*) to any one approaching one's
home was considered essential to good etiquette.

The saying last quoted shows that hospitality was not
always wholly spontaneous but was recognized and appreci-
ated as a human and social virtue. Friendliness and affection are a tonic and lubricant which constitute two chief
ingredients of the joyous temperament of our Hawaiian
people. They keenly sensed the crippling effect of the
opposite of *aloha*.

Na hana ku i ke aloha.   Work that fits love. Deeds
                              that express true love.

| **Aloha mai no, aloha aku: o ka huhu ka mea e ola ʻole ai.** | When love is given, love should be returned; anger is the thing that gives no life. |

Love begets love; hatred begets hatred.

GREETING.

The old Hawaiian mode of greeting was termed *honi*, and this referred to placing the nostril gently beside that of the person greeted. Kissing the cheek or gently touching lips to lips is recent. However, persons swept by sudden passionate affection are described in legend as " flying upon the neck " (*lele ʻaʻi*) of the beloved. In ancient Hawaiʻi joining hands (*papa lima* or *hoʻopapa lima*) was not a greeting but a taken or confirmation of agreement.[27]

> When I was a child men, women and children kissed each other, a common greeting for all. To refuse to kiss a kinsman was considered rude (*hoʻokano*). A person who avoided his friends and relatives was *hoʻokano*.
>
> A person who was friendly to everyone was said to be *ʻiʻike*, and such a person was well liked.
>
> Old time Hawaiians never " made love " in public, or even in the presence of relatives or friends. Kindly deeds, courtesy and affection in speech and action were all that were needed to show *aloha*.

[27] The expression " *paʻi a paʻi* " for a tie between two contestants in a game came from the way in which they made their agreement before the game was played. The contestants and their supporters discussed the points which would make one of them the winner and also the articles or amount of goods used in a wager between the two parties. Having agreed, one player held out his hand and the other lightly slapped it; then he in turn held out his hand to be slapped. This was called the *hoʻopapa lima* or hand touching. If the contest was a draw and neither player won, the expression " *paʻi a paʻi* " (slap and slap) was used. They remained equals as they were at the time they made their agreement. So, when two people were equal in skill, they were said to be *paʻi a paʻi*. But two equally handsome people were said to be " *like a like* " and never *paʻi a paʻi*, as physical charm was not an acquired skill.

The holding of hands was called *kuilima* or *kuikui lima*. When two people walked arm in arm, or hand in hand, this was *kuilima*. Holding hands in climbing or helping with some work where this was necessary was done in the olden days, but lovers never held hands, walked arm in arm, or kissed as they do today.—M.K.P.

There were several forms of greeting between relatives, of which the *heahea*, the *kahea*, and the *uwe* are described below.

INVITING.

The *heahea* was still a common practice in my childhood. Except in remote country places, it is now a thing of the past. It was a custom for an adult member of the family to come to the door, stand there and call a welcome to an approaching person, " Come hither, come " (*He mai! Mai! Mai!*). If the person was an acquaintance, a little more might be said, perhaps, " So it is you! The folks are here at home. Come!" (*O 'oe no ka keia. Eia no ka po'e o kauhale nei. Mai!*)

As soon as he was seated he was asked to have something to eat (*E 'ai*). If the stranger was hungry, he accepted, but if he was not, he declined. So with a good friend or relative who had come from a distant place, food was prepared as soon as he entered and he was asked to partake of it.

If a friend came to one's house and did not see anyone at the door, he would cry out " *O* ". This '*o* is a long drawn o-o-h-oh! with a drop of the voice at the end. This would be followed by the call: " Where are the people of the house?" (*Auhea kanaka o kauhale nei?*) As soon as the '*o* was heard, someone would hurry to the door to *heahea*, to call him to come in.

A dearly beloved kinsman or friend was welcomed, not only with the *heahea* but with a chant of welcome, *kahea*. For example:—

" Come!	*He mai!*
You are welcome, o lehua blossom of mine from the upland forest,	*He mai e ku'u pua lehua o ka wao,*
A blossom around whom the birds gather;	*I pohai 'ia e na manu o uka,*
My lehua that bloomed in the Ha'ao rain,	*Ku'u lehua i mohala i ka ua o Ha'ao,*
Light comes to our house, for you are here.	*Ua ao ka hale nei, ua hiki mai la 'oe.*
Come! come, we are here."	*Mai! mai! Eia no makou nei.*

There was no set chant of welcome; each person made up his own for the occasion. With favourite children and with chiefs, the *heahea* was followed by the name-chant (*mele inoa*) of that individual or of his family. This was to show that that favourite child possessed parent or grandparent to welcome him with this honour (*he mea makua* or *he mea kupuna*), or that the *Ali'i* possessed here a person to serve and love him (*he mea kanaka*).

The purpose of the *heahea* was to make a person feel welcome. When the *heahea* was lacking, a guest felt unwanted and ashamed to come. People would watch the host or hostess and whisper to each other, " Oh! he merely looks and does not *heahea*." (*Auwe! o ka nana wale mai no ka ho'i o ka maka, 'a'ohe heahea mai*.) A hospitable person was called a *kanaka heahea* or a *wahine heahea*.

WAILING.

If the guest was a dear friend or a relative who had been absent a long while, the *heahea* was followed by an embrace and a loud wail of welcome (*uwe*). The words of the *uwe* were spontaneous and not memorized, and they expressed the affection of the host for the returned traveller. Loved ones, home, the hills and the sea, places where they had been together, loved ones who had passed on during his absence might be mentioned. One person might do the wailing while others sat about and wept silently, or one adult followed another in uttering the *uwe*.

Children did not run around and make noise during the *uwe* but sat quietly near a parent or grandparent. Older ones, able to help with the preparation of food, hurried off to prepare and serve the guest as soon as the *uwe* was over. The younger ones waited to be called forward to meet the guest. Hawaiian children were quiet at times like this and did not prattle about this and that. When a child saw and recognized an approaching person, he did not dash out to talk to him but hastened to call his parents or grandparents so that one could come and *heahea* the coming guest.

After the *uwe*, the food would be ready for the guest to eat his fill.

In olden times Hawaiians removed their shoes before entering the house. They wore sandals made of dried *ti* leaves, banana or *hau* bark and other materials. In later times these were replaced by leather shoes or sandals, but the old folk always left them on the porch (*lanai*) before entering.

HOME.

How home was treasured and craved is made explicit in these sayings depicting the dread of homelessness and the unhappiness of being unwanted.

Hana a ka mea kama 'ole hele kuewa i ke alanui.	What a childless person will (eventually) do, is to wander about uncared for on the highway.
Ma'ewa'ewa i ka hale kuleana 'ole.	One receives abuse in a house without a relative.

Pitiful is the lot of one who dwells with those who do not care.

The sense of serenity and joy, the charm of familiarity, the happiness of companionship, as the essence of home, are distilled in the following:—

He lani i luna, he honua i lalo.   The sky above and the earth below.

Said to or of a person who has a home of his own.

Ua ʻike no makou i ko makou poʻopoʻo.   We know our own nooks.

We know all about our own family.

I wawa ia ka hale kanaka. Nawai e wawa ka hale kanaka ʻole?   Voices are heard around an inhabited house. Who hears voices around an uninhabited one?

Where people are, life is.

PARENT AND PROVIDER.

The home was centred in the parent and provider. The *makua* in the household was (and is) that person who is the responsible "head of the family," to use the English phrase. As such, he or she, irrespective of age or relationship (it often is a younger member by adoption or marriage) is in truth physically and spiritually the king-post of the house.

Pumehana ka hale i ka noho ia e ka makua.   Warm is the house in which a parent dwells.

Pohaku kaomi moena.   A stone to keep the strips of a newly made mat in place.

A person who likes to remain at home. A home body.

O ka makua ke koʻo o ka hale e paʻa ai.   The parent is the support that holds the household together.

Ka pouhana.   The main post.

Said of a person on whom others depended for leadership, guidance and help, the mainstay of the family or of a group.

In historic times at least, an industrious and devoted mother or grandmother has so often, single handed, been the support of her home and brood that this social phenomenon has become a recognized institution.

Luhi wahine 'ia.   Laboured over by a woman.

Said of a family reared by a widow or by any woman who, by her own labours, fed and clothed them. It was said in respect and admiration.

Inevitably, dependence was a natural consequence of the dependability of the true *makua*. We find coined in several sayings recognition of the psychological immaturity that may result in the children.

No ka 'ike no i ka makua.   Because he sees his parent.

Meaning that as long as there is a parent there the child feels no need to do anything for himself. (Said of a parent who remarks that his son or daughter will not do a thing for himself.)

Hele aku la a ahu, ho'i mai la no e omo i ka waiu o ka makua.   He goes, and gaining nothing by it, returns to nurse at his mother's breast.

Said of a grown son or daughter who, after going away, returns to his mother for support.

In the following we have an admonition to the woman to cherish her *makua* even after she herself becomes a housewife.

E malama i ka makua he mea laha 'ole, o ke kane he loa'a i ka la ho'okahi.   Take care of the parent for he is not replaceable, but a husband can be found in a day.

E malama i ka makua, o malama auane'i i ka ha'i elemakule.   Take care of your parent, before you take care of someone else's oldster.

In the following we have the contrast between the good provider and the negligent one:—

Na ke kino no, ono ka 'ai ana.   When the food belongs to a body, he can eat heartily.

| **E kanu i ka mea 'ai, i 'ole e nana na keiki i ka ha'i.** | Plant food-plants, lest your children stare at somebody else's food. |
| **Hele ka makuahine, 'alala keiki i kauhale.** | When the mother goes out, the children cry at home. |

Said of a neglectful mother.

FOOD PRODUCTION AND PREPARATION.

Offshore, reef and along-shore fishing was the function of men, while the collecting of shellfish, sea urchins, crabs and the like, and seaweed was done by women and children.

In planting, men alone planted the noble taro, while women as well as men cultivated the humble sweet potato and yam. Sugar-cane and gourds were cultivated by both men and women. In hard times everyone searched the forest for wild foods but under normal circumstances this miscellaneous foraging on and beyond the fringes of cultivated land, like the foraging for small marine life, was done by the women and children: men of action and dignity would scarcely " putter about " in this way unless times were hard.

Under the old system of *kapu*, requiring not only that men and women eat separately but that their food be cooked in separate ovens, the Hawaiian kitchen economy was somewhat complicated and certainly burdensome. It is small wonder that Kaahumanu's abolition of the *kapu* in 1819 was welcomed by the masses, if for domestic reasons alone. The Ka-'u rules were like those elsewhere. David Malo wrote (Chapter XI, p. 50) :—

> " The man first started an oven of food for his wife, and, when that was done, he went to the *mua* and started an oven of food for himself.
> Then he would return to the house and open his wife's oven, peel the taro, pound and knead it into *poi*, knead it and put it into the calabash. This ended the food cooking for his wife.
> Then he would return to the *mua*, open his own oven, peel the taro, pound and knead it into *poi*, put the mass into a (separate) calabash for himself and remove the lumps. Thus did he prepare his food ('*ai*), and thus was he ever compelled to do so long as he and his wife lived."

Though the mashing of cooked taro corms to make *poi* was normally the work of men every woman knew how to do it and would make *poi* for herself when left alone.

Certain foods were denied to women by reason of their sex. These particular *kapu* had nothing to do with prohibitions relating to guardian spirits (*'aumakua*), gods (*akua*) or particular nature spirits, either *kupua* or *'e'epa,* which might have family (or individual) personal psychic relationship to a woman or women in an *'ohana* or community. These foods were strictly forbidden to any woman unless it might be a high chiefess under particular circumstances, as when the mother of Kamehameha the Great craved, demanded, and received the eye of a tiger shark when she was pregnant, before giving birth to the great warrior chief and conqueror. To womankind these foods were *kapu*, for reasons given below:—

> Pork, because it was feast food for gods, chiefs and priests; and also related to the god Lono, as Kamapua'a.
>
> Bananas, because the banana tree was a body of Kanaloa.
>
> Coconuts, because the coconut tree was a body of Ku.
>
> *Ulua* fish (*Caranx* spp.), which was offered to the god Ku in his war ritual as a substitute for a human victim.
>
> *Kumu* (a red goatfish, *Pseudupeneus* spp.), which served as an offering in various rituals, such as consecration of the main post of a new sleeping house.
>
> *Niuhi* (The Great White Shark, *Carcharodon carcharias*) which is the largest and finest shark, a denizen of the deep sea, reaching a length of 30 feet. This shark was the symbol of the High Chief.
>
> *Honu* (sea turtle), probably a form of Kanaloa.
>
> *'Ea* (sea tortoise), probably a form of Kanaloa.
>
> *Nuao* (porpoise), probably a form of Kanaloa.
>
> *Palaoa* (whale), a form of Kanaloa. The whale's tooth was a sacred symbol of *ali'i.*
>
> *Hahalua* or *Hihimanu* (spotted sting ray, *Aetobatus narinari*), probably a form of Kanaloa.

LENDING A HAND.

By taking their part in so far as age and skill permitted in the respective activities of the older men and women of their household and of the *'ohana,* boys and girls acquired knowledge and skills by natural process, rather than by artificial means as in formal education. Young *ali'i* had guardians or tutors (*kahu*). In the simpler households, it was the grandparents of the respective sexes who were the tutors of the young, the transmitters of knowledge and lore. Hence arose the intimate sense of attachment between grandparent and grandchild which is recognizable today in the use of the affectionate appellative " *tutu* " for beloved elder.

The sharing and divisions of labour in all work (*lau-lima*)—in planting and fishing, in housebuilding and preparing feasts, in work on the irrigation ditches (*'auwai*), taro terraces (*lo'i*) and walls (*kuauna*), on ponds (*loko*) and in rituals, the *hula*, war—was also a way of education, for every one did his part. What one or another did was partly subject to the direction of the *Ali'i* and his or her priests and supervisors (*konohiki*) : but largely it was determined, according to status, age and sex, in accordance with traditional custom. Even the children had their duties, according to size.

Ka nui e pa'a ai i ka hue wai. The size that enables him to carry a water bottle.

About two years old. When fresh water was scarce and had to be brought from the upland, everyone helped; even the two-year-old was given a small gourd full to carry.

Ka nui e pa'a ai i na niu elua. The size that enables him to carry two coconuts.

About five or six years old.

Ka nui e 'auamo ai i ke keiki i ke kua. The size that enables him to carry a smaller member of the family on his back.

About ten years old. In ancient days the age of a child was not reckoned by years as we do today but by his physical ability to do something.

A man who planned to build or rethatch a house counted on his *'ohana* to lend a hand. His male relatives helped him prepare the foundation, get and prepare the timber and cords, erect the frame and thatch it, while the women-folk aided in collecting *pili* grass, pandanus or other leaves for thatching. The making of mats for the floors, the beating of *kapa* cloth for sheets were the work of women. Men made the wooden vessels used in eating and storing and both men and women worked on gourd containers and the nets used for carrying them. (These were generally acquired by exchange, however.)

ANCESTORS AND OLDSTERS.

Typical of Polynesia is the rearing of children by elders of the grandparent generation (*kupuna*), which leaves the young parents free to engage in the duties and pleasures of labour, travel and sociability. The child so reared was regarded as especially fortunate.

Ka moʻopuna i ke alo. The grandchild in the presence.

Said of a grandchild who was reared in the presence of a grandparent. Such a grandchild was made much of and was usually the one who learned the family lore and traditions.

I ulu no ka lala i ke kumu. The branches grow because of the trunk.

Without the ancestors, we would not be here.

Na ka mua, na ka muli. Belonging to the elder and belonging to the younger.

An explanation of the relationship of cousins.

The *kupuna* was regarded as equally fortunate when the child, in return, gave his devotion. It was recognized that this devotion might not always be spontaneously given, but the duty to cherish was plain.

Ola na iwi. The bones live.

Said of old folks to whom a grandchild is considerate and kind.

Oi kaʻakaʻa na maka. While the eyes are still open.

Advice given to young people often contains these words which mean to learn all they can from old folks while they are alive (eyes open) for it will be too late when the eyes are closed (*moe na maka*) by death.

He keiki e nana ana, he keiki e nana ʻole ana. Perhaps a child who will care, a child who will not.

Said to or of a person who raises a family: maybe some among them will care for the old folks and some among them will not.

Hana 'ino i ka ke kino 'ele-makule a ho'omakua aku i ka ha'i. To mistreat one's own oldster and care for someone else's.

Said to a rude and ungrateful grandchild or child.

The inevitability of old age, and the likely destitution of the childless one, form the theme of the following:—

He hopena luahine (or ele-makule). The ending into an old woman (or old man).

Said of a person who shows signs of old age.

He iwi koko. Blooded bones.

A living person.

He iwi koko 'ole. Bloodless bones.

A dead person.

Hana a ke kama 'ole, hele 'ope'ope i ke ala loa. A person who has never reared a child may travel with his bundle on a long road.

Said of a childless old person who has no one to care for him.

Dominant in the thinking of these ancestor worshippers was the thought of the elders who would soon be passing into the other world to join their forbears already in the realm of the ancestral guardians and nature gods. For the living the *kupuna* was likened to the root stock that is the source of the *'ohana* in this world.

Pili ma na kupuna. Related through grandparents or ancestors.

A more distant relationship that belonged to the grandparents' generation or before.

Make no ke kalo a ola i ka palili. The taro may die but lives on in its young offshoots.

The oldsters may die but live on in their descendants.

I maika'i no ke kalo i ka 'oha. The goodness of the taro is judged by the fine young plants it produces.

Parents are judged by the behaviour of their children.

Kalina ka pona, 'a'ohe hua o ka pu'e, aia ka hua i ka lala.	The potato hill is bare of tubers for the plant no longer bears; it is the vines that are now bearing.

The mother is no longer bearing, but her children are.

THE KAPU IN THE FAMILY.

In the matter of clothing, a general rule was that it was not right to wear clothing of anyone other than kin. But as between generations there were strict rules affecting this. A daughter's clothes might be worn by the mother, but not the mother's by the daughter, and the same rule applied as between aunts and nieces. The same *kapu* prevailed on the male side as between the generations. As affecting the sexes, there should be no sharing or exchange of clothing. All these *kapu* affected also adoptive (*ho'okama*) and fostering (*hanai*) relationship. In some parts of Hawai'i it was not good form for mother and daughter to wear at the same time clothing printed with the same design. This " trying to look the same " (*ho'ohalikelike*), involving the daughter's wearing the same design, was analogous to her wearing her mother's dress, which was forbidden.

The following are remembered as specific rules learned in childhood, relative to personal *kapu* typical of Ka-'u. They were observed with particular fidelity by those of *ali'i* or *kahuna* status.

A very near kinsman was indicated if a man said, " My *malo* he may gird about his loins " (*No'u ka malo, nana e hume*) ; or a woman said, " My skirt she may gird about her hips " (*No'u ka pa'u, nana e kakua*). Relationship by marriage, even the sealing of the union of two families by the birth of an heir (*puka-a-maka*), did not affect the clothing *kapu*. Marriage in other words was equivalent to the blood tie.

Contestants in games sometimes, however, exchanged loin cloths. If the contest had demonstrated equality in skill, and each admired the other, such exchange indicated that they had accepted each other as brothers. When any suggestion was made of another's wearing a *malo* other than that of his close *'ohana*, the answer was "The skin is different " (*A'ole i like ka 'ili*). It was *kapu* to use a sleeping mat for anything but sleeping upon; or a head pillow as a foot rest or to sit upon, or a seat cushion for the head to lie on; or to sit above anything containing food. It was *kapu* to use a mat one had sat upon over the food in the *imu;* so to preserve that *kapu* intact, the *kauewe* (*imu* mat) was hung up where no one would be likely to step over it (*a‘e*).

During retirement in the *hale pe‘a*, the menstruating woman used only her own worn-out skirts for pads. Clothing worn around the hips only, could be used for such pads but not those worn above the waist. Every girl or woman saved only her own old clothing for her period of retirement and never anyone else's, not even her husband's cast-off *malo* nor her sister's old *pa‘u*. Thus the daughters of the *kahuna* and the *ali‘i* upheld the personal *kapu*.

> The old time Hawaiians used to talk often, when I was a small child, of the terrible custom the Whites had of using a sheet sometimes to lie upon and sometimes to lie under—they (the Whites) did not seem to know that what belonged above (*ma luna*) should remain above and what belonged below (*ma lalo*) should stay below. There were in my time people who did use floor mats and bed *kapa* for *imu* covers, but generally this was not done, unless by very careless families; in the olden times, never.
>
> In a *hula* school conducted by my cousin ‘Ilala-‘ole-o-Ka‘ahumanu, one of the pupils thoughtlessly draped her skirt over her shoulder. The *hula* master spoke sharply to her, saying, " What belongs above should stay above, and what belongs below should stay below." (*Ko luna, no luna no ia; ko lalo no lalo no ia*.)
>
> One must never ask for a *lei* which another person was wearing. It was proper, however, if one were wearing a *lei*, to take it off one's self to garland a near relative or someone held in esteem. But a *lei* carelessly given, or left about after being worn, might fall into the hands of a sorcerer, and could result in ulcerations on the neck of the original wearer.
>
> Old, worn out clothing was disposed of by burying so that the *kapu* concerning their use might not accidentally be broken. Many a time I have seen my people soak old clothes in water that they might rot the faster after being put into the ground.

OBLIGATION.

In the extended family there should be giving and taking freely, without stint. But the selfish individual may pervert this good way of life by insistent demands.

'Ike aku, 'ike mai: kokua aku, kokua mai; pela iho la ka nohona 'ohana. — Recognize and be recognized; help and be helped; such is family life.

To thrive, a family life requires an exchange of recognition and help.

O ko-a-uka, o ko-a-kai. — The uplander, the lowlander.

The upland native gives his products to his lowland kinsman, and the lowlander to his upland kinsman.

No kahi ka pilikia, pau a pau. — When one is in trouble, without stint everyone gives aid.

I kua na'u. — A load for my back.

A request to a dying person, " Tell me what you want me to carry on with after you are gone."

Nana ka maka, hana ka lima. — What the eyes see, let the hands do.

Said to a person who sits where there is much work to do but does not offer to help.

Ho'okahi no la o ka malihini. — One is a stranger only for a day.

After that, he is a part of his host's family, and should share in all their doings.

The solidarity of the *'ohana* is its salvation: once broken it is difficult to repair.

He naha ipu auane'i o pa'a i ka hupau humu. — It isn't a break in a gourd container that can easily be mended by sewing the parts together.

A broken relationship is not as easily mended as a broken gourd and when the family is broken up the mutual support is ended.

Po'alo maka. — To scoop out the eyeballs.

To betray a friend or relative; as a woman who takes a friend's husband, or one who schemes to take a brother's position, or by insinuating oneself into a relative's good grace inherits at the expense of another.

That treachery could be expected even within the bonds of close relationship was recognized. Yet even evil speech towards a relative would be punished.

Make no o Pamano i ka 'i'o It was a near relative who
pono'i.   destroyed Pamano.

Pamano was a hero of an old legend, who met his death through his uncle, Wai-pu. The saying is used when a relative brings trouble.

Ka i ka waha.   Smites his mouth.

Having gossiped unkindly a person finds what he said happening to himself; as when a woman who gossips about her neighbour's daughter finds her own doing the same thing.

OFFENSE AND FORGIVENESS.

Hala is a wrong committed by or against one, and a *hala* is a binding thing, holding the wrong doer to the person against whom the wrong was done. One is bound by the fault he had committed, the other by holding the cord, if it may be called that, to the wrong doer. One is the debtor, the other, the person indebted to. The *hala* is the debt that lies between them.

If the one who holds the invisible cord does not wish to relax it but continues to bear the wrong in mind, he is said to *ho'omau hala*; hold fast the fault. This continuation makes him feel unhappy and dissatisfied; he is *ho'ohalahala*, literally " to make fault a fault."

The Hawaiian word " to forgive " is *kala*, that is, to undo, untie, unbind and set free. By *kala* the person to whom the wrong doer is indebted frees him of that debt. It isn't there any more.

The Hawaiians use the expression, " Unbound from the top of the head to the soles of the feet and throughout the four corners of the body." (*E kala 'ia mai ka piko o ke po'o a ka manea o ka wawae; a la'a ma na kihi eha o kona kino.*) The " four corners " are the two shoulders and two hips of the torso.

The *kala* works both ways, freeing forgiver and forgiven from the *hala*. I have heard this said in many a *ho'oponopono* (set to rights) ceremony: "I unbind you from the fault and thus may I also be unbound from it." (*Ke kala aku nei 'au ia 'oe a pela noho'i 'au e kala ia mai ai.*)

Huikala (all together freeing) is to take all and every fault, remembered and forgotten, secret or open, and combine them (*hui*) into one. Then with the *kala,* all faults, big and little are entirely done away with.

The *kala* required prayer and ritualistic acts of various sorts, according to circumstances, often involving the symbolic use of the *kala* seaweed (*Sargassum*).

POLITENESS AND HOSPITALITY.

It was polite to greet any person one met on the road, acquaintance or not. If a man in a nearby food-patch saw a stranger going by, he might call out, "*Aloha e ka malihini.*" The stranger returned the greeting, after which the native would say, "Let us go home to have something to eat!" (*E hoi kakou i kauhale e 'ai ai!*") If he was not hungry, he declined the invitation, but if he was, he accepted. Then the two talked as they walked to the native's house. He learned where the stranger had come from by the politely indirect: "You must have come a long way in this warm sun." "Yes, I have. It has taken me two days' walk from my home in Kahalu'u."

As they neared the house, seeing his wife busy at some household task, the native called to her and said, "I have a guest." (*He malihini ka'u.*) Looking up, she hurried to the door and called: "Come! Come! Come inside here." (*Mai! Mai! Komo mai maloko nei.*) Then, "Sit down and rest till your weariness is gone from you, then have something to eat." (*E noho iho a ku'u ka luhi, hele e 'ai.*) In the meantime food was being prepared in the eating house and the guest was taken there to eat.

The polite way of asking one to eat was to say "*E 'ai!*" in an urgent and sincere tone. It was not polite to say, "Hungry? Perhaps you will like something to eat?" (*Pololi, ea? E 'ai paha?*") This was embarrassing to the guest and sounded reluctant on the host's part. "Yours is the house" (*Nou ka hale*) was a courteous way of telling the guest that he was very welcome. "Do not be bashful." (*Mai ho'ohilahila.*)

When the guest was ready to leave he said to his host, "I am going." (*E hele ana au.*) Then the host was expected to reply, "You may go." (*O hele.*) If two or more people were departing, he would say, "*E uhaele*" instead of "*O hele.*"

Once a foreigner complained that a guest kept telling him that he was going but made no move to do so. Later he learned that the man was too polite to do so without his host's permission. Yet the foreigner was too polite to say the " Depart, then," for which his guest was waiting!

Once a person had started out, it was an annoyance to him to call him back (*kahea kua*). He would give up his plan of going, for it was a sign of bad luck to be called back.

There was beach ettiquette, too. When one went to talk to a fisherman and found him sitting on the sand, picking the trash out of his net, then the polite thing to do was to sit down and help him as they conversed. It was bad manners, because bad luck, to take bananas or *hala* to a fishing place. It was equally impolite to cross hands behind one's back, step over the net or ropes, break wind, wear anything red, or ask the fisherman about his plans for the next fishing trip.

There is still need to guard the tongue in those respects with the few oldsters that remain. What may be an innocent remark to a modern person may be an offense to an old timer. In admiring a pretty object belonging to a friend, one should only point out its fine features but should never say, " I wish I had one like that." Such a remark was called *ho'omaoe* (a hint for) and politeness required that the owner give it to the rude admirer.

A friend or relative should never say " What a pretty child you have." Instead, one should say, " A homely child!" When gently spoken, this was a compliment; when harshly said it was not.

One never spoke of the amount of food a person ate, only that he had a wonderful appetite: " How he relishes his food!" (*Ono kana 'ai!*)

Past favours should never be recalled and told, such as, " I was the one who helped her by doing this, that or the next thing." This was called *helu* or counting. Sometimes the person so offended would return every gift given to her and would replace others she had used.

A person, skilled in humorous expressions and witty remarks (*'olelo ho'oka'au*), in the use of figurative speech and in making similes (*'olelo ho'opilipili*), was always well liked. How I remember listening to the Hawaiians of my childhood! Skilled were they in using the *'olelo ho'opilipili* to make their conversation or their sermon interesting and comprehensive. Such choice of words! Poetic and beautiful and never offensive—even when directed at a person's faults. The point of the dart was so well wrapped in the velvet of fine speech that it left not even a tiny prick. Instead it created a feeling of pleasure and a desire to do better. In the olden days, a wit, who had humour and wisdom, found his way to the court of the chief.

Hospitality was typical of all Hawaiians on all of the islands. My own parents, our relatives, friends and associates were always glad to share whatever they had, be it little or large. The best sleeping place, was for the guest. People going from

Ka-ʻu to Hilo, and from Hilo to Ka-ʻu, in the days of the horse drawn vehicle, often stopped at my aunt's to pass the night—usually unexpected. There was no market at Glenwood and whatever of fish and meat there was, was salted. Back of the house was a wide field of taro, in the bins were rice and flour, so there was actually no lack, but sometimes visitors might come when the *poi* was low and after night had descended The family gave the *poi* to the guests, and the best salted meat, even if it was the last; for the guests were always very welcome even if unexpected and the time most inconvenient to have them! I still remember the running around and the hustling to prepare sleeping places for them and then retiring, tired, to sleep on the floor with other members of the family. No matter what, there was no complaining, no grumbling.

Cowboys came too, tired and hungry, to share the salted fish, or meat with *poi*. Sometimes, they came with a portion of a wild bullock or pig—then there was fresh meat But only for that meal: the rest had to be salted for preservation, to be eaten later with vegetables.

ADMONITIONS.

Admonitions relating to manners and behaviour are sometimes direct and sometimes, to the non-Polynesian, oblique.

Hoʻoke a maka.   **Deny the eyes.**

One who looks toward no one else; a selfish person who gave to his own children and refused to share with those of his relatives and neighbours.

Keke.   Literally, " the teeth are exposed."

A sharp admonition to a girl. A girl so warned will not sit so that she exposes herself. " Keke!" A small girl, hearing it, pulls down her skirt or changes her sitting position.

Piapia.   (A common expression.)

Maka piapia means that one's eyes are so thick with mattery substance that he cannot see well; a very rude expression.

Misbehaviour, even in the little child, will bring bitterness to the parent or elder.

Liʻiliʻi kamaliʻi, ʻawahia ke au.   Though the child is small, the gall is bitter.

Said of a rude, impudent child.

Mentioning the shortcomings of an *'ohana*, and tall talk, and reckless speech, all are bad manners.

Holehole iwi.   To strip the bones of flesh.

To speak disparagingly of one's relatives.

Ho'onuinui.   Make big-big.

The dire threat of a husband, wife or parent which is used only to frighten, but never carried out.

BAD MANNERS AND INHOSPITALITY.

Politeness and good manners were carefully, even severely taught, but as in all civilizations there were the impolite and the ill-mannered, and special types of rudeness in all grades of society. These were recognized and so labelled.

It showed a lack of good manners to stand talking to a person with hands on hips. This posture, *ku 'aha'aha*, signified a sense of superiority.

It was rude to stand with hands crossed behind the back (*'ope'a kua*), for this was a sign that the person who did so wished a load of trouble to descend upon the back of the beholder.

It was bad manners for a visitor to stand in the doorway (*ku i ka puka*) of a house. While waiting to enter or to depart he stood a little to one side. The doorway was never obstructed for any length of time. Nor was it proper for members of the household, or outsiders, to sit in the doorway (*noho i ka puka*). That was an obstruction, hence an annoyance, to the family *'aumakua* (ancestral spirits) who might want to go in and out freely.

To break wind (*puhi'u*) in the presence of anyone was not only bad manners but insulting. If one did so accidentally, he apologized immediately. To break wind while someone was eating, working with his fishing gear, discussing business or praying was the height of rudeness. He guarded against giving offense to others through carelessness in speech. He was not bluntly outspoken (*ho'opuka ku*) nor did he make rude remarks (*kikoi*).

Sometimes an action or remark that a foreigner did not consider rude was very much so to a Hawaiian; as for instance a teacher's playfully pulling a child's hair, or (as a matter of discipline) threatening to slap her face. Because the head was regarded as sacred, this threat could cause instant rebellion from otherwise mild-mannered Hawaiian children, who felt the sting of unbearable insult in the threat.

To compare human beings to animals was also insulting. I have not forgotten how angry my aunt Kamakolu was when her son was called " a wild goat of Puna " (*ke kao 'ahiu o Puna*). Another form of rudeness in speech was *kiko'ola* (literally, reaching for the sun) : speaking to another in a manner to imply that one regarded himself as superior.

A third form of rudeness in speech was to break the peace of the moment with a loud and nasty remark, termed *kikaho*. It was like dropping a rock in a quiet pool.

Hawaiians did not take the names of their gods in vain, but they were experts in using insulting language, both figurative and direct. No part of the human body was spared in the *kuamuamu*. To call a person " shrimp-headed " (*po'o 'opae*) was *kuamuamu*. (The eliminative organs of the shrimp are in its head, and so a remark like this meant that one's head contained only excreta.) The word *pilau* is very freely used today, but in olden times Hawaiians were taught never to call anyone that. *Pilau* is a stench like that of a decomposed body. Another humiliating word carelessly used today is *kauwā*, " outcaste " (see the section on *kauwā*). The term *kauwā* applied to one who was not of *kauwā* ancestry was an insult that was bitterly resented.

A person who liked to hurt another by prodding his feelings (*pahupahu*, jabbing) was generally avoided. For example: " So you had to go to So-and-So's home—Well, who do you think you are to expect welcome there?"

Lawe 'olelo and *holoholo 'olelo* are practically the same thing: to bear tales from person to person, which often resulted in fights (*ku kau hakaka*). Such a person was certainly unpopular.

There were some people who liked to have a reckoning (*ho'oku'i*) when they heard anything said about them that was not to their liking. Such a one would hurry to seek the person who was believed to have made the remark and ask him why he said such things, and so forth. My wise old grandmother used to say to her children: " Let the matter go; we shall see in time what it is all about." (*Ho'oku'u aku, na ke au e nana.*)

The *ho'ona'aikola* or *ho'aikola* was behaviour that expressed one's contempt for another and it could take several forms. One was the *ho'opohopoho*, or bending over with the rump towards another, a sign of defiance and contempt. Another was the *ho'opu'ukahua*, a thrusting of the thumb between the index and middle finger, also as a sign of contempt. It signified the female genitalia. Sometimes the hand was thrust forward with the words " *Eia kau!* This is what you'll get!"—that is, misfortune. Sometimes a similar gesture was made toward the face and the eyelid drawn down (*ho'ohelei*). As it was a sign of bad luck to meet a person with eyelids drawn down (*maka helei*), this was equivalent to wishing one bad luck. A person, blessed with a sense of humour, would merely cry out in amusement, "A 'ula!" (Ah! a red one!) at such bad manners, but others would feel insulted.

To double the fist and raise it with a quick bend of the elbow (ho'opanau) was the male sex sign, equivalent in significance to the female sign mentioned above, and with the same contemptuous meaning. To spit (kuha) resoundingly at or to one side of a person was a gesture of utmost contempt. To thrust out the tongue (ho'opake'o) or to "make faces" (haikaika) meant contempt and defiance. Among friends the protruding tongue meant not defiance but an impudent "I don't care!" And, when certain persons were mentioned, a swaying of the chin and a twist of the mouth meant, "I certainly care nothing for those people!" A quick wrinkling of the nose meant "no," the quick elevating of the eyebrows "yes"; and a quick lift of the chin was a question: "What did you say?" With a slight inclination of the head toward a third person it meant "Who is he?"

Any of these gestures of contempt might be sufficient cause for an offended person to consult a sorcerer by way of revenge, so children were taught that such behaviour was rude, offensive and might bring serious consequences, even death.

Treating a parent, a relative or friend with utter disregard for their feelings was also termed ho'ona'aikola. To fail to heed the teachings of parents and grandparents and to be wilful and headstrong, was called ho'oki'eki'e, to elevate oneself above others.

To break into or interrupt a conversation was called kaha maha (literally—to thrust in the temples) and children were taught that this was a rude thing to do. Likewise to behave in a bold manner toward strangers, asking for things, going through the premises of others without permission, claiming something that is not one's own—all such behaviour was called maha'oi (literally, temples thrust forward).

It was also rude to ask too many questions (niele). Instead, one should observe what was being done and how, and if there were things he did not understand, then he might ask.

Claiming relationship to the ali'i or trying to be the equal of one's superiors was to be pi'ikoi (straining to ascend) and a person who did this was regarded with scorn.

Hukiku means to pull against the others, to be contrary and want one's own way instead of co-operating with them. When this unmannerly attitude becomes contentious, then it is hukihuki, to keep pulling in the opposite direction. When members of a family disagree with each other over a piece of property, each one desiring to have his way, that is hukihuki. A child over which various members of the family would dispute (hukihuki) as to who would have the right to rear it, would sicken and die unless the dispute was quickly brought to an end.

A person is termed paweo when he pretends not to see an acquaintance approaching and looks or walks in the opposite direction to avoid speaking to him. It was regarded as equally rude to walk up to an aquaintance and say " Oh what a pretty *lei*. Give it to me." That is *noi ku*, to ask point blank, indulged in only by the very ill-mannered.

Old fashioned courtesy demanded that we do not ask, " Give me this " or " Give me that." If one had need, let him say, " Have you such and such to spare? If you do, I would like to have some." Then at a later date, bring to the donor something that he may not have.

When one had been given a gift of something in a bowl or dish, the container was kept for a few days at least, then filled with something and returned. To return something in the container immediately after receiving a gift in it, savoured of trade or *ku'ai*. This trading back and forth at once was called *ku'aku'ai*. It spoiled the pleasure of the first giver, therefore it was not polite.

The *kuhilani* was also impolite, that is, to say to others, " Do this for me " or " Go and fetch that." Literally, the word *kuhi* meaning to point and *lani* meaning a chief, the expression means to give orders like a chief.

Inhospitality was so rare that a case would be discussed with horror for years. Nevertheless, there were of course some who were stingy and avaricious. Here are several stories showing how such folks were treated.

A story is still told in Puna of some stingy natives who were peeling cooked breadfruit when a missionary with his native helpers who had walked a long distance and were tired and hungry came along and asked if they might have some to eat. " Oh no," said the natives, " we have only enough for ourselves and the pigs."

Soon after that the people of this village took sick with a strange malady resembling leprosy. Those who died first were buried, but those who died later were left unburied. The hungry pigs came in and ate some of them. " Thus," the story was told, " they were saving for the pigs!"

Being so seldom met with, when a case of inhospitality was found, it was noised abroad and discussed with derision. A victim of any meanness practised often paid back in the same coin, as in the following story, long told with satisfaction.

A Hilo man went on a visit to Puna and expressed a desire for coconuts. " Come to my place," said a Puna man, " and I'll give you all you want." When they reached his place, the Puna man pointed to some very tall coconut trees and said, " There they are, help yourself." The Hilo man was unable to climb and so he went without the nuts. A few years later the Puna man

needed a canoe and inquired where he could find one and was told
that the Hilo man was the best canoe maker there. His request
was kindly heard by the Hilo man, who took him to the upland
where the logs were already cut but not yet dubbed out into
canoes. "There you are," said the Hilo man pointing to the
logs, "take your pick of the canoes."

I remember a case in my childhood of a man in Ola'a noted
for inhospitality who refused lodging to a traveller one dark and
rainy night, only to discover him the next day, at a neighbour's
along with several pack-mules loaded with bundles of sea food
and dried goat's meat. The neighbour's wife was cooking goat
meat and on the table were some fish, all from the stranger.
"Woe is me," the Ola'a man exclaimed aloud. And then to the
stranger: "As you are not going home today, come up and stay
with us for the night!" But the stranger refused to accept.

MANNERS IN EATING.

Hawaiians ate when hungry. The one cooked meal a
day was eaten before sundown lest hungry ghosts be
attracted. Hands were rinsed in the washbowl (po'i wai
holoi), or when water was scarce, as often in Ka-'u, they
were wiped on wet ferns or leaves. A long, narrow mat
(pa kaukau) laid on the floor with food set in readiness for
eating was the papa 'aina (a term later applied to the dining
table). A poi bowl was set between each two persons facing
each other, and a meat dish between each two persons sitting side by side. Favourite children and kapu ali'i had
their private dishes.

Men sometimes dipped poi with one finger. Generally
two fingers were used, dipped to the first joints only when
eating daintily, to the second joint for the hearty appetite.
A deft twist ('awili) on the way to the mouth gracefully
retained the semi liquid paste on the fingers. "One finger,
two finger and three finger poi" is a modern notion. Dipping
with one finger used to be regarded as a sign of stinginess
(pi); and eating with three fingers was greedy. The old
hand-pounded poi was uniform in consistency, not pasty or
liquid as mechanically milled or watery poi may be today.

To be finicky in picking from the meat dish was termed
kama lani (behaving like an ali'i's child). It was proper to
eat what came to hand, and to consume all of it. Smacking
the lips (muka) to show appreciation was good manners.
To sit cross legged was approved; but for women and girls
to sit with knees together and to one side was preferable.

Host or hostess should continue eating till the guests were satisfied; and never should the *poi* clinging round the sides of the bowl be scraped down (*kahi*), a sign of intended removal, while a guest was still eating. "Eat your fill!" (*'Ai, 'ai a maona*) ; "Do not be bashful, the food is yours!" (*" Mai ho'ohilahila, nau ka 'ai!"*) were generous expressions of hospitality.[28]

We come now to a convention in the old Hawaiian household in relation to eating which shows the reverence that was felt for the Provider of the staff of life. In a very real sense, the bowl or bowls of *poi* round which family and guests were gathered on ordinary or festive occasions, was to the Hawaiian household what to the Greek and Roman family the hearth represented. It was from the first-born child of Heaven and Earth that all taros descended. In remembrance of this, all taro, *poi*, and the bowl of *poi* were reverenced.

> The ancestor of the chiefs and the people was Haloa. This Haloa was the son of Wakea by his daughter Ho'o-hoku-ka-lani. But this Haloa was the second-born: the first-born was Haloa-naka-lau-kapalili (Longstem-shaky-leaf-trembling), which came forth a shapeless mass, but when buried close to the wall of Wakea's house grew into the first taro. Haloa was named in honour of this elder brother.

> This explains why, when the *poi* bowl was open, there must be no haggling, quarrelling, arguing, for this was displeasing to Haloa. Eating around the *poi* bowl was the time for pleasantness and heartiness. Nor should any serious business be discussed until the *poi* bowls were covered. "Haloa will nullify it" (*Ke ho'ole mai nei o Haloa*) was the warning that would be voiced by an elder if some child mentioned any work or undertakings while the family was gathered round the *poi* bowl.

WISDOM.

A very great number of the deft sayings of Hawaiians express the age-old folk wisdom of this people. We have selected a few that seem to relate particularly to family relationship and social ethics.

The wisdom of turning an attentive ear to one's elders is the theme of the following.

---

[28] In the above commentary I wish to acknowledge having briefed, with her permission, some detailed notes made by Miss Margaret Titcomb in conversation with Mrs. Pukui about old Hawaiian "table manners."—E.S.C.H.

Mai kapae i ke a'o a ka makua, aia he ola malaila.
Do not ignore the teachings of a parent, for there is life in them.

I lohe i ka 'olelo a ho'oko, e ola auane'i a laupa'i.
He who heeds good counsel, will live to see many descendants.

Pungent advice against idleness, procrastination, gadding and gossip are found in these next.

E ho'ohuli i ka lima i lalo, mai ho'ohuli i luna.
Turn the palms of the hands downward (in work) and not upward (in idleness).

Ako 'e ka hale a pa'a, a i komo mai ka ho'oilo, 'a'ole e kulu i ke kuaua o Hilinehu.
Thatch the house beforehand, so when winter comes, it will not leak in the rainy month of Hilinehu.

Do not procrastinate. Prepare for the future now.

Mai hele wale i ko ha'i ipuka, o pa i ka leo.
Do not make it a habit to go to the doors of others, lest you hear a remark (to hurt your feelings).

Nahu no oia i kona alelo.
He bites his own tongue.

A man has talked so much against a certain thing, then turns around and does it. Or perhaps after insulting a girl with all the names he could think of, he marries her. Or after lecturing his brothers and cursing them roundly for drinking, he does the very same thing.

There are many having to do with the all important matter of sustenance, of which a few have been quoted in previous sections and others are added here.

E 'ai i ka mea i loa'a.
Do not be particular.
What you have, eat.

Wae aku i ka lani.
Do your picking and choosing when you get to heaven.

This is no time to be finicky.

Mai hana 'ino i ka 'ai, o huli   Do not wilfully waste food,
mai no e nana.   lest some day it turn and
stare at you.

Waste breeds want. The time may come when food will
keep its distance.

Hana kapulu ka lima, 'ai 'ino   Careless work with the
ka waha.   hands produces dirty food
for the mouth.

Some that have reference to food are figurative, as in
this pungent reference to family scandal:

E kopi no i ka i'a a 'eu no   No matter how much one
ka ilo.   salts fish, maggots are
bound to crawl.

Others have reference to the unwisdom of affronting
the listening *akua* or *'aumakua,* as described in the section
on Haloa, the elder brother of man (page —).193

Ke ho'ole mai nei o Haloa.   Haloa will nullify it.
Said of business discussed over the *poi* bowl.

STATUS AND PRESTIGE.

Hawaiians of the old order had a strong sense of status,
but likewise a very definite sense of modesty with respect
to it, and of contempt for those who made unwarranted
pretensions.

Mai kaula'i na iwi o kupuna   Do not put the bones of
i ka la.   your ancestors out in the
sun to dry.

Do not discuss the ancestors too freely with strangers,
for it is like bringing their bones out of their hiding
places for everybody to stare at.

E noho iho i ka puweuweu,   Stay among the clumps of
mai ho'oki'eki'e.   grasses and do not elevate
yourself.

The teachings of grandparents and parents: Do not put
on airs; remain peaceful, quiet and unassuming.

He pili nakeke.   A relationship that fits so
loosely that it rattles.

Said of one who claims a very questionable relationship.

Keiki a ka pueo.   Child of an owl.

The child begotten on the wayside, whose paternal lineage
is unknown to the mother.

Socially, political and ceremonial status and prestige
were theoretically determined by genealogy. The *'ohana* of
a particular lineage depended on an elder who was known
as the *Mea-pa'a-ku'auhau* (Person-firm-in-knowledge-of-
genealogical-history) ; or, briefly, this person was the
Ku'auhau. The last word refers to genealogy and pedigree
in the context of history: The knowledge of the names of
ancestors as such was not enough: the family genealogist
must be also an historian, whose knowledge of facts (traditional and mythical) relating to the forbears was " firm "
(*pa'a*), i.e., accurate, sound. This was no casual matter.
Error in craftsmanship or ritual was inacceptable to the
vigorous, hard thinking Hawaiians. The canoeman's and
fisherman's very life, as well as his livelihood, depended upon
accuracy and soundness of tested materials and techniques.
The same accuracy was required in the all important science
of oral verbal documentation of pedigrees which comprised
the basis of legal, social, political and ceremonial status,
prestige, rights and obligations. Possibly one reason the
Polynesians relied entirely on accuracy of memory rather
than upon any of the various mnemonic devices they used
occasionally for other purposes was because it was safer to
have the *ku'auhau* in the private and secret repository of a
trustworthy elder's mind than to record it by means of some
simple mnemonic or graphical device, which would lay it
open to inaccuracy and possibly to misappropriation. The
ku'auhau for persons of rank was the most precious of all
heritages, requiring as careful guarding as the bones of the
dead, for the names and the bones had a related, and equal,
intimate relationship to the *'uhane* of the individuals who
were forbears.

GENEALOGIES.

True to old Polynesian folkways, Hawaiians in Ka-'u
who had any claim to distinction memorized and passed on to
their following generations their genealogies, and these had
a very important function in the determination of precedence
and right. With the *ali'i* class, genealogy was, in fact, a

carefully and critically guarded historical science: order and right in the matter of succession, formal marriage of aristocrats, and claims to relationship with the high-born had to be proven genealogically. Such matters were authoritatively and legally determined in the *'Aha Ali'i* (councils of Ali'i) subject to judgment of the experts in genealogy (*po'e ku'auhau*) of the lines involved. The matter of precedence, that is to say, whether an individual belonging to *kaikua'ana* (elder) or *kaikaina* (younger) lines, was of course registered in the genealogies.

Mo'o or *kuamo'o* means succession, *mo'okupuna* the succession of ancestors, and *mo'oku'auhau* the story or telling of genealogy. *Ku'auhau*, as we have said above, was also the term for one skilled in genealogy and traditional history. *Hanauna* or " Birthings " means a generation. The imagery of *mo'o* (lizard, with vertebrae visible) and *kua mo'o* (vertebrate backbone) is apt and obvious as a simile for sequence of descendants in contiguous unbroken articulation.

The *mele ko'i honua* (adzed earth chant) was one in whose verses were woven genealogy, place names and history. Such " earth-wrought " chants, composed only for the high-born, were tokens of rank and prestige. They had ritualistic and magical potency, were imbued with *mana* (spiritual power).

There are interesting sections in Malo indicative of the place of genealogy in the polity of the *ali'i*. The *Hale Naua*[29] was a house built on occasion by a ruling *Ali'i*, where his family experts in genealogy tested the claims of persons who claimed to be kin of the *Ali'i*, in accordance with a formal mode of challenge and examination. The institution and its functioning are described in some detail by Malo and Emerson (pp. 253 ff.). What is here described by David Malo, a native of Kona, was true for the neighbouring *moku* of Ka-'u.

A number of the words that were used with reference to family reveal the conception of human propagation and the growth of the generations as similar to that of the plant world. The Hawaiians in many instances thought of plant

---

[29] We refer here to the old purely native *Hale Naua*, not to that instituted by King Kalakaua in Honolulu in the late nineteenth century which combined ceremonial akin to Masonic lodge ritual with elements and conceptions of the old.

forms in anthropomorphic terms: yet their imagery shows us that they thought, too, of human kind figuratively as botanomorphic. *'Oha* means specifically the sucker or shoot growing from the corm of the taro plant: the family as a group was termed *'oha-na,* which literally means " all the offshoots." *Pulapula,* which was applied to human offspring or descendants, literally means offshoots of a plant. *Kupuna,* or ancestor, is probably the substantive, formed by the suffix *na* affixed to the root *kupu,* to grow. *Laupa'i,* which means specifically the first leaves put forth by the newly planted *taro,* is used figuratively to describe a family that is growing, producing many children. A person who had no grandchildren of his own and who is in danger of having no descendants was *lala make,* a " dead branch." One with living descendants was a " living branch " (*lala ola*).

> Keli'ihue, when she was an old lady, came to her cousin's home one day with her great grandson, Likeke, and said, " *E Pa'ahana, he lala ola 'au, he lala make 'oe* " (Pa'ahana, I am a living branch and you are a dead one). Pa'ahana had no grandchildren then. But a year later, Pa'ahana held out her new born granddaughter to Keli'ihue and said, " *Eia 'au la! He lala ola, 'a'ole 'au he lala make* " (Here I am now, a living branch, not a dead one).

SAYINGS OF THE ALI'I.

We are including these following sayings relating to the *ali'i* because the Paramount Chief (*Ali'i Nui*) fulfilled the role of father to his people. All the people of Ka-'u felt their blood kinship to him and to his relatives, who were the aristocracy of senior and junior lines: in other words, the relationship of commoners to chiefs was but an extension of the social custom based upon *'ohana* folkways. Also numerous sayings reflect what was proper behaviour for persons of *ali'i* descent, as members of that *'ohana* which ranked at the top of the social order by reason of primacy in genealogical prestige.

Status.

As the first-born in the line from the gods, the person of the *ali'i* was as sacred as that of a god. The paramount chief was not regal, he was divine; and he was supreme.

Kuneki na ku'auhau li'ili'i,
    noho mai i lalo; ho'okahi
    no o ko ke ali'i ke pi'i i ka
    'i'o.
	Set aside the lesser genea-
	logies and remain humble;
	let only one be elevated,
	that of the chief.

Said to members of the junior line of chiefs: Boast not
   of your lineage but elevate that of your chief.

The scion of the royal house was the most precious of all
children to all the people.

He liko ali'i.	A royal leaf bud.

A child of a chief.

The high ranking female *ali'i* was too sacred to rear her
infant.

He 'uha kapu.	A sacred lap.

Said of a person whose *kapu* forbade the carrying of
   babies lest the lap be wet by them. Such a *kapu* woman
   was often unable to rear the children she bore. Such
   children were usually adopted and reared by others.

The concomitant of the sacredness of the chief was his
power.

He mano holo 'aina ke ali'i.	A chief is a shark that travels on land.

Like a shark, a chief is not to be tampered with.

Those related to the chief did not boast of it abroad,
though they served in his household; nor did those of
aristocratic ancestry speak of their pedigree unless they
were insulted or challenged.

Ma loko o ka hale, ho'opuka
    ia ka pili, a ma waho o ka
    hale he haku ia.
	Inside the house, the rela-
	tionship may be men-
	tioned but outside your
	chief is your lord.

Those who served inside a chief's home were usually
   blood relatives of a junior line; they were taught from
   childhood not to discuss the relationship and always to
   address him as " *ku'u haku* " (my lord), *ku'u ali'i* (my
   chief) or *ku'u lani* (my heavenly one), and not by any
   relationship term.

Aia a pa'i ia ka maka, ha'i 'ia kupuna nana 'oe. Only when your face is slapped do you tell who your ancestors were.

Never boast. Only when slandered or called a worthless offspring of worthless ancestors may one mention one's lineage to prove that the slander is baseless.

Proud and zealous were those relatives of the *Ali'i* who were of his entourage.

O ka 'ilio kahu no ka 'ilio hae. A dog who has a master is the dog who barks most.

Said of a chief's servant who resents any disparaging remarks concerning his lord.

Ho'okahi mea mana'o nui a ka 'ohua o ka hale, o kahi mea mai ka lima mai o ke ali'i. There is one thing all members of the household look to: whatever they are given by the hands of the chief.

All members of a chief's household are dependent on him.

Ke kaena a ka noho hale. The boast of the stay-at-home.

The boast of the people for their own local chiefs and home land.

Rectitude.

Certain sayings point out the fact that good comes neither to the chief nor to his people out of weakness on the part of the *Ali'i*. Uprightness (*pono*) must be the foundation of good rule.

'A'ohe e nalo ka iwi o ke ali'i 'ino, o ko ke ali'i maika'i ke nalo. The bones of an evil chief will not be concealed but the bones of a good chief will.

The people will not care for a bad chief who does not care for their welfare and, if he dies, will not take too much trouble to hide his bones. It is the good chief that the people will faithfully serve.

'A'ohe ola o ka 'aina i ke ali'i haipule 'ole.   The land can not live under an irreligious chief.

He ko'oko'o haki wale.   A staff that breaks easily.

A weak leader, one who hasn't the strength to assume the responsibilities of his position.

The following are admonitions to the wise *Ali'i*:

E malama i ke kanaka nui, i ke kanaka iki.   Take care of the big man and the little man.

Advice to a chief to take care of his lesser chiefs and commoners alike, for together they are the strength of his rule.

E 'opu ali'i.   Have the stomach of a chief.

Be as kind and as generous as a chief should be.

He halau na 'I.   A long house belonging to 'I.

'I was a wise and generous chief and because he was an ancestor of many, he was referred to as a long house in which many were sheltered.

I ali'i no ke ali'i i ke kanaka.   A chief is a chief because of his subjects.

A chief without followers is no chief at all.

And these are admonitions to his subjects:

Eia ka lua huna o na ali'i o ka waha.   Here is the secret cave of the chief, the mouth.

" I refuse to discuss the affairs of my chief to satisfy any one's curiosity."

Minamina ka leo o ke ali'i i ka ha'ule i ka puweuweu.   It is a pity to allow the voice of the chief to fall among the clumps of grass.

The commands of the chief should not be allowed to go unheeded.

He lohe ke ola, he kuli ka make.   To heed is to live; to disobey, death.

He ki'i kanaka noho wale o kahi ali'i.   Only an image does no work in the household of a chief.

In a chief's home, everybody but the chief works.

The Ali'i and the People.

Next in hoonur to the *ali'i* and the priestly orders of Ku and Lono (whose pedigrees ranked second to the high chief's) were the able warriors who had won fame in warlike games and the favourite sport of the *ali'i*, the game of war. These heroes, whose name, *koa*, is taken from the magnificent hardwood forest tree (*Acacia koa*), sometimes called Hawaiian mahogany, were revered by the people because they were the defenders of the homeland and the valiant guard of the beloved *Ali'i*. Their prowess gained for their families fame and wealth in lands and gifts and, in conquest, loot.

He maka lehua no kona one hanau. One who has the face of a warrior for his birthplace.

Said of a person who wins honour and praise for his homeland.

Ke kaulana pa'a 'aina o ke ali'i. The famed landholders of the chiefs.

The best warriors received the best land grants.

'Ike no ke ali'i i kona kanaka, a 'ike no ke kanaka i kona ali'i. The chief recognizes his man and the man recognizes his chief.

At the other extreme of the social order were the despised *kauwā*, who were outcasts compelled to live in a barren locality apart from the tribesmen or people " belonging to the land " (*ma-ka-'aina-na*), and whose only function and destiny was to serve as human sacrifices to the *Ali'i's* war god Ku when a Luakini or war temple was dedicated in anticipation of a season of fighting. Not so despised but held in contempt were worthless fellows referred to in the following saying:

He 'unu pehi 'iole. A pebble to pelt a rat with.

An insignificant person, worth no more than a pebble.

Such ne'er-do-wells sometimes made a great fuss about pretended prowess and status:

He kohu puahiohio i ka ho'olele i ka lepo i luna. Like a whirlwind, whirling the dust upward.

Said of a commoner who makes an attempt to elevate himself so that he would be regarded as of chiefly blood.

There were various sayings which aptly described the humble place of the hard working farmers and fishers who were serfs of their overlords and yet were proud to belong to their chief and their homeland.

He ma‘ona ‘ai a he ma‘ona i‘a ko ka noanoa.   The commoner is satisfied with fish and food.

The commoner has no greater ambition than success in fishing and farming. It is the chief who plans the wars.

‘A‘ohe nana i ko lalo ‘ai i ka papa‘a, nana i ko luna ‘ai i ka ‘ahulu.   Never mind if the taro at the bottom burns, but watch out that that at the top is not under-cooked.

It matters little what happens to commoners: look out for the welfare of the chiefs.

The wise chief well knew, and the people knew, that it was these humble folk upon whom the *Ali‘i* and his entourage depended:

I lele no ka lupe i ke pola.   It is the tail that makes the kite fly.

It is the number of followers that raises the prestige of a chief.

He mai‘a ua pa‘a i ke ko‘o.   A banana tree well supported by props.

A man well supported by his followers.

These had their recognition and reward on occasion at the home and at the hands of their *Ali‘i*:

He pololi kali ko kahi o na ‘li‘i.   At the place of a chief one must wait for hunger to be appeased.

One must wait for the will and favour of a chief. No one is independent in his presence.

Ho‘i pu‘olo no o kahi ali‘i.   One returns with a bundle from the place of a chief.

When one visits the home of a generous chief, one always has a gift to take home.

Under the authority of a forceful chief, the proud and the humble alike must be alert to heed the least command of their lord:

Ho'okahi no leo o ke alo ali'i.   A command is given only once in the presence of a chief.

The commoner at least enjoyed a certain security in that he ran less risk of giving offense than those in high places in the entourage of the *Ali'i*.

Ko luna pohaku no ke ka'a i lalo, 'a'ole hiki ko lalo pohaku ke ka'a.   It is the stone that is high up that can roll down but a stone that is down can not roll.

When a chief is overthrown, his followers move on but the people who have lived on the land from the days of their ancestors, continue to live on it.

THE OUTCASTE CLASS.

The aristocrats (*ali'i*), experts in priestcraft of one kind or another (*kahuna*), and tribesmen of the land (*maka-'aina-na*) were proud of being one stock, native to Ka-'u. But there was an outcaste group whose origin is subject to speculation.

A part of Ninole, in Ka-'u, was set apart for the *kauwā* people; a people so despised that they were never allowed to mingle even with the commoners nor to marry anyone but a *kauwā*. Should any forbidden union take place and offspring result, the baby was put to death.

Should any person walk on land set apart for the *kauwā*, he or she was regarded as being defiled and was put to death. A *kauwā* was allowed to go to the place of the chief who was his lord and nowhere else. In travelling, the head was covered with a large handkerchief of *kapa*, and the eyes kept downcast in humiliation.

When there was no law-breaker or war victim to offer as human sacrifice in the *heiau*, the *kahuna* went near the boundary of the *kauwā* land and selected a man, as one might select a fowl in a barnyard. A *kauwā* could not refuse, and followed the *kahuna* who called him. If he were not to be put to death immediately, he was given an elongated gourd to wear, suspended from the neck with a string, which was referred to as " garland for waiting " (*lei i ke 'olo*). To say to one that his ancestor had worn the 'olo gourd, was the equivalent of saying that he was a person of no consequence. For a person to refer to himself as his chief's *kauwā* was all right, because it implied a properly humble spirit. In Christian times the expression *kauwā o ke Akua*, God's humble servant, came into use. But in other than Bible language we prefer to speak of servants as *kanaka hana* (work man) or *kanaka lawelawe* (*lawe*: to carry, serve).

With the overthrow of the *kapu* system the segregation of the *kauwā* was done away with. It was no longer compulsory for them to wear distinguishing marks tattooed in the middle of the forehead or at the outer corners of the eyes. They mingled with the people in general and were lost sight of. Some married outside of their own group, thus mixing *kauwā* blood with that of others.

In our homeland lived a man in whose veins ran the blood of chiefs and of the *kauwā*. One of his daughters became intensely interested in genealogy and went to question him. He would only mention the chiefly side but of the *kauwā* side he was silent. To his daughter's plea, his one reply was, " What do you care about such smutty nosed people?" (*He aha ka nana ia po'e ihu papa'a?*)

At one time my mother's brother fell in love with a pretty girl who lived in Pahala. She was industrious, well mannered and the kind of person who would have made an excellent wife. Plans for the coming marriage went on until my grandmother learned that she was of *kauwā* ancestry. The engagement was broken at once and all plans laid aside! Excellent though the girl was, she was absolutely not acceptable as a new addition to the family.

It is my own belief that the despised *kauwā* were early settlers, who fought against those who migrated hither at a later date, were badly defeated, greatly reduced in numbers and forced by their conquerors to live a segregated life on a tract of land allotted to them—despised and regarded as the very lowest of the low.

HO'OPAU PONO (FINIS).

The *'ohana* study ends here. We remind our readers that the task we set ourselves was that of sheer description, not analysis; nor comparison, even with other areas in the Hawaiian Islands. We have drawn to the best of our ability an accurate picture of a phase of old Hawaiian civilization now well nigh extinct, namely the old Polynesian family system of Ka-'u. This we have done with the utmost brevity compatible with thoroughness. The task has not been a simple one: it would have been easier and would have taken less time and effort had we compiled voluminously from

notes and knowledge available. Each topic has been reduced
to bare essentials, generally with a single example, and sometimes not even that, as in the case of many relationship
terms: these alone, if fully discussed and illustrated would
have made a book-full in themselves. The same is true of
the subject matter of each chapter.

It is for others to analyze and compare in accordance
with their interests and knowledge.

Pa'i ana na pahu a ka hula le'a.   Let more famous chanters beat their own drums.

O ka maua hula no KEIA!   'Tis ours, indeed, THIS ONE!

—M.K.P. and E.S.C.H.

VIII.

KA-'U, HAWAI'I, IN ECOLOGICAL AND HISTORICAL PERSPECTIVE

By Elizabeth Green Handy.

NOTE.—The following section is in no sense an independent contribution, but has been wrought in constant consultation with Dr. Handy and Mrs. Pukui, with whom the author has collaborated both in the field (Ka-'u in 1935 and after) and since in literary research over the years.—E.G.H.

GEOLOGY.

Geologically, Ka-'u is certainly one of the most interesting localities in the chain of volcanic Hawaiian islands. There exist today the vestiges of very ancient volcanoes along the great fissure in the floor of the Pacific, which extends south-eastward for a distance of over 1,600 miles, from Ocean Island in the north-west, through Midway to the island of Hawai'i in the south-east end.

Kure (formerly called " Ocean Island ") is a mere dot on a map. East by south, twenty minutes by plane, there is another speck, called Midway, a man-made " flat-top " practically at sea level, notable in the annals of World War II. Midway was an active volcano in Tertiary times, probably before any land existed where now the Hawaiian islands stand, and before the ancestors of the human inhabitants of these islands were humanoid. The great fissure in the ocean floor is in process of lengthening south-eastward.

The island of Hawai'i is the present focus of vulcanism, the only member of the Hawaiian chain now active. Ka-'u district, in which is located Kilauea volcano, the most youthful of the active volcanic " domes " on Hawai'i, is literally the active " growth point " of the island and the chain.

Native mythology likens the island of Hawai'i to a great tree with spreading branches:

> Born was the island—
> It budded, it leafed, it grew, it was green,
> The island blossomed on the tip; 'twas Hawai'i . . .
> Unstable was the land, tremulous was Hawai'i . . .[30]

South-east of the shores of Ka-'u and Puna new land is growing, as shown by seismographs and by soundings. There lies the tip of the most vigorous lateral root of the tree that is Hawai'i. Small wonder that its population became inured to cataclysms of cosmic dimensions, and to the jolts and reverberations of earthquakes. The magnitude of the earth drama that is literally "under foot" for every Ka-'uan, night and day, was a dominant factor in conditioning the character of the people of Ka-'u.

The slopes and plains of Kamao'a, which include Ka Lae (South Point), and adjacent *'ili* (land strips) represent a type area in whose basalt, lava and soil geologists can identify every phase in the long story of the growth of the island of Hawai'i.

There have been two ancient geologic stages or eras, and Ka-'u and Puna are now in the throes of a third. Before the birth of the two immense volcanic domes, rising over 13,000 feet above sea level—Mauna Kea and Mauna Loa—there had previously risen, in Tertiary times, two older domes. The remains of one, at the north end of the present island, form the mountain and slopes of Kohala and contiguous eroded areas. The remains of the other are revealed in the hills of Pahala in eastern Ka-'u.

These hills (Makanau and Pu'u 'Enuhe) are vestiges of a very ancient volcano out of which flowed the basalt that is found beneath the deep surface soil of Kamao'a and Ka Lae. That soil is almost entirely ash or dust from pumice and spun volcanic glass (obsidian, " Pele's hair ") drifting from countless lava fountains in the course of a million and more years.

Mauna Kea was the chief source of this ash. In Pleistocene times this majestic mountain rose as the primary dome during the second stage of the growth of Hawai'i. Then rose Mauna Loa, whose southern slopes lift like a vast parabola behind and above Ka-'u. Mauna Kea is believed to be

[30] Fornander, Abraham, " Collection of Hawaiian Antiquities and Folklore." B.P. Bishop Mus., *Mem.*, vol. VI, p. 363.

extinct. Mauna Loa it is that in historic times sends lava down upon Ka-'u and Kona. This lava has partially filled the canyon-like valleys between the hills that remain as vestiges of the more ancient Pahala or Ninole Dome. On Kamao'a and over surrounding areas recent lava flows have inundated the surface soil of ash which had been laid down upon the basalt originating in the Pahala extrusion of magma. There are other ash, cinder and olivene deposits which come from eruptions of Kilauea, the very young dome now in process of formation, in a position relative to Mauna Loa, comparable to Mauna Loa's position relative to Mauna Kea when the Mauna Loa dome was in an early stage of eruption.

The soil, then, which the *'ohana* of Kamao'a cultivated was (except for a thin layer of humus created by vegetation, and some deep pockets of humus in " *kipuka* ") a deep bed of ash laid down upon drifted dune sand and massive basalt not only before man came to Hawai'i, but probably before fully evolved man existed on earth. The forbidding black brow (Ka Lae) of South Point and the cliff known as the Kahuku Fault that forms its western edge (Palikulani), is basalt older even than man's anthropoid ancestors.[31]

The effects of time on the original deposits of wind-blown ash and sand are described by Stearns and Macdonald as follows:

> In most areas weathering has altered the ash to a fine-grained aggregate of palagonitic clay minerals. The originally sandy texture has been largely lost in wet areas and clay-like properties dominate. Black humus layers, ancient surfaces formerly supporting vegetation are fairly common. A few of them carry plant fossils.[32]

The process of soil formation continues today, as does likewise wind and water erosion, and the drifting of marine sand before the powerful winds that sweep across the plains of Kamao'a and South Point.

> During eruptions on the north-east rift of Mauna Loa, accompanied by trade-wind weather, Pele's hair and small fragments of pumice, sufficient to give the sky a straw colour, drift toward the Pahala area. Pele's hair with droplets of glass attached are common in Kau at such times. Similar material settles in Kau from summit and south-west rift-zone eruptions

[31] Stearns and MacDonald, *Geology and Ground-Water Resources of the Island of Hawai'i*, pp. 69-72. Honolulu, 1946.
[32] Stearns and MacDonald, op. cit., p. 74.

when the wind is in the right direction. Although such deposits during any one eruption are too small to measure, the 30,000 years of Recent time, with several eruptions each decade, must have produced an accretion of ash measurable in feet in the leeward *kipukas*.[33]

PREHISTORIC PERSPECTIVE.

The natural setting of Ka-ʻu and contiguous areas of the southern tip of the island of Hawaiʻi, when it was first colonized by the forbears of the Polynesian *ʻohana,* was quite different from what was seen from offshore in 1779 by Captain Cook. And that of 1954 is wholly different from what Cook saw.

Legendary and archaeological studies both justify the assumption that Polynesian settlers from *Kahiki* (which means " a foreign land," not necessarily Tahiti) were migrant *aliʻi* who came about a thousand years ago and colonized Ka-ʻu. To visualize the landscape that they saw from the sea, and the shores they landed upon and the country they gradually peopled, we must " peel off," so to speak, the various eras that have since changed the face of the *ʻaina* (land).

Our opinion is that these earliest settlers found Manukā (the western *ahupuaʻa* or district of Ka-ʻu) habitable, though it is now, along with the whole adjacent coastal area a deso-lation of recent and older lava. This seems a reasonable assumption, in view of the fact that large sections of these adjacent areas, including Kahuku and Pakini districts, are known to have been cultivated garden spots before their devastation by historically dated lava flows; while others were traditionally so referred to prior to 1800.

As the map shows, Manukā, Kahuku and the lower western part of Pakini are isolated from Kamaoʻa *ahupuaʻa* and the remainder of eastern Ka-ʻu by a sharp and sheer cliff, the result of a geological fault. That this slip occurred after Hawaiian settlement may be inferred from the fact that the fault line bisects the *ahupuaʻa* of Pakini. If the *pali* had been there when the land divisions were first origi-nated by Hawaiians, *ahupuaʻa* boundaries would, we believe, have followed the line of the cliff, which actually today makes upper and lower Pakini inaccessible from each other except by a difficult trail clambering up its sheer face.

[33] Stearns and MacDonald, op. cit., p. 75.

Eastward of Pakini the windswept plain which slopes very gradually up from South Point toward Mauna Loa is Kamao'a district, the homeland of the *'ohana* who were Mrs. Pukui's forbears.

When the early Hawaiian colonizers first came upon this land it was very different from what was seen by the European "discoverers," for by that time the Hawaiians had, in the course of their millenium or more of habitation, cleared much of Kamao'a and the South Point area of their prehistoric vegetation, in order to make way for the subsistence plants which they had brought with them. (Yet within the living memory of old timers, before Kamao'a became ranch land there was still much forest and brush right down to Ka Lae.) It therefore may be presumed that at the time of colonization the endemic flora gave a continuous cover of forest and brush, between spots of prairie where the grasses grew.

This would mean that it was less windy; and undoubtedly, with such cover, there was much more rainfall, mistfall and dew, in comparison with the modern dessication of bare, windswept, sunbaked plain flanked now to east and west and north by recent black lava which condenses the sun's heat and dries the air above it. The winds come in off the sea over the flank of the mountain, and in trade-wind season (March to November) would normally have been saturated with moisture from spray, when not dessicated in passing over arid land as now. The winter storms from the south still bring heavy rains.

Peculiar to this region even today is the cold mist-laden breeze (*kehau*) that pours down from the wet or snow-clad heights of Mauna Loa. A hundred and twenty-five years ago, and later, travellers described snows on Mauna Loa in July and August. (In modern times the snow cap is less constant.) [34] Even as recently as fifty years ago, after severe deforestation both on the seaward slopes and in the upland had taken place, dewfall was a recognized source of moisture, where it condensed off vegetation and cool rocks and dripped

[34] The regularity of this evening mist is commented on by a visiting scientist in Ka-'u in 1846: see Journal of Chester H. Lyman in the Hawaiian Islands, 1846, '47; MS. Book IV, p. 15 and elsewhere. Manuscript copy in the Hawaiian Mission Children's Society Library, Honolulu, Hawai'i.

into low-lying holes to be collected in gourds for drinking and for watering nearby plants.

Furthermore, it is not to be doubted that there was anciently more flow in underground streams and more percolation into and from lava tubes, which fed springs like that of Wai-o-Ahukini and deep rock pools like the famous waterhole Wai-a-Palahemo near South Point. Old timers today point out that earthquakes are known to have shut off some underground streams in historic times, and that introduced trees such as the eucalyptus may have clogged underground waterways with their root mats.

It may therefore be assumed that the first Polynesian colonists found a much more favourable habitat so far as fertile soil, favourable climate and water supply are concerned, than their descendants were obliged to learn to live with after continuing volcanic destruction and subsequent deforestation had materially altered the aspect of their land; and that those climatic factors presented them, at the time of settlement, with a well-established and valuable flora, which botanists give us reason to picture as giving Ka-'u a fairly continuous cover.

THE ETHNO-BOTANY OF KA-'U IN HISTORIC PERSPECTIVE.[35]

The endemic flora described below is what the colonizing Polynesians encountered in Ka-'u, as their settlements spread inland from the seacoast: an Oceanic sub-temperate high-volcanic-island wilderness, with many plants already well known to them, but others until then unknown.

The descendants of these colonists utilized *some part of every plant here described*: many were essential components of their equipment for living. The appraisal of the local ethno-botany is, then, as essential to a comprehension of the life of the *'ohana* of Ka-'u as is that of ocean, land, weather

---

[35] The standard botanical authorities consulted are: Rock, Joseph F., *The Indigenous Trees of the Hawaiian Islands*, Honolulu, 1913; Neal, Marie C., " In Gardens of Hawai'i," *Bernice P. Bishop Museum Special Publication No. 40*, Honolulu, 1948; Degener, Otto, *Plants of Hawai'i National Park*, 1945; Hubbard, Douglass H. (Park Naturalist), *Ferns of Hawai'i National Park*, Honolulu, 1952; Handy, E. S. Craighill *et al.*, " Outline of Hawaiian Physical Therapeutics," *B.P. Bishop Museum Bulletin 126*, Honolulu, 1934. All taxonomic identifications at the Bishop Museum are subject to the authority of Dr. Harold St. John, Curator of Botany. Mrs. Pukui has been the final authority on Hawaiian names and uses.

and climate. Within the limitations of their knowledge, ingenuity and cultural heritage, these native Hawaiians' utilization of their available natural assets was well-nigh complete—infinitely more so than that of the present commercial era which ruthlessly exploits the few things that are financially profitable for the time being, neglecting and often obliterating the rest. Modern scientific conservation seeks to remedy this situation.

KO KAHA KAI (along shore) :

POHUEHUE (*Ipomea*), the beach morning-glory. The long roots and vines were eaten sparingly in famine time. The vines, exuding milky latex, were used to slap the breasts of a mother lacking in milk. The long, tough, leafy vines also served to drive fish into nets.   PA'U-O-HI'IAKA (*Jacquemontia*), a small trailing plant with fleshy inch-long leaves and small blue flowers. The legendary name (Hi'iaka's skirt) comes from the coastland of Ka-'u, where the volcano goddess Pele laid her baby sister, Hi'iaka, while on a fishing trip, and returning found the creeper spread over the child to shade her from the hot sun. Used medicinally.   AUHUHU (*Tephrosia*), a low-growing woody-stemmed herb. The pounded leaves, whose juice contains tephrosin, were scattered on the surface of inshore and off-shore pools to stupify fish.   NAUPAKA (*Scaveola*), a shrub with thick downy leaf-clusters, spreading in bright green medallions on tough but brittle stalks, compact and wind-resistant, and growing to a height of four or five feet at the shore. It bears distinctive clusters of small whitish half-flowers, and large pulpy white berries, good food for birds but not for man. The bark was used medicinally.
HINAHINA (*Heliotropium*), a tiny, low-spreading, silvery-leafed native heliotrope with fragrant flowerets. Leaves were dried and brewed as tea, and used medicinally.
KAUNA'OA (*Cuscuta*), a dodder whose slender leafless tendrils attach themselves to other vines and shrubs, forming seasonally a network of golden yellow over dry areas. Used medicinally it is boiled in water to be used for a hot, soaking bath, to counteract insomnia.   'ILIMA (*Sida*), a tough-stemmed creeper with downy gray-green leaves and a profusion of round, orange-golden, delicately scented flowers prized by the *ali'i* for garlands. The stems were plaited into

rough baskets called *kiki*. This plant is a form of Kane 'Apua, the healer and patron of taro planters, whose shrine is on the high plain of Pakini some miles above South Point. The flowers chewed by the mother, were used as a purge for newborn babies.   PALA (*Marattia*), a small fern growing along shore where sunshine penetrates deep moist lava pits. The thick, spongy frond base was eaten raw or cooked in famine time. Sliced and soaked, the juice mixed in the water was laxative. Fronds, fragrant when crushed, were prized for wreathing with *maile* vine for *lei*. *Pala* was also used ceremonially in the *heiau*.   KO'O-KO'O-LAU (*Bidens*), a tall herb with small leaves (*lau*) sparsely placed on jointed stalks (*ko'o-ko'o*). A medicinal tea, steeped from its leaves, was drunk as a tonic.

KO KULA KAI (on the seaward slopes) :

Here was found PILI (*Heteropogen*), the straw-like grass, growing in small tufts, carpeting all the open lands toward South Point and along the elevated lower slopes toward Puna. It became the universal thatching for the wind-and-weather-tight sleeping house (*hale*). The seed are " stick-tights " (*pili*).   KOALI 'AWAHIA (*Ipomea*), the blue-flowered morning-glory. The latex was a drastic cathartic. Poultices made of pounded stems and roots mixed with salt were applied as a counter-irritant to stimulate healing of contusions, dislocations and broken bones. KOALI 'AI has pink to purple flowers. The large tuberous roots and main stems were famine food. The milky latex was used medicinally to increase milk flow. The long tough vines of both species, plaited, served for heavy cordage for canoes, etc.   KAKALAIOA (*Caesalpinia*), a climbing bramble with " fish hook " thorns (*kakala*) bearing spiny pods whose marble-like hard seeds sprout, after rains, within cracks or broken lava chunks. A favourite for seed *lei*. The seeds yield a powder resembling quinine, medicinally, and containing the tonic bonducine; used in Hawai'i as a strong purgative; known in India as " fever nut."   'ALA-'ALA-WAI-NUI (*Peperomia*), a small herb with succulent leaves and stems, growing on and amongst rocks and on exposed tree roots in moist, sheltered places. Medicinally, the juice is used as a tonic and healing agent in lung diseases and disorders affecting the inner ear.   PUA KALA (*Argemone*), the Hawaiian prickly poppy, growing in dry, sandy soil, with grey stem and foliage and handsome white orange-centred blossoms. Seeds and gummy yellow sap were used as a narcotic and analgesic agent for toothache, neuralgia and ulcers; the juice was applied to remove warts. This is a body (*kinolau*) of Kane, as were likewise the spiny seaweed, *limu kala* (*Sargassum*), and *kala* or unicorn fish.

KO‘OLOA ULA (*Arbutilon*), a " hoary shrub " with heart-shaped leaves and dark red flowers somewhat resembling hibiscus, a favourite flower for the hair in Ka-‘u. 'ILIMA KU KULA, the bush *'ilima* (see *'ilima ko kaha kai*, above) flourished here. In housebuilding, stems of this tough plant were woven into a lattice-like base for thatch, or for inner wall covering. PA‘U-O-HI‘IAKA is here the companion of *'ilima,* as alongshore. ‘AUHUHU was found here also, as was KO‘O-KO‘O-LAU (see above). ‘A‘A-‘LI‘I KU-MAKANI (*Dodonaea*), whose name means " rooted like a lord standing erect in the wind," grows as a shrub on the windswept plains and even on *a‘a* lava flows. Its yellow, red or brown fruit clusters were plaited with fern for head wreaths. It was sacred to Laka, patron of the *hula*. A Ka-‘u boast: " I am an *'a‘a-'li‘i* shrub; no wind can blow me over." AKIA (*Wikstroemia*). *Akia 'awa* (bitter) growing on the *'a‘a* of the Ka-‘u desert, is a many branched shrub with tough bark and orange-red fruits. Decoctions of root and bark were deadly, used for killing and suicide. Bark and leaves, pounded and packaged in coconut sheath, were thrust into rock holes to stun fish and eels (a method called *hola*). There is also *'akia manalo* (benign), another one of the many species of *Wikstroemia*, which is said by Mrs. Pukui not to be poisonous. PUKIAWE (*Styphelia*), a crackling dry ground cover found on arid lava flows, where it is stunted. NAIO (*Myoporum*), or " false sandalwood," a shrub whose wood (fragrant when dried) was used in the construction of the grass house. ALAHE‘E (*Canthium*), a shrub belonging to the coffee family growing in dry places. Scrapers and short fishing spears (*'o*) were made from its strong wood. ILIE‘E (*Plumbago*), a small shrub with white flowers used medicinally, whose sap served to stain tattoo designs. WILIWILI (*Erythrina*), a tree which thrives on coral, lava or almost any sand or soil not salt-saturated, having a thick spiny trunk and spreading branches. Its claw-like blossoms may be brilliant crimson, orange, yellow or white. The shiny red bean-like seeds were strung as *lei*. The very light soft wood, durable in seawater, served as outrigger and net floats, and for light surfboards. Abundant in Ka-'u, *wiliwili* wood was exchanged for Kona *koa* for boat hulls.   KAUILA (*Colubrina*), a sturdy-trunked tree growing up to 35 feet tall on ancient lava, whose very hard, heavy dark-red wood was prized for spears, *kapa* beaters and *kahili* standards. A similar tree of the same name but distinct botanically (*Alphitonia*), having equally durable close-grained wood streaked with black, was abundant in Ka-'u, where it was used to cover and partially seal blow-holes along shore-side planting areas (to eliminate salt spray) ; the logs, laid criss-cross with rocks piled against them, were also used to seal the openings of burial caves. 'OHI'A LEHUA (*Metrosideros*), the characteristic hoary-barked tree of the volcanic regions, one of the first to appear, gnarled and stunted, on fresh lava flows, whose brilliant red flower pompoms (*lehua*) are associated with the volcanic deities Pele and Hi'iaka. Its hard reddish wood was used for spears, mallets, etc. *Liko lehua*, the flower buds, were prescribed as a tonic to stimulate appetite and digestion for a debilitated child. The *'ohi'a* is a " body " of the warlike *akua*, Ku : images in the *Luakini* or war temples were *'ohi'a* logs carved in conventional style depicting ferocity.

KO KULA UKA (on the upland slopes) :

Here was found KUKAEPUA'A (*Digitaria*), a native crab-grass growing thickly around trees in woods where wild hogs dwell. The name means " hog's excrement." Its stem is hairy like a hog's leg. A *kinolau* or form of the hog-god Kamapua'a, it could be used as an offering in place of pig in religious ceremonies. Its juice was used medicinally to heal birth lacerations.   PUA KALA and 'ALA-'ALA-WAI-NUI (see above) were here also.   'APE-'APE (*Gunnera*), a marsh plant with large leaves looking like rhubarb, is peculiar to the Hawaiian islands.   MOA (*Psilotum*), a very ancient almost leafless small plant, growing on rocks and tree trunks, moist or dry, whose stems were brewed into a tea and used as medicine for thrush (*ea*) in infants, and a laxative; its oily spores were used under the *malo* like talcum to prevent chafing; it was taken internally to counteract diarrhoea.   WAWAE-'IOLE (*Lycopodium*), a club moss descriptively named " rat's foot," which was boiled in water for bathing as a remedy for rheumatism. ULUHE (*Dicranopteris*) or false staghorn fern, which spreads in impenetrable thickets, growing over its own dead branches and engulfing other plants, and becoming, with its brittle undergrowth, a source of devastating fires.   An infusion from its fronds was drunk as a laxative.   'AWA-PUHI (*Zingiber*), the native ginger plant, whose modest and deep green leaf stalks bearing small blooms grow prolifically in the *kuahiwi* (wet uplands).   The rhizomes were powdered and sprinkled among the bed *kapa* for fragrance, the juicy stems were squeezed over the hair to perfume it, and the leaves were used in the *imu* to flavour the meat. 'ILIMA (see above), which at this altitude becomes a four-foot shrub, known as *'ilima 'apiki* (likewise called *kanaka maika'i*, " good man," i.e. Kane 'Apua, patron of husbandry and healing) the roots and flowers of which had medicinal uses.   A close relative called *'ilima makana'a* grew as straggling bushes on old lava flows and were pulled and piled up to make beds in caves or other temporary shelters. KO'O-KO'O-LAU (see above), the widespread native herb found from shoreline to an altitude of 8,000 feet, was also here.   KUPAOA (*Railliardia*) is an herb or shrub with purplish leathery leaves which thrives on open dry ridges; its fragrant root was used to perfume *kapa* and feather mantles.   PUKIAWE (see above), one of the most characteristic shrubs of the dry slopes, with bracken-like straggling branches four to five feet high, fine, stiff-leaved, and fruited with dry multi-shaded berries, white through pink to red at any one time.   Its branches and leaves when burned give off a creosotish smudge which was, according to the historian Malo, used ceremonially to divest an *ali'i* of his *kapu* on certain occasions, and for cremating the bodies of outlaws.   'ULEI (*Osteomeles*), a tall shrub thriving on *'a'a* lava flows, up to 4,000 feet in altitude.   Its strong, pliable stalks were used as rims for fish nets, and for the musical bow, the *'ukeke*.   PAPALA (*Charpenteria*), a shrub whose light, gummy wood was highly inflammable and used for " fireworks " displays.   The gum was smeared on sticks for snaring birds.   The upland region in Ka-'u known as Ka-papala, now a ranch, was named for this prevalent shrub.   'A'A-'LI'I, a shrub at lower elevations (see above), becomes a sizable tree on upland slopes. Its hard wood was found useful for tools, and its red seed capsules made a dye for *kapa*.   KAUILA (see above) here grew up to forty or fifty feet high, a single tree thus giving a valuable supply of heavy hard wood for its many uses.   WILI-WILI (see above) grew in the drier upland areas, though more plentifully on the hot plains.   MAMANE (*Sophora*), a small tree peculiar to the Hawaiian islands, in Ka-'u being especially abundant at Ka-papala and Ka-pali-i-uka. It was notable for its golden yellow flower clusters and hard bitter seeds, and for its durable wood, a substitute for the rarer *ka'uila* wood for tools, *holua* sled runners, and ceremonial uses. Its branches, thrown into a muddy stream, were said to have the property of causing the mud to settle and the water to clarify. There is a Ka-'u proverb: *Uhiuhi lau mamane ka wai o Ka-papala*, meaning to let the mud of scandal settle as silt sinks in the waters of Ka-papala.

NAIO, the false sandalwood (see above) is here a tree of forty-five or fifty feet, and its fragrant wood was used for main house timbers.   'OHI'A LEHUA (see above) is prolific and larger in the uplands. Hawaiians distinguished several local varieties, these they named *lehua mamo* " royal scion " (orange flowering), *lehua lauli'i* (" small leafed "), *lehua ku-makua* (" parent erect "), *lehua puakea* (" white flowers "), etc.   'OHI'A HA (*Syzygium*), generically unrelated to *'ohi'a lehua*, resembles it except in its smooth bark and its profusion of red berries in summer. It is a small shrub-like tree on exposed ridges. Its hard wood was used in housebuilding and for fuel, and its bark rendered a black dye for *kapa*.   MAMAKI (*Pipturus*), a small tree with long drooping branches thriving in wet uplands up to 4,000 feet, was the most abundant source of the native bark cloth and was said to make a finer, softer cloth than did the *wauke* (*Broussonetia*) which later Polynesian colonizers brought with them. The *mamaki* was especially plentiful in the forest zone above Na'alehu, Ka-'u, where it grew to thirty feet in height and a foot in diameter. In addition to its strong fibrous bark (light brown in colour) it was sought out for its berries, which were used as a digestive tonic for children, and (being slippery when chewed) were said to be good to stimulate bowel action.   KOA (*Acacia*), a stately upland tree found in Polynesia only in the Hawaiian islands, and after the *'ohi'a lehua* the most widespread. Notable in the forest for its grey-barked massive trunk and slender, hard, crescent-shaped, olive-green " leaves " (which are flattened elongated petioles) growing thickly on spreading branches. Its tough wood is the most beautiful in colour and grain of any native tree, and for old Hawai'i its primary use, because of size and durability, was for boat hulls. It was also sought for images in the war temples (*koa* means warrior), for spears, bowls, spittoons, and other utensils.

THE WAO (or upland jungle) :

The most prevalent feature of the rain forests was the variety of ferns, from tiny delicate ground cover to the majestic tree ferns. Among the many small species that the Hawaiians named, which we will not attempt to differentiate descriptively here, were the LAU-KAHI (" single leaf ") or Cliffbrake; the PALAI-LAU-LI'I (" little leaf ") ; PALAI-HINAHINA ("lying flat") ; KIHI ("angular") ; WAHINE NOHO MAUNA (" mountain-dwelling-woman ") ; PAI (a bracken) ; all air plants; the WAWAE-'IOLE ("rat's foot"), or clubmoss, called by botanists " a living fossil "; a group of small " elephant-tongue " ferns all named 'EKAHA by Hawaiians (as was also the very large "birdnest fern," *Asplenium*, found usually in tree crotches) ; the filmy 'OHI'AKU (" upright *'ohi'a* "), KILAU, OWALI'I and 'IWA'IWA (maidenhair). Among the more distinctive larger fern clumps were the PALA'Ā, whose stems yielded a red dye; PAMOHO, which hangs curtain-like over wet cliffs and cavern mouths; 'AKOLEA, a broad-fronded lacy fern; NI'ANI'AU, a group of closely related sword-ferns; two lacy ferns, PALAPALAI, sacred to Laka and essential for the *hula* altar, and PALAPALA-'A, sacred to Hi'iaka (her magical skirt was made from it), whose juices were used for dye and for medicine; WAIMAKA-NUI (" great tears ") ; HO'I'O, whose young leaves were edible. Other well-known but less spectacular ferns were the A'E, LOULU, KIKA-WAIO, PI'IPI'I-LAU MAMANA (" branching climbing leaf "), and the PALA.

Among the " vines " we note two that are unique. MAILE (*Alyxia*), peculiar to the Hawaiian islands, is more

properly described as a twining shrub, whose fragrant bark
and thick close-growing oval leaves made it desirable for
wreathing as *lei* and for ceremonial or festive decoration,
particularly on the *hula* altar, as it was associated with the
goddess Laka; there are many legends about the four *maile*
sisters. The second " vine," *'IE-'IE*, a climbing *Freycinetia*,
is a handsome forest denizen whose long saw-edged leaves
growing in spirals resemble those of the *hala* or pandanus
(a very useful economic plant brought in by the colonizing
Polynesians). The endemic *'ie-'ie* also had many uses: the
strong, durable roots were woven into tight carrying baskets
and into fine meshed funnels for shrimp traps, and were also
plaited to make a strong foundation for the feathered war
helmets (*mahiole*) ; the stem fibres were pounded and made
into binding twine for house rafters and canoe outriggers.
'Ie-'ie branches formed part of the stipulated wildwood
offerings on the *hula* altar.

MAU'U-HO'ULA-'ILI or MAU'U-LA-'ILI (*Sisyrinch-
ium*) is a yellow-flowered native grass found from median
to high altitudes in boggy places, whose juice was used to
burn designs on the skin. A native lily-like sedge called
'UKI-'UKI is common here and was gathered for house-
thatch; it is identified as *Vicentia* and differs from the
'uki-'uki (*Dianella*) found elsewhere in these islands. The
large-leafed marsh-plant 'APE-'APE and the herb 'ALA-
'ALA-WAI-NUI thrive here as at low altitudes. 'AKU-
'AKU (*Cyanea*) has lettuce-like leaves liked by bird and
man.   'OHELO (*Vaccinium*) is a relative of the blue-
berry and the cranberry, but our Hawaiian species is
peculiar to volcanic areas of Mauna Loa on Hawai'i and
Haleakala on Maui, where its juicy, edible red berries were
identified with the volcano goddess Pele. Another variety,
called *'ohelo kau la-'au*, grows up to six feet high and has
bitter berries.   NAUPAKA KUAHIWI is a shrub of
more compact growth than shoreline *naupaka*, having thick,
smooth bright green leaves. It has the characteristic white
half-flowers, but black fruit. False staghorn, ULUHE,
proliferates massively in the uplands, a useless pest except
for occasional use as temporary thatch. It stifles other vegetation.   'AMA'U fern on the other hand, widespread in
the *wao*, is a generous host to seeds of other plants, particularly the *'ohi'a lehua*, whose seeds lodge and sprout in frond

bases of the ‘ama‘u stalks. The leathery fronds served for
thatching upland shelters, for house decoration, and mulch
for unirrigated forest taro patches. The starchy pith of
the stalks, and young shoots, were famine food. The fire-
pit of Kilauea Volcano (in the forest surrounding which it
grows abundantly) is named *Hale-ma‘u-ma‘u*, house of the
‘ama‘u fern—possibly because cooled lava outpourings in the
vicinity often have a striking resemblance to the fern fronds.
KOA in the rain forest develops a straight, massive bole,
branching forty feet above ground, the best for canoe hulls.
‘OHI‘A LEHUA is here abundant, and large.   MAMANE
attains a height of forty feet.   ‘A‘ALI‘I, a shrub on the
plains is a thirty-foot tree at 6,000 to 8,000 foot elevation.
KUPAOA, an herb or shrub in lowlands, becomes here a
twenty-foot tree.   PUKIAWE grows fifteen feet high.
‘ALANI (*Pelea*) is known only in the higher forest of the
Hawaiian islands. Its generic name *Pelea* is bestowed in honour of the volcano goddess, Pele. A smallish tree with leathery leaves, its nut, used medicinally, contains a fragrant oil
reminiscent of that found in orange rind.   OLOPUA
(*Osmanthus*), the Hawaiian olive, having yellow flowers
and bluish olive-like but inedible fruit, is abundant on the
leeward lava slopes of Ka-‘u where it attains to sixty feet in
height. The hard dark-brown wood was prized for making
the *o‘o* or digging stick, as well as for adze handles.
KOLEA (*Suttonia*) is a small tree with very thick leaves,
whose wood was favoured for *kapa* anvils, while its red sap
was used as a dye.   KOPIKO (*Straussia*), is glossy-
leaved and magnolia-like in form, handsome but useless.
A‘E (*Sapindus*) or “ Soapberry ” whose fruit lathers in
water, is a tall deciduous tree (sometimes eighty feet high)
native only to the island of Hawai‘i, having a smooth light-
brown bark which scales off in large patches. The large
black seeds are prized for making necklaces.   The ‘OHA
(‘*oha-wai* or ‘*oha kepau*), is a *Clermontia*, a genus peculiar
to the Hawaiian islands, having a tall straight stalk topped
by a crown of slender, dark, glossy leaves and pendant waxy
flowers producing dark globular fruits. The sticky, milky
sap (*kepau*) of the leaf branches was employed as bird lime.
HAPU‘U (*Cibotium*) are giant ferns, of which there are two
forms. The *hapu‘u i‘i* trunk attains twenty-five feet in
height, with fronds rising fifteen feet higher; the term *i‘i*

describes the stiff bristles on the stalks, suggestive of those on a hog's leg—hence this fern was a " form " of Kamapua'a, the hog god. The *hapu'u pulu* is slightly shorter and has soft down (*pulu*) surrounding budding fronds. The *pulu* was packed into body cavities in embalming, and used for other purposes. But the prime value of *hapu'u* was in the starch core of the trunk which was eaten as famine food. 'ILIAHI (*Santalum*), or sandalwood, thriving best at 5,000 feet or more altitude in open drier areas, was prized for its heartwood (*la'au 'a'ala,* " fragrant wood "), which was powdered for perfuming bark cloth bed coverings.

THE COLONISTS LAND.

So the colonists landed. They were not numerous. There were possibly already a few settlements of some pre-Polynesian Hawaiians brought by drifts from Micronesia, the islands or mainlands of east or north-east Asia or the west coasts of the Americas. Mrs. Pukui believes that the outcasts known as *Kauwā* (later doomed to die as human sacrifices), who were kept on a reservation consisting of the west half of the subdistrict of Ninole, may have been descendants of some conquered local tribe who resisted the colonizing *ali'i* and their clansmen in the period of early Hawaiian settlement. There was perhaps an era like that described by Te Rangi Hiroa in *The Coming of the Maori*, when the 14th century fleet of Maoris settled the coasts of New Zealand: The colonists fighting with tribes of an older indigenous population; border quarrels and battles with advancing colonists of their own *maoli* (native) breed as population expanded on the west (Kona district), east (Puna and Hilo) and north (Hamakua).

The most likely original landing place was the hospitable beach at Punalu'u. Other likely beachheads for these invading colonists were Ka-'ili-ki'i, west of Ka Lae; or Ka'alu'alu, a small bay along the shore north-east of Ka Lae. Inland, between and beyond these two points favourable for landing, are the plains and valleys of Kamao'a, Pakini and Waiohinu. Honu'apo is the landing most accessible to Na'alehu and Waiohinu.

Their Subsistence Economy.

The plains and the lower forested hills of Manukā, Kahuku, Pakini and Kamao'a, and the lush sheltered valley

of Waiohinu must have looked like a veritable land of
promise to the keen-eyed early Polynesian colonists who
were skilled horticulturalists, accustomed to appraise an
Oceanic landscape from the sea in terms of its habitability.
The great current called Ke Au a Halali'i, sweeping south-
westward from Ka Lae like the wake of a ship, made plain
to these men, who sharply watched every sign of ocean and
air, the fact that here the flow (*au moana*) of ocean around
the island came together from east and west alongshore,
pushed by whatsoever wind—trade winds (*ko'olau*),
southerlies (*kona*), north-westerlies (*kiu*). And they knew
that here ran the big fish they treasured most for subsistence
—'ahi (tuna), *aku* (bonito), *'a'u* (swordfish), *ulua* (*Caranx*)
and *mahimahi* (dolphin fish), and the smaller but much-
relished *'opelu* (mackerel).

There were serious drawbacks, of which they were
aware at first glance. There was no reef; there were but
tiny coves, few beaches; and this meant few squid, mullet,
goatfish, parrotfish and the like along and offshore in
shallows; few shellfish and crustaceans, a dearth of *limu*
(seaweed)—all food items of prime importance for these
tropical Oceanic islanders, undoubtedly well acquainted with
the dietary wealth of the lagoons of reef-rimmed high
volcanic islands and coral atolls. Yet the land was both a
challenge and a promise. They settled; they spread " like a
gourd vine " over the plain. They cleared their plots and
planted all that they had carefully transported from the old
homeland.

The Polynesian horticultural complex established by
these settlers included: taro, sweet potato, yam (*Dioscorea*),
banana, sugar-cane, breadfruit, coconut, paper mulberry,
gourds, ti, candlenut. Hogs, edible dogs, and chickens were
the Polynesian farmer's "livestock." The *kou* tree (*Cordia*),
flowering hibiscus, *hala* (pandanus), *milo* (*Thespesia*), *hau*
tree (a Hibiscus) and *kamani* (*Calophyllum*) were planted
and tended for use and beauty. There are some botanists
and some natives who believe that the old Hawaiian *hala
Kahiki* ("foreign pandanus") or pineapples were introduced
by early Hawaiians. On the *kula* slopes, or hillsides and
mountainsides above the plains, and in the lower forests,
upland taro and yam, arrowroot, turmeric, bamboo, *olonā*
(*Touchardia*), and *'awa* were planted in arable clearings.

The Endemic Wilderness Retreats.

The old Hawaiian endemic flora and fauna of the plains were slowly eliminated from areas capable of cultivation. Patches of old wilderness remained only in barren rocky places and in some *kipuka* (holes or patches of old soil and vegetation surrounded by a lava flow). Some *kipuka* were used, especially those that were deep and cool where moisture condensed; others were too rough or too dry. For the rest, the plains of Pakini, Kamao'a and neighbouring areas slowly came under relatively intensive cultivation and use.

The median forest zone was unquestionably profoundly modified by use and exploitation on the part of the Hawaiian population, and by secondary effects of their increase and spread in Ka-'u. *Koa* trees were felled in quantity for canoes and wooden utensils, *ohi'a, ka'uila, mamaki, wiliwili* and countless other endemic trees were utilized to a considerable extent. In famine times—which were frequent if historical conditions of weather and terrain are anything like the prehistoric—the several fern trees, with their starch-filled cores, other edible ferns large and small, wild edible morning-glory, and many weeds, nuts, were avidly sought by all families throughout the land. The bird population was undoubtedly greatly reduced by the various methods of hunting: snaring, noosing, netting, etc. (See the second paragraph below.) During long droughts, fish vanished from the shores and offshore currents into more distant waters, and coast-bound marine fauna was " fished out " by every known means. Consequently, survival in times of severe drought and famine meant living in and off the jungle, and must have seriously depleted it.

How much effect on the forest in old Hawai'i wild hogs, chickens and rats, which came along with the voyagers, may have had is a question worthy of consideration. At times of drought, wild hogs root everywhere in the forest zone, wild chickens pick everything that chickens eat, and wild rats gnaw all roots, barks, fruits and seeds edible to a rat, above and below ground. Unquestionably the virgin jungle of Mauna Loa's slopes was profoundly changed by Hawaiian Polynesian populations before the coming of the white man.

The avifauna of Hawai'i was very extensive. Here we list those birds known to the folk of Hawai'i. The list is not complete. *Seabirds*: Albatross, shearwater, petrel, tropic bird, booby, frigate bird. *Swamp, pond and stream*: heron, native wild goose, duck and mud hen. *Shore and lowland*: coot, golden plover (winter migrant), curlew, tattler, turnstone, sanderling, stilt, tern. *On slopes and in* lower forest: hawk (*'io*), owl, rail, crow, thrush (all endemic). *Upper forests*: *'elepaio* (*Chasiempis*), various honey-eaters, honey creepers, *'ula-'ai-hawane* (*Ciridops*), *'amakihi* (*Chlorodrepanis*), creepers (*Paroreomyza*), *'akepa* (*Loxops*), *'akialoa* (*Hemignathus*), *'o'u* (*Psittacirostra*), *palila* (*Loxioides*), *hopue* (*Rhodacanthis*.) The meaty, flavourful large birds were regularly hunted for food, others only in famine time, except those that are *kapu* like hawk, owl, *'elepaio*, *'ula*. All figured in lore, many in mythology, symbolism and ritual.

" DISCOVERY."

Captain James Cook.

The first view of this district to be recorded by Europeans at the period by them labelled " discovery," occurred in February of 1779 when Captain James Cook first sighted Ka-'u. Of the devastation he saw Lt. James King, chief officer on Captain Cook's ship *Resolution,* records the following impression:

> The coast of Kaoo presents a prospect of the most horrid and dreary kind: the whole country appearing to have undergone a total change from the effects of some dreadful convulsion. The ground is every where covered with cinders and intersected in many places with black streaks, which seem to mark the course of a lava that has flowed, not many ages back, from the mountain Roa to the shore. The southern promontory looks like the mere dregs of a volcano. The projecting headland is composed of broken and craggy rocks, piled irregularly on one another, and terminating in sharp points.[36]

Because of the wealth of food offshore, the *'ohana* of Kama'oa revered even these desolate seaward zones, ingeniously finding ways and places for cultivation, adapting themselves in some places to an almost desert existence in order to live close by the best fishing grounds. This proud and independent Ka-'u song (translated by Mrs. Pukui)—a name-chant for a beloved chief, Kupake'e—bears witness to their spirit:

[36] King, James, *A Voyage to the Pacific Ocean.* Vol. III, p. 104, Captain James Cook's Voyage . . . G. Nicol, London, 1784. First ed.

I do not care for Kona,
For Ka-'u is mine.
The water from Ka Lae is carried all night long,
(Wrung) from tapa and from sponges.
This land is heard of as having no water,
Except for the water that is waited for at Manā and Unulau,
The much-prized water found in the eye-socket of the fish,
The water prized and cared for by the man.
Even the child carries a gourd container in his arms.
The voice of the water gourd is produced by the wind,
Sounding like a nose flute at midnight,
This long-drawn whistling of the gourd we hear,
Hearken, how fortunate you are!
There is no going back; ways now are different.
In childhood only does one regret in secret,
Grieving alone.
(Look) forward with love for the season ahead of us!
Let pass the season that is gone!

It was in the course of his survey of this coast that Captain
Cook

> . . . sent Mr. Bligh, the master in a boat, to sound the coast
> . . . and to look for fresh water . . . When he landed, he found no
> stream or spring, but only rain-water, deposited in holes upon the
> rocks; and even that was brackish, from the spray of the sea;
> and that the surface of the country was entirely composed of
> [stone] flags and ashes, with a few plants here and there inter-
> spersed.[37]

This would appear to be descriptive of the tiny bay of
Ka'alu'alu, on the eastern side of South Point. But none of
these officers who then commented upon the barren aspect of
Ka-'u had penetrated inland, and the fertile valleys and lush
uplands of this region, thickly populated and well cultivated,
were unseen and unknown to them. We must wait another
forty-odd years for a full description here.

First Missionary Description.

In 1823 a tour of Hawai'i was undertaken by resident
missionaries and William Ellis, a scholarly English missionary from the Society Islands.[38] The party travelled overland,
across the dry, hot, lava-strewn zone of Manukā where, save
for

> . . . here and there, at distant intervals . . . a lonely house . . .
> with a solitary shrub of thistle struggling for existence among
> the crevices . . . All besides was one vast desert, dreary, black
> and wild.[39]

[37] King, op. cit., p. 545.

[38] Ellis, William, *A Journal of a Tour around Hawai'i, the Largest
of the Sandwich Islands.* Boston, 1825.

[39] Ellis, op. cit., p. 95.

After two exhausting days along the coastal trail under the hot sun of July, sleeping in the open on the rough terrain where " the land-wind, from the snow-covered top of Mouna Roa, blew keenly down," they turned inland from " Tairitii " (Kaʻilikiʻi), a populous shore village.   This is in Ka-ʻuʻs most westerly district of Manukā.   Their way led " over a bed of ancient lava, smooth, considerably decomposed, and generally covered with a thin layer of soil " but adjacent to a more recent stream of lava, "rugged, black, and appalling." Then, after a half-hour's climb by a winding path up the 300-foot face of a steep precipice (the cliff along the fault scarp of Kahuku) :

> A beautiful country now appeared before us, and we seemed all at once transported to some happier island, where the devastations attributed to Nahoaarii and Pele had never been known. The rough and desolate tract of lava, with all its distorted forms, was exchanged for the verdant plain, diversified with gently rising hills and sloping dales, ornamented with shrubs, and gay with blooming flowers. We saw, however, no streams of water during the whole of the day; but, from the luxuriance of the herbage in every direction, the rains must be frequent, or the dews heavy.[40]

Then on, through a similarly lovely land, cultivated and with a " numerous, though scattered population," where " the prospect was delightful."

> On one hand, the Pacific dashed its mighty waves against the rocky shore, and on the other the *kua hevi* (mountain ridge) of Kau, and snow-topped Mouna Roa, rose in the interior, with lofty grandeur.[41]

The travellers describe the " mountain taro " of this region, growing in " a dry, sandy soil, into which our feet sank two or three inches, every step."   This was in the district named Pakini.

Much of this " fertile plain " and these " farms of varied extent, scattered over the whole face of the country " as seen in 1823, are now covered by the lava flows of 1868 and 1881.   Other scenes that these men recorded a century ago, though menaced by flows in 1926 and 1950, are still preserved in natural beauty.   After climbing toward the forest zone, the missionaries' path suddenly turned south-eastward and presented to their view " a most enchanting

[40] op. cit., p. 100.
[41] op. cit., p. 101.

valley, dotted with verdure " and " open toward the sea . . .
adorned with gardens even to the summits of the hills . . ."
This was the dramatically lovely valley of Waiohinu. Beyond
Waiohinu their course led toward the shore to Honu'apo, a
miniature bay formed by a tongue of lava jutting out into
the sea, which they describe as " an extensive and populous
village, standing on a level bed of lava." So great was the
excitement of the inhabitants that the visitors concluded
that they had seldom if ever seen foreigners before.

Beyond Honu'apo they crossed a " rugged tract of lava
. . . most violently torn to pieces, and . . . in some places
heaped forty or fifty feet high," thereafter arriving at the
" pleasant village " of Hilea, some miles inland. From here
was pointed out to them the hill " called Makanau " where
the last native chief of Ka-'u finally surrendered to the
usurping forces of Kamehameha the Great.[42] Here the trail
returned to the sea, along the black pebbled beach and small
village of Ninole, and the adjacent fishing town of Punalu'u.

As they again, on the following day, directed their steps
mountainward and away from the coastal villages, they
travelled over " a rich yellow-looking soil of decomposed
lava," the same sort of " verdant country," with " large
fields of taro and [sweet] potatoes," and sugar cane and
bananas " growing very luxuriantly "—the whole area " in
a high state of cultivation " as they approached the uplands
of Kapapala (not more than twenty miles below Kilauea
crater on the south-east slope of Mauna Loa). Hereabout
the surface of the earth seemed to them to have remained
undisturbed for " ages," with a considerable depth of
" prolific soil, fertile in vegetation," in contrast to a new
volcanic rift which they visited but five miles distant at
" Poonahoahoa," where within the eleven moons just past,
according to kama'aina, an earthquake had suddenly produced two chasms from which smoking lava was now oozing,
threatening for this " smiling " area the desolation that had
been witnessed elsewhere.[43]

So did Ka-'u present itself to these careful observers
from England and New England during the first quarter of
the 19th century—in all its characteristic and contrasting
aspects of grandeur and desolation, lush natural beauty and

[42] op. cit., pp. 102, 104, 110.
[43] op. cit., pp. 114-15, 120.

thrifty cultivation, under the stringency of a stern climate and the ever-present threat of seismic ruin. As yet its aspect was untouched by the oncoming human and cultural wave of which these men themselves were the forerunners.

KA-'U MISSIONIZED.

Ka-'u, remote, with few safe canoe landings, and approachable by land only by the most arduous mountain, shoreline or desert paths, was the last major district in the islands to receive a resident missionary. The Rev. Cochran Forbes, stationed in South Kona in 1831, made occasional tours thither to carry the Congregationalist message to Ka-'u folk; and the Rev. Titus Coan, from his base at Hilo from 1836 on, preached in the villages of Keauhou adjoining Puna, which was his charge.

Actually the first resident missionary was French Catholic Father Marechal who settled there in 1841,[44] and soon had a church " near the center of Kau . . . under the foothills of Mauna Loa."[45] In three months he had 900 converts. The sturdy Congregationalist Coan remarks upon the indefatigible, the " bold and defiant " young Catholic's proselytizing.[46] It is said that the district was " two-thirds Catholic " by 1843 or 1844;[47] and a discouraged new Protestant missionary arriving at Waiohinu in 1866 writes, " This is a R.C. parish."[48] Neither statement takes account of the two decades between 1843 and 1866 or of Protestant contacts since 1823 (Ellis *et al*).

In January of 1842, a few months following the Catholic priest's arrival there came the Rev. John D. Paris, a Presbyterian of Virginia, to live and work in this " most inaccessible district in the Islands," " single-handed and alone " to labour " among a wild, savage, independent people," who nevertheless turned out to be toward him gentle and eager

[44] Yzendoorn, *History of the Catholic Mission in Hawaii*, p. 183. Honolulu, 1927.

[45] Coan, Rev. Titus, *Life in Hawaii, an Autobiographic Sketch— 1835-1881*, p. 95 ff.

[46] Coan, loc. cit.

[47] Yzendoorn, op. cit., p. 184.

[48] Pogue, MS., Report to General Meeting, 1867; H.M.C.S. Library, MSS. files; Honolulu.

for a teacher.[49] Arriving at Ka'alu'alu by schooner, he and
his goods were landed on the *pahoehoe* (smooth lava) shore
of the small cove.

> The shore was lined with hundreds of natives as our little
> boat neared the shore. I was taken up by a great strong native
> Samson, whose entire dress was a *malo* and who was tattooed
> from head to foot. He looked fierce, but set me gently down on
> the *pahoehoe* amid a crowd of natives . . . Then came greetings
> from the multitude, some kissing my hands and some taking hold
> of my feet. A joyful " *Aloha ino!*" with a low wail, rose from
> the aged ones.

The missionary spent his first night in the chief's *hale
ho'okipa* (house of refreshment and rest), a grass house
three miles inland, and was served a bountiful feast.

> . . . two strong men, tattooed from head to foot, came in
> bearing a huge whole hog, baked entire minus hair and entrails.
> These bearers were followed by others, dressed in the same style
> bringing calabashes of various sizes filled with fish, poi, potatoes,
> then came melons, bananas, and sugar cane, and little gourds
> filled with goat's milk. All was spread out in royal Hawaiian
> style—a dozen *kukuis* burning and *kahilis* waving to and fro.[50]

Quite evidently the Protestant pastor was receiving both an
official and a popular welcome. The next day he proceeded
on horseback to Waiohinu, to find evidences of spontaneous
welcome.

> Here the good elder and teacher, Kema or Shem, put a new
> grass house which he had built for himself at my disposal as long
> as I wished to occupy it. The house was built on a huge pile of
> *aa* or lava stones, about fifteen feet square, with one door about
> four and one half feet high.[50]

Some weeks later his delicate wife and infant daughter
came from Kona to help found a church and a school and to
build a home in which to live and labour " for nearly nine
years, under the pillars of cloud by day and of fire by
night—the fiery cloud over Kilauea to be seen from Waiohinu . . ."[51] During the first five of these, he says: " There
were no foreigners in the district of Kau . . . except the
French priest who hated us with perfect hatred for our
work's sake."[51] But in addition to loneliness for his own

---

[49] Paris, Rev. John D., *Fragments of Real Missionary Life*, p. 12;
collected extracts from private MSS. and from *The Friend*; published
Honolulu, 1926.

[50] Paris, op. cit., pp. 14, 17.

[51] Paris, op. cit., pp. 29, 59.

kind, Mr. Paris' journals record no complaints of his situation save that " our cisterns were cracked by repeated earthquakes."[51]

Ka-'u in the 'Forties.

Reversing the Ellis tour, twenty-three years later, Chester H. Lyman in 1846 coming through the forest of tree ferns and 'ohi'a below Kilauea, passed through the beautiful country of Kapapala, where he encountered dwellings and canoe-making sheds, the first such to be seen on descending the mountain. He was impressed with the green hills, the moist state of the soil, the " several horses with cattle and goats " feeding near the chief's house; and " the fires of Kilauea which shone up magnificently on the clouds like the light of a conflagration at evening."[52]

Punalu'u village he found " romantically situated on the beach, shut in in part by a rough lava stream." Continuing along the shore, he passed the black-pebble beach of Ninole and found "a succession of small villages" whose inhabitants were " extensively engaged in fishing." The coastal road, across the streams of lava southward to Honu'apo, was improved since Ellis' time,

> . . . it having been built with great labour by levelling a path 4 or 5 feet broad, lining it on each side with a wall of some two feet high, and covering it with a layer of sand from the neighbouring beach.

He refers to the " peculiarly striking " mountain scenery behind this stretch of coast, and to the pleasant village and canoe landing of Honu'apo set amid its coconut grove.

> The hills back of it are cultivated with potatoes, taro, etc., as also are the sloping hills which lie back 2 or 3 miles from the coast all the way from Punaluu, from the base of which the lava streams . . . seem to have burst forth, as I could see no marks of their having descended from the more distant hills.

Striking inland from Honu'apo through a beautiful and fertile country he came to Waiohinu, still the lush valley described by Ellis; and there he found " Bro. Paris' " dwelling set " in a green nook in the hills."

Later, travelling westward from Waiohinu through "delightful" country—soil good and "vegetation abundant"

[51] Paris, op. cit., pp. 29, 59.
[52] Lyman, Chester H., MS. pp. 9, 10. H.M.C.S. Library, Honolulu.

—he continued to retrace the path of the Ellis tour in reverse, climbing down the steep *pali* of the Kahuku Escarpment, through " a forest of Ohia and other trees and shrubs " on ancient lava to Manukā, and making an evening journey over clinkery lava to Kapu'u, " pleasantly situated in a cove of the sea."[53]

It is notable that he makes no mention of plantations or villages beyond Waiohinu, but only of " abundant vegetation."

THE SHIFTING HUMAN SCENE.

Captain Cook's officers at " discovery " and the early missionary travellers some forty years later speak of the " populous " villages and the widely cultivated plains and valleys of Ka-'u. In 1833 a missionary census estimated the population to be between 5,000 and 6,000. Fifteen years later, in 1848 it was reported that " the work of depopulation has gone on with fearful rapidity "; in 1866—" the land is almost desolate."

What were the forces operating to bring about this melancholy change in a little over half a century, in a district remote and scarcely touched by the new contacts, compared with such ports as Honolulu, Lahaina, even Hilo? For the most basic and perhaps the most potent cause we must go back in time behind the foreign " invasion," to a primary effect more subtle than physical disease or disaster.

The time and the event merged in the conquest of the island of Hawai'i by Kamehameha the Great. The effect in Ka-'u was—the broken spirit of a proud and fiercely independent people, who lost at one treacherous blow the entire flower of their native *ali'i* and came under the hated rule of the conqueror. *Ka-'u makaha*—" Ka-'u the Fierce," was humbled, their proud title brought to shame. The grandparents of oldsters yet living will attest to the withering character of this thing. Songs, chants, stories bear witness; even the naming of children commemorates their shame. Small wonder that with the betrayer of their lost *ali'i* sent in by the conqueror to govern them, the spirit of the people was snuffed out, their ambition killed. Disintegration was accelerated. They inevitably became more vulnerable to introduced disease, an easy prey to other catastrophes

[53] Lyman, op. cit., MS. pp. 11, 20.

soon to follow, which repeatedly decimated the population, then led to flight from their land.

Political Changes.

Kamehameha I was in many ways a wise and just ruler. But the very process of welding into one kingdom the widely separate and individualistic islands of this chain, and of creating a governing hierarchy which would include (though carefully dispersed) the several conquered *moi* and their sub-chiefs, wrought great changes in established customs and ways of life—including re-apportionment of feudal land holdings. Still, the new *Moi* had a real feeling for the welfare of his people and endeavoured to ground his new system firmly upon *pono*—"the right." It was not until after his death in 1819 that disastrous disintegration of the well-wrought ancient culture set in.

By that time contact with foreigners—on naval vessels, merchantmen and whaling ships—had excited in the *ali'i* a lust for trade, foreign goods and liquor—new wants and to a limited extent new values. It had also considerably undermined their loyalty to the sense of their own personal sanctity and obligation to law based on sacred *kapu*. In 1820 the new *Moi*, Liholiho, at the behest of the ambitious Ka'ahumanu, Kamehameha's favourite wife, had ordered priests and householders to burn all tribal, clan and family *ki'i* (symbolic "images") in public and domestic temples and shrines. With "idol worship" went the orderly times of rest from work, and of worship, in four periods during each moon. More disastrous socially was Ka'ahumanu's abolition at the same time of all *kapu* affecting eating. Thereafter, domestic life, which had hitherto followed patterns evolved through millenia requiring women and small children to eat apart from men, and isolation of men engaged in serious labour, and of menstruating women, became helter-skelter, and neither man, woman nor child any longer knew order, status or authority in the household. The first missionaries had not yet arrived. The old order was null and void: it would be decades before a new order, based upon New England Congregationalist and French Roman Catholic *mores* was really comprehended.

One of the most immediate consequences was the rapidly growing indifference of many of the *ali'i*—each

anciently the fostering head of his 'ohana—to the welfare of
their people. Their own personal desires and demands now
became paramount. This would be particularly true in
Ka-'u. Equally important as a cause of social and moral
dissolution was the substitution, under the new system and
the alien governor, of konohiki, or supervisors of sub-districts
and fishing grounds, for the native junior ali'i (the ali'i 'ai
ahupua'a) and the haku or functioning master, the senior
male director of the affairs of the 'ohana or kinship group.
(See pages 5, 6.)

Before this time, and particularly during the career of
the first Kamehameha, an ali'i's need of and dependence
upon loyal warriors dictated a policy of care, if nothing else
did. The prevalence of warfare in the decades before and
during Kamehameha's rise and reign had taken heavy toll of
the population of the islands. New weapons and modes of
fighting introduced by the first foreign ships and eagerly
sought by the warring chiefs, from iron for daggers and
spearheads to guns and gunpowder, had made warfare vastly
more deadly. In Ka-'u where the warfare had been pro-
longed and violent the effects upon the population must have
been especially severe.

But now came, generally speaking, a time of peace; and
the desires of the Moi and his sub-chiefs were turning toward
the many fascinating things that could be acquired through
foreign trade: no longer mere items of curiosity and
personal adornment, but ships, materials for "civilized"
houses, furniture and luxuries of every sort. The trading
captains were only too eager to supply these things in return
for precious cargoes of sandalwood for the China trade, or
for the promissory notes of the ali'i.

It was the people who suffered for this. They suffered
in two ways, and their alien ali'i seem to have had little
thought or compassion for either their present suffering or
its later consequences. Logging the sandalwood was a
gruelling task—the heavy labour of felling the trees in the
cold, wet, upland forests, the back-breaking toil of dragging
them down for long distances over rough terrain to the
seacoast.

This was bad enough, but as the desires of the chiefs
and the pressure of the trading captains grew, more and
more people were put to the task, fewer and fewer were left

for the normal duties of everyday living; in many areas planting and fishing virtually ceased, and for a season thereafter there would be little harvested beyond the needs of the *ali'i* and their *konohiki* (supervisors). It was the people who went hungry. Contemporary writers and the historian Kuykendall,[54] looked upon it as one of the prime causes of famine, sickness, and depopulation throughout the kingdom before 1829 (when the sandalwood resources were practically exhausted).

Fundamental Cultural Changes.

Closely related to these political changes which reflected themselves so disastrously in the attitudes of the chiefs, were the profoundly dislocating effects of the abandonment of the old cultural pattern, with its fixed relationships, its reciprocal duties and benefits, its fixed seasons for fishing, planting, harvesting, ceremonial, warfare and games. The result may well be described as the paralysis of a once integrated culture.[55]

Warfare, with its rigorous disciplines, had ceased. The gods of the harvest were no longer honoured in the great winter festival of the Makahiki, at which time the produce of the land had been ceremonially divided between the gods, the *ali'i* and the people. The long season of labour no longer culminated in the refreshing and invigorating social season of athletic games and dancing. The demands of a careless (now often debauched and hated) *ali'i* were unpredictable and never-ending, instead of being reasonably fixed and accountable. Planting, therefore, except for immediate needs, became desultory and unplanned, even when not interfered with by such exorbitant labour demands as the sandalwood trade. The observance of inshore fishing *kapu* at spawning time lapsed, and the breeding grounds were fished out. Without direction much deep-sea fishing, which is of necessity a team enterprise, lapsed also, resulting in a lack in this essential element of nutrition. But most disastrous of all was the factor which underlay all these things—the slackening of the co-operative will, and of that sense of well-being within a secure social frame which attends a right relationship between governor and governed.

[54] Kuykendall, Ralph S., *The Hawaiian Kingdom, 1778-1854*; p. 89. University of Hawai'i, Honolulu, 1938.
[55] See Handy, E. S. C., *Cultural Revolution in Hawaii*. 1932.

Foreign Impact.

Upon a people already bewildered by breakdown and change came now the impact of total innovation. Ka-'u felt the actual impact of foreigners less (and later) than neighbouring Kona, and much less than did the main ports of the islands of Maui, Oahu and Kauai. But inevitably its people early felt the indirect effects. In Kalaniopu'u's time the *Moi* and his warriors made expeditions to Maui and return, and his court alternated between Kona and Ka-'u. In Kamehameha's time the earlier isolation was quite broken, as first conquering armies and then the court itself moved from island to island and back again. Coming in contact with the growing numbers of foreign crews ashore in the larger ports, and with the native women of those port towns, two vicious introductions made inroads in both army and court— venereal disease and alcoholism, both disastrous among a folk hitherto untouched by either. These were the foremost influences which undermined the native physique at that time. Others followed.

Thus, inevitably, foreign addictions and ailments were carried back to the *'ohana,* even in isolated Ka-'u, there to become virulent diseases among an unsophisticated folk. Measles, whooping cough, fevers, " lung inflammations " in turn ravaged the population everywhere, " fearfully mowing down by annual thousands " (before the eyes of the despairing early mission workers) " those for whom the work was undertaken."[56]

The Rev. Titus Coan,[57] first missionary to be established in Hilo and Puna (1835), passed the remainder of his long life in those districts, doctoring bodies as well as souls. He observed the effects of a " too rapid change of national habits " as disastrous to the native health, particularly emulation of foreign dress styles in place of the healthful *malo* and *kapa* mantle. He describes the church-going Hawaiian of an early day fantastically garbed in " two pairs of pantaloons over a thick woollen shirt, with tight boots, and a thick coat . . . over all . . . panting with heat and wet with perspiration " rushing home to throw off all but a shirt or *malo* and fall asleep in the chillest breeze to be found. Such was often the prelude to " consumption, fevers, and other diseases

[56] Bingham, Hiram, *A Residence of Twenty-one Years in the Sandwich Islands;* 1855; p. 169.
[57] Coan, op. cit., pp. 258, 259.

which almost decimate a community," diseases unknown in their old life in Nature. As the grass *hale* was discarded, the new hot and unventilated " civilized " dwellings which replaced them became " charnel houses," in his phrase.

Barrenness among women became a serious source of depopulation—a condition beginning to be prevalent, where previously it had been common only among court followers in consequence of the practice of abortion. Coan and other missionary historians ascribe the new sterility chiefly to the introduced " vile disease." Other commentators of the time, such as the Englishman Alexander Simpson,[58] regard it as a deplorable by-product of new religious attitudes toward breaches of chastity, shame and heavy social penalties now attending upon " the many Magdalenes " which gave new stimulus to the practice of abortion, with increasing sterility as the inevitable result. The general decline in sports was a prime factor in weakening the splendid physique of the native Hawaiian, hence rendering him more vulnerable to disease. This had many causes: the cessation of games in connection with ritualistic practices, already referred to; the impressment of all adult commoners into the *ali'i's* service, first for procuring trade goods, later, after missionary influence began to be felt, into the schools; the widespread adoption of " civilized " dress, and no doubt, a certain amount of missionary disapprobation, as most games involved gambling. Hiram Bingham,[59] however, pays tribute to Hawaiian physical dexterity and prowess, particularly in aquatic sports, and deplores their decline.

Epidemics.

Coan says there was a native account in his district of a " pestilence like a plague " which " swept off multitudes " long before the arrival of the missionaries. There are also, in a report sent to the Board of Foreign Missions in Boston in 1833, accounts given by oldsters of the dreadful " camp pestilences " which attended the wars of Kamehameha the Great—wars of long duration and involving the movements of numerically greater armies than any previously remembered.

[58] Simpson, Alexander, *The Sandwich Islands: Progress of Events Since their Discovery* . . ., p. 16. London, 1843.
[59] Bingham, op. cit., pp. 190, 193, 335, 370, 401, etc. See also other missionary accounts.

Of a later era we have more exact knowledge. We know
that all quarters of the island of Hawai'i suffered in 1848
from " a fearful epidemic of the measles " which " carried
off . . . a tenth of the whole population "; and that leprosy
was a " persistent unrelenting plague."[60] Leprosy came in
from China with the first contract labourers during the reign
of Kamehameha III, and spread alarmingly, being known to
the natives as the *ma'i Pake*, the Chinese disease.[61]

In 1849, Ka-'u, in common with Hilo, Puna and Kona
districts, suffered from an epidemic of influenza with many
fatalities. Dr. Charles Wetmore,[62] first physician stationed
on the island, regards the prevalence of this disease as due
to the weakened lungs of those who survived the previous
year's measles epidmic; to " their imprudence " thereafter,
which led to whooping cough; and to an unusually long wet
winter season following. Rev. Henry Kinney[63] in his 1849
report for Ka-'u speaks of the suspension of schools for
several months as " parents, teachers and children were all
prostrate." In a later letter for that year he further refers
to " the ravages of those diseases, which within a few months
have swept off scores of the members of this church " (at
Waiohinu).

A similar letter written by the Rev. J. D. Paris in the
previous year, on the point of his departure from that
station, says: " Since the year 1845 the work of depopulation in Kau has gone on with fearful rapidity." Owing to
this decrease the number of schools was reduced from 20
to 12 during three years. " The people of this remote and
scathed and often oppressed district," he writes, " are
emphatically poor," and yet he praises their industry and
their benevolence.[64] (He then refers to other causes which
will be discussed in the following section.) Fr. Marechal
had recorded on arrival in Ka-'u in 1841 that the " heathen "
were for the most part " exceedingly poor, often living days
without food."[65]

[60] Coan, op. cit., pp. 258-9.

[61] Kuykendall, *A History of Hawai'i*, p. 227. 1926.

[62] Wetmore, Charles, Collected MSS. Letters, 1848-1899. H.M.C.S.
Library, Honolulu.

[63] Minutes of General Meetings of the Hawaiian Mission, 1838-
1853. Vol. I, 1849, p. 6. Honolulu.

[64] Minutes of General Meetings . . ., etc. Report for the year 1848.

[65] Yzendoorn, op. cit., p. 183.

Disasters.

Mr. Paris mentions first " the distressing famine which prevailed in 1845-46," due to many months of drought, which drew after it " a dark train of disease and death, the marks of which are still visible."

Some of these physical " marks " then still visible on the face of the country, were vividly described by the visiting scientist Chester H. Lyman in his journal of 1846-47.[66] He found the usually lush country below Kapapala (and extending as far as Waiohinu) " recently burned over, the black roots of the tufts of grass, the wilted and blackened shrubs, and the smoked stones [presenting] a most dismal prospect for many miles." Later at Waiohinu he learned that this was the consequence of an accidental fire which caught and raged through the drought-stricken dry grass of the plains and up through the tinder-like staghorn fern of the uplands, leaving only " the blackened stalks of ti trees, burnt fern stumps " and like desolation in the vegetative realm, and sweeping away whole hamlets of grass houses in its path.[67] Natives of the Waiohinu district told Mr. Lyman that there were two subsequent fires in other adjoining areas; and that previously in 1830 or 1831 there had been " a like burning over of nearly the whole district, producing great distress among the inhabitants." In 1846 this devastation, together with the famine, " drove many people to other parts of the islands," says Mr. Paris; and on those who remained:

> The effects of the sufferings then experienced have not yet ceased. The early and the later rains have returned in their season; the hills and vallies are clothed with verdure and beauty; and food abounds through all the district. But the graves are multiplied. The silent work of death, the fruit of extreme suffering, has been going forward. The old and the gray headed are seldom seen in our borders. They sleep beneath the clods of the valley.

Mr. Paris was no longer in Ka-'u when the next great disaster struck his parish, but he has left a description of it from nearby Kona. In 1867 a drought followed by famine had prevailed, so that the people were obliged to " subsist in a great measure upon ti and fern roots."[68] But in 1868

[66] Lyman, op cit., MS. Bk. IV, pp. 10, 14. H.M.C.S. Library, Honolulu.

[67] See also Paris, op. cit., pp. 26, 27. ·

[68] Minutes of Hawaiian Evangelical Association—1854-1863. Report for 1862, p. 6. Honolulu.

"came the great disaster, the overturning of Kau with the earthquake and the tidal wave destroying the villages from Punalu'u to Ka'alu'alu."[69]

This was a truly cataclysmic disaster, "a series of terrific earthquakes" during which "for three weeks the earth seemed to vibrate all the time,"[70] culminating in the most destructive of all remembered shakes in Ka-'u, when great chasms opened in the earth, swallowing houses and cattle, and many human lives and thousands of cattle, goats and sheep were lost in the volcanic flow of mud and lava west of Waiohinu which overwhelmed and devastated the lovely valley of Wai-o-ahu-kini at the base of the Kahuku Scarp.

But by far the greatest devastation at that time was wrought by the accompanying tidal waves in the fishing villages along the rugged south-eastern coast of Ka Lae, the cape.[71] In all of these the loss of life was great, and in many the physical destruction was such that they were no longer habitable.[72] These marks of alteration or desolation are still notable in most. None ever recovered their former prosperity.

Dislocations.

Such a disaster, in addition to the outright deaths, had its secondary effect in the scattering of the remaining population. So it had been after the famine and fires of 1846. So it was now, to an even greater extent. Uprooted, homeless, deprived of their potato and taro patches and other means of subsistence, these survivors now became drifters; many of them, when and as they could, left the district entirely, to seek livelihood in some more favourable locality.

Factors other than physical disaster had already been contributing to the dislocation of life and population in Ka-'u, ever since the Kamehameha conquest. During the heyday of the whaling era Ka-'u had contributed its quota of

[69] From MSS. report of the pastor, J. Kauhane, at Kapaliiuka, Ka-'u, for 1867-68. In H.M.C.S. Library, Honolulu.

[70] Paris, op. cit., p. 55.

[71] Reports of eye-witnesses in the newspaper *Kuokoa*, April 11 and 18, 1868, translated by Mrs. Pukui.

[72] Mrs. Pukui's grandmother was a survivor of the devastation wrought at Waikapuna, her home being on a slightly higher ground; but the valley and the fresh springs were ruined for any subsequent cultivation, by the tidal waters and heaped-up sands. Her home was later moved *mauka*, to the uplands above Na'alehu.

adventurous males to the ships putting in at Kealakekua and Kailua for provisions, whose masters did systematic recruiting for able-bodied Polynesian crewmen. Even before this, and as soon as the fur trade between the Northwest Coast of America and China developed, in the 1790's, the sailing ships which broke their voyages at the Sandwich Islands frequently took "kanakas" away with them, often out of interest, occasionally by impressment. Some returned, some did not.[73] Increasingly, as the years passed and more ships plied between Hawai'i and the other islands, curiosity led the young and unattached to "seek their fortunes" in the ports of Honolulu and Lahaina. Mr. Paris' letter of 1848 referred to these "influences operating to draw the people from this district," and commented sadly that "a very large proportion" were the youth of the land—"from the ages of eight to eighteen."

By 1859 there came about a new type of dislocation. The *pulu* trade had taken the place of the vanished sandalwood, and the rain forests of Mauna Loa were being ransacked for the hairy down (*pulu*) which encases the stems and the young opening fronds of the tree fern. This was being sought in great quantity by the Honolulu merchants to be shipped to California factories as mattress stuffing. This traffic, which lasted intensively from 1859 to 1885, actually threatened the magnificent fern forests of these lower mountain zones.[74] According to the Rev. William Shipman, then resident at Waiohinu, an even worse fate threatened the people of the district who forsook their homes and settled pursuits to engage in this exciting new form of barter for "needless" trade goods. Families were scattered, "all agricultural pursuits, even . . . the culture of taro" neglected (always a forerunner to famine) and the countryside lay as though dead.

"Houses are deserted, education neglected, meetings forsaken, and the people going back to barbarism," he wrote.[75] A gloomy, but perhaps not an overly pessimistic view; for where family dislocation takes place all the routines of society are apt to suffer.

[73] Kuykendall, 1938, op. cit., pp. 21, 22.

[74] Degener, Otto, *Plants of Hawaii National Park*, p. 29, 1945.

[75] Minutes . . . 1854-63 (op. cit.). Report for 1859, p. 10.

The Changing Face of Nature.

Perhaps the most significant evidence, and effect, of social dislocation (other than that reflected in individual character) is observable in the changing face of nature during the fifty years after first description.

The valley of Waiohinu, according to early foreign observers, was the heart of the cultivated area of Ka-'u. Verdant and blossoming, watered by a stream and by "never-failing springs," it was the centre of wet cultivation for the district. As late as 1833, according to the missionary surveyors,[76] there were twenty sizable plots (*lo'i*) of irrigated taro in Waiohinu village requiring constant flooding by flowing water, diverted from the stream in ditches ('*auwai*). This indicated both an abundance of water (considering the needs of the two or three thousand people estimated to be dwelling within the valley) and an intensive use of it in conjunction with fertile soil. In upland areas, away from flowing water, other varieties of taro were grown by dry cultivation methods. Along the gulches of Pakini and in areas of deep soil on the Kamao'a plain a special variety of taro known as *paūa* was extensively planted. And all across the plain, unwatered save by rain, and in moist crannies in the lava, sweet potatoes ('*u'ala*) were the staple. Everywhere in pockets of good soil bananas, sugar cane, gourds and other supplementary foodstuffs flourished. The early visitors saw the fertile sections of this now largely barren lower land as " one continuous garden."

As we have seen, this picture soon began to deteriorate, due first to the sullenness of the *kama'aina* under alien governors and next to the inactivation of the once co-operative society, after the old ceremonies and *kapu* had been cast aside; then to preoccupation with the gathering of trade items (sandalwood, *pulu*) ; finally under the effects of long droughts and serious depopulation. But there were other influences at work; the introduction of new plants,[77]

---

[76] *Sandwich Island Questionnaire*, 1833.

[77] Apart from house plots and gardens, where almost everything from Orient, Australasia and Occident, has been tried, the growth that one becomes familiar with in the wilds includes prominently the following trees and shrubs of which the last eight named have become more or less serious pests: algaroba, monkeypod, eucalyptus, casuarina, mango, *pamakani* (*Eupatorium*), bracken fern, Java plum, guava,

many of which spread rapidly as pests—and plant diseases; and most markedly the introduction of animals. Vancouver, with purposive generosity, in 1793 and '94 presented small herds of cattle to Kamehameha and these he ordered released into the uplands where they roamed and multiplied in the wild. Goats were another early introduction which soon proliferated in the mountains as they escaped from domestication. Both breeds, in addition to becoming economic staples, meantime wrought destruction amidst the natural growth of the land, and on native plantations.

The missionaries very early sought means of amplifying the subsistence economy of the district by introducing temperate-zone garden produce and fruits. Don Francisco Marin had already brought in oranges and grapes and other products of Mexico, but for a long time none of these were other than dooryard novelties. He had also made molasses and sugar from the native cane, for his own use. The missionaries as soon as they settled were prompt in beginning to grow their own coffee and in hand-milling their own sugar. They likewise attempted cotton growing and the spinning and weaving of cotton cloth, for their own use and as a supplement to the native industry. But these new things were very late in reaching Ka-'u, and seem to have had no great spread there. In the 1850's an Agricultural Society was formed with a view to improving the impoverished condition of the people, and in 1858 the Protestant Mission incumbent could report: " The temporal condition of the people is improving. Farms are fenced, lands and roads improved. About 150 acres of wheat is growing, and promises well."[76] Corn, as a commercial crop, had been tried previously, but failed, for lack of distribution facilities to a ready market; and by 1859 the promising wheat crop had

cactus, lantana, castor bean (*Ricinus communis*), klu (*Acacia Farnesiana*), blackberry, Australian wattle or *koa haole*, Christmas berry (*Schinus terebinthifolius*). Over 175 grasses, sedges, and herbs have been introduced, such as plantain, purslane, groundsel, chick-weed, dandelion, pigweed, Australian saltbush, milkweed; most of the grasses have been purposely brought in for pastures, including many clovers, pigeon pea, and other legumes, foxtail, Australian blue grass, red top, Bermuda grass, Wallaby grass, etc. (See *Vegetation Zones of Hawaii*, by J. C. Ripperton and E. Y. Hosaka, Hawaiian Agricultural Experiment Station, Bul. No. 89, Univ. of Hawai'i Press, Honolulu, 1942.)

[78] Minutes, Hawaiian Evangelical Association, 1854-1863. Report of 1858, p. 5.

come to nought because the *pulu* traffic which began in that year had " put an end to all agricultural pursuits." (See footnote 75.)

In 1862 Mr. Shipman's successor, Mr. Gulick, reported[79] that taro culture had been exceptionally poor during the previous year, " owing to the drought *and to the free range of cattle*." By that time there were individual holdings of cattle on the plains, but with a common run.

In 1865 and '66 Mr. Pogue, the new Protestant missionary at Waiohinu, reported[80] two *haole* sugar enterprises in the Waiohinu area, with tracts of cane already under cultivation and mills in course of building, but he does not name the entrepreneurs. (It is said that after the violent earthquakes and tidal waves two years later many famished survivors took refuge in these canefields and subsisted on the cane for a time during the food shortage subsequent to the disaster.[81])

The Lands are Apportioned.

These enterprises had become possible because now foreigners could secure land by means other than direct grant from the King or a lesser *aliʻi*. The old feudal system of land tenure was superceded during the 1840's as the result of a series of conferences between King and Chiefs and resident foreign advisors. What is known as the Great *Mahele* (division) was agreed upon, by which lands were set aside as Crown Lands, Government Lands, lands for the chiefs, and lands for the commoners. Those who had previously occupied and cultivated small plots under their local *aliʻi* were confirmed in their tenure and could, by application to the new Land Board and payment of a small fee, obtain absolute ownership of their plots (*kuleana*).

In Ka-ʻu we note from Mission reports that the people were slow to understand and avail themselves of this new privilege. But the more responsible native leaders slowly began to set an example and gradually most of the tenants took the necessary steps to acquire royal patents on their lands. This patent carried, of course, the right to lease or sell, and so set the stage for a rapid shift of characters in

[79] Minutes, op. cit., Report of 1862, p. 6.
[80] Manuscript Missionary Reports in H.M.C.S. Library, Honolulu.
[81] MS. " History of Hutchinson Sugar Plantation Co." Courtesy H.S.P. Co. office, Naʻalehu, Ka-ʻu, Hawaiʻi.

the prevailing land drama of the district. As late as 1858 Mr. Shipman could say of Ka-'u, " Our foreign community is small, and exerts no influence over the natives."[82] (The census of 1853 lists seven only; 26 in 1860.) In 1866 Mr. Pogue reported that " the *haoles* " were increasing. (The census of that year lists 46.) In 1869 the pastor J. Kauhane referred to widespread drunkenness due to the distilling of liquor from *ti* root by " michievous persons of the camps of the *haoles*,"[83] camps which had sprung up here and there, probably in connection with the *pulu* trade.

Obviously a marked change had occurred in the *haole* population within the decade under consideration. The Rev. Pogue mentioned the presence of several new *haole* couples in the community, some of whom attended church and some not, whereas previously all had had connection with the missions. He likewise mentions *haoles* from Honolulu who had recently leased land and come to Waiohinu to live. In 1870 there is a record of the sale by one Lazarus Ahi of 225 acres of land in the Na'alehu area (adjacent to Waiohinu town) for sugar planting purposes, and in the next few years land transactions included both sale and lease of various parcels for similar purposes.

So, obviously, enterprising whites had arrived. At first the newcomers were mainly Americans—planters and ranchers—with a sprinkling of British and Europeans. (At least one Italian, John Costa, was briefly an early sugar entrepreneur.) But by 1872 Chinese coolies had been brought in as plantation labourers (numbering 22), and only a short time was to elapse before the population in Ka-'u had radically changed its composition, the chief agency in this latest change being the sugar industry.

Sugar.

As to what exactly was the relation of the first experimental planting in this field, on Ka-'u, to its next phase there seems to be no sure information. But in May of 1870 an American, Alexander Hutchinson (previously connected with the Honolulu Iron Works), came to Waiohinu and in association with John Costa bought the 225 acres of land at Na'alehu before referred to and there " laid down " a sugar

[82] Minutes Hawaiian Evangelical Association. Reports for 1858 and 1866, p. 5.
[83] MSS. Missionary Reports in H.M.C.S. Library, Honolulu.

mill and built the manager's residence. The partnership was short-lived, and within the next few years Costa left and Hutchinson was vigorously adding to his holdings and extending the cultivation of cane.

The only connection we find with the earlier experiments lies in the fact that Charles N. Spencer of Waiohinu, who was known to have planted 10 acres of cane there in 1867,[84] was head overseer of Hutchinson Sugar Plantation in 1874, and that in 1877 he and Hutchinson were partners in a new sugar enterprise at Hilea, where a new mill was built and put in operation the following year. The Hutchinson interests had also acquired by this time a plantation and mill in Waiohinu started by Costa and developed by others. In 1879 the site for still another mill was purchased by Hutchinson at Honu‘apo, a much nearer and more convenient ship's landing and loading place, once the road and wharf were built.

At the beginning of the enterprise all building materials and plantation necessities had been landed at Ka‘alu‘alu and carted up over the *pahoehoe*, much as Mr. Paris' household possessions had been some thirty-five years earlier, except that now bullocks did the hauling. There was by this time a fairly frequent schedule of small steamers calling at Puna-lu‘u, Honu‘apo and Ka‘alu‘alu (as early as 1862 Rev. Gulick was deploring that the Sunday steamer arrivals had become " an ever-returning temptation to Sabbath desecration." See Mission Report of that year.) The receipt of freight and the shipment of sugar, was, however, a never-ending risk and uncertainty for the Plantation manager, as were the periodic years of drought—an unfailing feature of the terrain—and the complex problem of labour.[85]

The Labour Scene.

The first labour force for the new plantation was supplied by the local Hawaiian population. For the mill, expert boiler-tenders, carpenters and coopers (the sugar barrels were coopered on the site) were imported from

---

[84] MS. " History of Hutchinson Sugar Plantation Co.," H.S.P. Co. office, Na‘alehu, Ka-‘u, Hawai‘i.

[85] Reference is here made to the Letter Press volumes of the years 1876 ff. in the Office of the H.S.P. Co. at Na‘alehu, on which the following summary is based, and for access to which we are indebted to the courtesy of Mr. James Beatty, present manager, and his staff.

Honolulu—already a cosmopolitan town. By 1876 Mr. Hutchinson had in addition a group of contract field labourers from China living in a camp beside the Na'alehu Mill. The correspondence of this period with W. G. Irwin Co., Agents in Honolulu, bristles with problems: runaways, breaking their contracts; quarrels " continually " between " the Chinamen and natives "; Chinese complaints over occasional rice shortages (all rice had to be imported); " serious rows " over " the new 9 hr. law "; Chinese opium-smoking, frequent illnesses and deaths (some the manager complained were " half-dead " on arrival); desperate need to recruit dwindling labour supply among " any returning whalers, natives or South Sea Islanders that come along."

In 1877 there was " a coloured man " as *luna* (overseer) at Waiohinu Plantation; and another " coloured man " from Wailuku, Maui, made application as Sugar Boiler for the new mill (it is presumed from the names that these were American Negroes)—so here was another new, if minor, element. In June of that year the question of field labour became especially acute. Over 115 acres of cane was spoiling to be taken off, over 120 acres requiring immediate stripping, 50 acres of young cane overgrown with weeds, and new acreage to be planted. While " to do all this and run the mill, wood, carts, etc.," there was only " a gang of 73 Kanakas and 45 Chinamen, which is very small indeed " for the work to be done. These basic needs were never more than partially filled until in 1878 the first group of Portuguese arrived, giving considerable satisfaction. In the spring of 1879 Mr. Hutchinson reports on a new labour influx: " I am well pleased with the Darkies and would like some more of the same class." Probably these were Gilbert Islanders, a group of whom were known to have been brought to Hawai'i about this time. (The next Census, that of 1884, lists 85 " South Sea Islanders.")

By the time the Census of 1884 was taken (14 years after the first plantation was started), Ka-'u's labour population included 568 Chinese and 933 Portuguese, and there were 116 *haoles* in the district. The native Hawaiians and part-Hawaiians numbered 1,543 out of a total population of 3,483. (Twelve years earlier, the native element had numbered 1,829 out of 1,865.)

In the year 1866 the Government of Japan entered into

an agreement with the Government of Hawai'i for the con-
tracted entry of Japanese labourers into the islands. That
same year Hutchinson Plantation Co. at Na'alehu began
receiving groups of Japanese, in what numbers we do not
know; but 476 appear in the Ka-'u Census report for 1890,
whereas the Chinese and Portuguese figures for that year
were considerably decreased.

The Economic Scene.

By the beginning of that decade (1890) it was obvious
that the sugar plantations had become the dominant factor
in the life of central Ka-'u. Cattle raising by Hawaiians
was also growing in importance, due perhaps in part to the
needs of the plantation for beef and for work bullocks (both
of which had at first been supplied from outside the district)
and the shipment of beef, tallow and hides had become a
considerable asset. But clearly sugar was dominant.
Hutchinson Sugar Plantation Co. had bought or leased large
tracts of land from Hawaiian owners. It had flumed water
into Waiohinu from the springs that once irrigated the
valley's taro *lo'i,* and had tapped other upland water sources
for its ever growing needs. It was a new source of livelihood
for the community, either as workers on the plantation pay-
roll or as contract planters furnishing cane to the mill. It
had brought in varied new population elements (and was to
bring in more), and had introduced new skills to the native
population. But it was not for long a factor in holding the
remaining Hawaiians of the district to their homeland.

In the first place, Hawaiians appeared to be tempera-
mentally unsuited to the sort of labour regimentation
essential to a big scale plantation enterprise—in " all-out "
heavy labour undertakings they were magnificent (and
enthusiastic) conjoiners; for day-after-day routine drudgery
they had no preference. Furthermore, there were not enough
of them available to supply the increasing demand; and they
did not get on well with the new importations. By 1890 they
had almost drifted out of the Plantation picture, except in
special types of employment.

In the second place, they found it more profitable (at
least in the short range) to lease their lands to the plantation; and more interesting to seek employment elsewhere.
The H.S.P. Co.'s correspondence files for those years of

expansion are filled with matters relating to native land transactions—leases, mortgages, cash advances, efforts to purchase certain tracts and the refusal of the offer of others. It is significant, too, that most of these transactions were carried on with owners who had already removed to Honolulu, or with those at a distance who had fallen heir to family lands heretofore persistently held by old folks until their death.

Turn of the Century.

The three decades between 1870 and 1900, despite great changes in the population picture, nevertheless constituted something of a heyday for those native Hawaiians who had stubbornly clung to their homes in the district during previous vicissitudes. These families still held preferred place, as *kama'aina*, children of the soil. From among them were recruited the various appointive officials. Sheriffs, police officers, wharf officials, school superintendants, teachers, pastors—these were Hawaiians. On the plantations, while native field labour was fairly soon supplanted by imported contract labourers, many Hawaiian men held the more responsible jobs, and quite a good number of Hawaiian women were married to *haole* men in upper-bracket positions of comparative affluence and prestige, from minor technicians to *luna* (supervisor) and manager. Life in the 'eighties and 'nineties is remembered as gay and good by oldsters of today, an interesting blend of Hawaiian ways of livelihood and pleasure with the new, but with native song, dance and storytelling still prevailing.

While Hawaiian men did not take kindly to routine field labour, they responded zestfully to the vigorous excitement of ranch life. From the beginning of the domestication of wild cattle in the district, as elsewhere in the islands, the *paniolo* (cowboys, so named for the first " Españolos " brought in from Mexico to teach the art) were Hawaiians. As the big commercial ranch ventures were undertaken— first on Princess Ruth's Kamao'a lands, then under *haole* management at Kahuku, Ka'alu'alu, Kapapala — the Hawaiians were the ones who became famous for their daredevil riding over the rough lava-bedded terrain, and indispensable for their strength and skill in handling cattle. Others were equally famous as runners in the goat roundups—an important adjunct to the cattle ranching of those days, where goat-meat was a valued commodity, and thousands of hides were regularly shipped out in foreign trade.

At the turn of the century, however, various events contributed to bring this easy-going and comparatively prosperous era to a close. The dying monarchy gave place to United States Annexation—with the preliminary brief interlude of the Republic. In the realms of government existing institutions were considerably shaken. On the local industrial scene the more or less benevolent relationships were altered and management at Hutchinson took on a more hardheaded, hard-fisted and totally uncomprehending attitude under a new " boss "—Prussian in his mentality and probably in his training, to judge from his ruthless methods and military regimentation. Although this state of affairs could not and did not prevail, it lasted long enough to create a general rebellion, in the course of which a large majority of the Hawaiians and part-Hawaiians connected with the Plantation walked out of their jobs—many of them leaving the district entirely; and it created a long-lasting sense of enmity in those who did remain in the neighbourhood.

More and more, after this, did other plantations, or seafaring, or Honolulu with its political opportunities and its congenial waterfront jobs, entice away the youth of Ka-'u from the increasingly meagre living at home. The World War of 1914-1918 caused further dislocation. The schools, still taught for the most part by Hawaiian women, were smaller and had fewer and fewer Hawaiian pupils. The fishing villages were almost deserted; the once-numerous taro planters along Pakini gulch had left their homes and plots to desolation; the homesteads on Kamao'a plain and above Waiohinu were neglected; ranch and plantation had almost completely taken over the broad terrain, and Waiohinu town was now only half populated.

Mid-Century.

Meantime the second and third generation of Japanese and Portuguese plantation workers were coming onto the scene; and a new element had been added to the contract labour camps—the Filipinos. (The earlier Chinese had largely drifted away—although a few remained, for the most part as storekeepers; and there is still an intermixture of Chinese blood in the local population.)

Among the native-born children of immigrant stock, adaptation in the direction of Hawaiianization and Americanization has gone on apace, accelerated by the environment, the education system, industrial policy, and the ambition of the immigrant elders. America's part in the Second World War, 1940-1946, likewise helped the process. Today, in mid-century, and save for a few old-timers, the political figures in Ka-'u are elder *haoles* and younger Japanese; the ranchers are largely Portuguese and Portuguese-Hawaiians; the fishermen are mainly Japanese, as are also the commercial truck-gardeners and banana-growers, the storekeepers and garage mechanics. The skilled plantation workers (as distinguished from the field labour) and the trained business-office employees of the plantations are for the most part the sons and daughters, or grandsons and granddaughters of early Japanese contract labourers, born on the plantation, graduates of High School, University, or Business College in the Territory. The top figures in management are *haole*—American and Scotch.

The district is fairly populous again; but both the pattern and the composition of the population is entirely different. It is largely concentrated in the two plantation towns of Pahala and Na'alehu (Hutchinson), with a scattering in and around adjacent Waiohinu town, a mere handful on the beach at Punalu'u and Ninole. The broad plain of Kamao'a, Pakini, and adjacent districts, is now inhabited almost exclusively by cattle, all the way down to Ka Lae, with only a few widely dispersed ranch homes. The grassy slopes of Kapapala to the north-east—just below the Volcano National Park—are likewise given over to cattle range and ranch buildings. All across the great fertile uplands, stretching above the descending plains, away through the rainfall region to the forest zone on Mauna Loa's southern flank, one sees neat, vast, scientifically farmed fields of waving, rustling cane, wide smooth plantation roads for the gigantic mechanical equipment of modern industrial farming. One accustomed to studying small farming, Hawaiian, *Haole* and Oriental, has a sense of awe at the magnitude, the perfection, and the beauty of this achievement of our pioneering race within the span of a century.

Envoi.

It may be of interest to note that the most ancient Polynesian ancestor, Kane, is said in native mythology to have been white-skinned. Sugar cane, according to Hawaiian lore, was brought to Hawai'i by this primordial ancestor, Kane, and is a *kinolau* or form of Kane. Luxuriant cane varieties created by the *Haole* by means of artificial selection, hybridization, irrigation, cultivation and fertilization now cover all these uplands of Ka-'u which anciently were the traditional domain of Kane-i-ka-wai-ola (Kane-of-the-water-of-life). Gone is the land-grabbing, vengeful war god, Ku-ka-'ili-moku. The rocks of his last temple have been rudely thrust aside by a bulldozer to make more ground for open furrows. From its site on the crest of Makanau hill one looks out on thousands of rolling acres of flourishing cane, on peace, and plenitude nourished by " waters of life " from springs and from clouds over the flank of Mauna Loa. In this favoured locality Kane, the male procreator and god of peace, is lord.

Even fiery Pele the Earth-shaker has not in any recent geologic time been able to threaten his sovereignty here, for the very conformation of these high lands, created by a vastly more ancient volcanic upheaval, has protected its wide-stretching deep-soiled terrain from the ravages of all her lava flows from Mauna Loa and Kilauea rifts and craters within historic times. Her earth-rumblings are still a gigantic force in the land; the fascination of her fiery displays and the threat of fresh desolation are never remote from the minds of Ka-'u dwellers—exerting their potency today as of old upon the character and temper of the children of her soil, whatever their race. But it seems probable that this thriving green heart-land of tumultuous Ka-'u will long remain Kane's primordial domain and, whether in sugar cane or some subsequent economy, will continue to contribute bounteously to the well-being of man.

> " There is no going back; ways now are different . . .
> Look forward with love for the season ahead of us!
> Let pass the season that is gone !"[86]

---

[86] For Chant of Kupake'e, see p. 226.

INDEX TO HAWAIIAN WORDS AND NAMES

TALES OF THE PACIFIC

JACK LONDON

Stories of Hawaii by Jack London
Thirteen yarns drawn from the famous author's love affair with
Hawai'i Nei.
$6.95   ISBN 0-935180-08-7

The Mutiny of the Elsinore by Jack London
Based on a voyage around Cape Horn in a windjammer from
New York to Seattle in 1913, this romance between the lone
passenger and the captain's daughter reveals London at his
most fertile and fluent best. The lovers are forced to outrace a
rioting band of seagoing gangsters in the South Pacific.
$5.95   ISBN 0-935180-40-0

South Sea Tales by Jack London
Fiction from the violent days of the early century, set among
the atolls of French Oceania and the high islands of Samoa,
Fiji, Pitcairn, and "the terrible Solomons."
$6.95   ISBN 0-935180-14-1

HAWAII

Ancient History of the Hawaiian People by Abraham
Fornander
A reprint of this classic of precontact history tracing Hawaii's
saga from legendary times to the arrival of Captain Cook,
including an account of his demise. Originally published as
volume II in *An Account of the Polynesian Race: Its Origins and
Migration,* this historical work is an excellent reference for stu-
dents and general readers alike. Written over a hundred years
ago, it still represents one of the few compendiums of precontact history available in a single source.
$7.95   ISBN 1-56647-147-8

Hawaii: Fiftieth Star by A. Grove Day
Told for the junior reader, this brief history of America's fiftieth state should also beguile the concerned adult. "Interesting,
enlightening, and timely reading for high school American and
World History groups."
$4.95   ISBN 0-935180-44-3

A Hawaiian Reader
Thirty-seven selections from the literature of the past hundred years, including such writers as Mark Twain, Robert Louis Stevenson and James Jones.
$5.95   ISBN 0-935180-07-9

Hawaii and Its People by A. Grove Day
An informal, one-volume narrative of the exotic and fascinating history of the peopling of the archipelago. The periods range from the first arrivals of Polynesian canoe voyagers to attainment of American statehood. A "headline history" brings the story from 1960 to 1990.
$4.95   ISBN 0-935180-50-8

True Tales of Hawaii and the South Seas Edited by A. Grove Day and Carl Stroven
Yarns from the real Pacific by 21 master storytellers, including Mark Twain, W. Somerset Maugham, Robert Louis Stevenson, and James A. Michener. This anthology comprises some of the best nonfiction writing about the South Pacific.
$5.95   ISBN 0-935180-22-2

A Hawaiian Reader, Vol. II
A companion volume to *A Hawaiian Reader*. Twenty-four selections from the exotic literary heritage of the Islands.
$6.95   ISBN 1-56647-207-5

Kona by Marjorie Sinclair
The best woman novelist of post-war Hawai'i dramatizes the conflict between a daughter of Old Hawai'i and her straitlaced Yankee husband. Nor is the drama resolved in their children.
$4.95   ISBN 0-935180-20-6

The Wild Wind, a novel by Marjorie Sinclair
On the Hana Coast of Maui, Lucia Gray, great-granddaughter of a New England missionary, seeks solitude but embarks on an interracial marriage with an Hawaiian cowboy. Then she faces some of the mysteries of the Polynesia of old.
$5.95   ISBN 0-935180-3-3

Claus Spreckels, The Sugar King in Hawaii by Jacob Adler
Sugar was the main economic game in Hawai'i a century ago, and the boldest player was Claus Spreckels, a California tycoon who built a second empire in the Islands by ruthless and often dubious means.
$5.95   ISBN 0-935180-76-1

Remember Pearl Harbor! by Blake Clark
An up-to-date edition of the first full-length account of the effect of the December 7, 1941 "blitz" that precipitated America's entrance into World War II and is still remembered vividly by military and civilian survivors of the airborne Japanese holocaust.
$4.95   ISBN 0-935180-49-4

Russian Flag Over Hawaii: The Mission of Jeffery Tolamy, a novel by Darwin Teilhet
A vigorous adventure novel in which a young American struggles to unshackle the grip held by Russian filibusters on the Kingdom of Kauai. Kamehameha the Great and many other historical figures play their roles in a colorful love story.
$5.95   ISBN 0-935180-28-1

Rape in Paradise by Theon Wright
The sensational "Massie Case" of the 1930's shattered the tranquil image that mainland U.S.A. had of Hawaii. One woman shouted "Rape!" and the island erupted with such turmoil that for 20 years it was deemed unprepared for statehood. A fascinating case study of race relations and military-civilian relations.
$5.95   ISBN 0-935180-88-5

Mark Twain in Hawaii: Roughing It in the Sandwich Islands
The noted humorist's account of his 1866 trip to Hawai'i at a time when the Islands were more for the native than the tourists. The writings first appeared in their present form in Twain's important book, *Roughing It.* Includes an introductory essay from *Mad About Islands* by A. Grove Day.
$4.95   ISBN 0-935180-93-1

The Trembling of a Leaf by W. Somerset Maugham
Stories of Hawai'i and the South Seas, including *Red,* the author's most successful story, and *Rain,* his most notorious one.
$4.95   ISBN 0-935180-21-4

Hawaii and Points South by A. Grove Day
Foreword by James A. Michener
A collection of the best of A. Grove Day's many shorter writings over a span of 40 years. The author has appended personal headnotes, revealing his reasons for choosing each particular subject.
$4.95   ISBN 0-935180-01-X

Pearl, **a novel by Stirling Silliphant**
In a world on the brink of war, the Hawaiian island of Oahu was still the perfect paradise. And in this lush and tranquil Pacific haven everyone clung to the illusion that their spectacular island could never be touched by the death and destruction of Hirohito's military machine.
$5.95   ISBN 0-935180-91-5

Horror in Paradise: Grim and Uncanny Tales from Hawaii and the South Seas, **edited by A. Grove Day and Bacil F. Kirtley**
Thirty-four writers narrate "true" episodes of sorcery and the supernatural, as well as gory events on sea and atoll.
$6.95   ISBN 0-935180-23-0

HAWAIIAN SOVEREIGNTY

Kalakaua: Renaissance King **by Helena G. Allen**
The third in a trilogy that also features Queen Liliuokalani and Sanford Ballard Dole, this book brings King Kalakaua, Hawai'i's most controversial king, to the fore as a true renaissance man. The complex facts of Kalakaua's life and personality are presented clearly and accurately along with his contributions to Hawaiian history.
$6.95   ISBN 1-56647-059-5

Nahi'ena'ena: Sacred Daughter of Hawai'i **by Marjorie Sinclair**
A unique biography of Kamehameha's sacred daughter who in legend was descended from the gods. The growing feelings and actions of Hawaiians for their national identity now place this story of Nahi'ena'ena in a wider perspective of the Hawaiian quest for sovereignty.
$4.95   ISBN 1-56647-080-3

Around the World With a King **by William N. Armstrong, Introduction by Glen Grant**
An account of King Kalakaua's circling of the globe. From Singapore to Cairo, Vienna to the Spanish frontier, follow Kalakaua as he becomes the first monarch to travel around the world.
$5.95   ISBN 1-56647-017-X

Hawaii's Story by Hawaii's Queen **by Lydia Liliuokalani**
The Hawaiian kingdom's last monarch wrote her biography in 1897, the year before the annexation of the Hawaiian Islands by the United States. Her story covers six decades of island history told from the viewpoint of a major historical figure.
$7.95   ISBN 0-935180-85-0

The Betrayal of Liliuokalani: Last Queen of Hawaii 1838-1917 by Helena G. Allen
A woman caught in the turbulent maelstrom of cultures in conflict. Treating Liliuokalani's life with authority, accuracy and details, *Betrayal* also is tremendously informative concerning the entire period of missionary activity and foreign encroachment in the Islands.
$7.95   ISBN 0-935180-89-3

HAWAIIAN LEGENDS

Myths and Legends of Hawaii by Dr. W.D. Westervelt
A broadly inclusive, one-volume collection of folklore by a leading authority. Completely edited and reset format for today's readers of the great prehistoric tales of Maui, Hina, Pele and her fiery family, and a dozen other heroic beings, human or ghostly.
$5.95   ISBN 0-935180-43-5

The Legends and Myths of Hawaii by David Kalakaua
Political and historical traditions and stories of the pre-Cook period capture the romance of old Polynesia. A rich collection of Hawaiian lore originally presented in 1888 by Hawai'i's "merrie monarch."
$7.95   ISBN 0-935180-86-9

Teller of Hawaiian Tales by Eric Knudsen
Son of a pioneer family of Kauai, the author spent most of his life on the Garden Island as a rancher, hunter of wild cattle, lawyer, and legislator. Here are 60 campfire yarns of gods and goddesses, ghosts and heroes, cowboy adventures and legendary feats among the valleys and peaks of the island.
$5.95   ISBN 1-56647-119-2

SOUTH SEAS

Best South Sea Stories
Fifteen writers capture all the romance and exotic adventure of the legendary South Pacific, including James A. Michener, James Norman Hall, W. Somerset Maugham, and Herman Melville.
$6.95   ISBN 0-935180-12-5

Love in the South Seas by Bengt Danielsson
The noted Swedish anthropologist who served as a member of the famed Kon-Tiki expedition here reveals the sex and family life of the Polynesians, based on early accounts as well as his own observations during many years in the South Seas.
$5.95   ISBN 0-935180-25-7

The Blue of Capricorn by Eugene Burdick
Stories and sketches from Polynesia, Micronesia, and Melanesia by the co-author of *The Ugly American* and *The Ninth Wave*. Burdick's last book explores an ocean world rich in paradox and drama, a modern world of polyglot islanders and primitive savages.
$5.95   ISBN 0-935180-36-2

The Book of Puka Puka by Robert Dean Frisbie
Lone trader on a South Sea atoll, "Ropati" tells charmingly of his first years on Puka-Puka, where he was destined to rear five half-Polynesian children. Special foreword by A. Grove Day.
$5.95   ISBN 0-935180-27-3

Manga Reva by Robert Lee Eskridge
A wandering American painter voyaged to the distant Gambier Group in the South Pacific and, charmed by the life of the people of "The Forgotten Islands" of French Oceania, collected many stories from their past—including the supernatural. Special introduction by Julius Scammon Rodman.
$5.95   ISBN 0-935180-35-4

The Lure of Tahiti selected and edited by A. Grove Day
Fifteen stories and other choice extracts from the rich literature of "the most romantic island in the world." Authors include Jack London, James A. Michener, James Norman Hall, W. Somerset Maugham, Paul Gauguin, Pierre Loti, Herman Melville, William Bligh, and James Cook.
$5.95   ISBN 0-935180-31-1

In Search of Paradise by Paul L. Briand, Jr.
A joint biography of Charles Nordhoff and James Norman Hall, the celebrated collaborators of *Mutiny on the "Bounty"* and a dozen other classics of South Pacific literature. This book, going back to the time when both men flew combat missions on the Western Front in World War I, reveals that the lives of Nordhoff and Hall were almost as fascinating as their fiction.
$5.95   ISBN 0-935180-48-6

The Fatal Impact: Captain Cook in the South Pacific by Alan Moorehead

A superb narrative by an outstanding historian of the exploration of the world's greatest ocean—adventure, courage, endurance, and high purpose with unintended but inevitable results for the original inhabitants of the islands.

$4.95   ISBN 0-935180-77-X

The Forgotten One by James Norman Hall

Six "true tales of the South Seas," some of the best stories by the co-author of *Mutiny on the "Bounty."* Most of these selections portray "forgotten ones"—men who sought refuge on out-of-the-world islands of the Pacific.

$5.95   ISBN 0-935180-45-1

Home from the Sea: Robert Louis Stevenson in Samoa, by Richard Bermann

Impressions of the final years of R.L.S. in his mansion, Vailima, in Western Samoa, still writing books, caring for family and friends, and advising Polynesian chieftains in the local civil wars.

$5.95   ISBN 0-935180-75-3

Coronado's Quest: The Discovery of the American Southwest by A. Grove Day

The story of the expedition that first entered the American Southwest in 1540. A pageant of exploration with a cast of dashing men and women—not only Hispanic adventurers and valiant Indians of a dozen tribes, but gray-robed friars like Marcos de Niza—as well as Esteban, the black Moorish slave who was slain among the Zuni pueblos he had discovered.

$5.95   ISBN 0-935180-37-0

A Dream of Islands: Voyages of Self-Discovery in the South Seas by A. Gavan Daws

The South Seas... the islands of Tahiti, Hawai'i, Samoa, the Marquesas... the most seductive places on earth, where physically beautiful brown-skinned men and women move through a living dream of great erotic power. *A Dream of Islands* tells the stories of five famous Westerners who found their fate in the islands: John Williams, Herman Melville, Walter Murray Gibson, Robert Louis Stevenson, Paul Gauguin.

$4.95   ISBN 0-935180-71-2

His Majesty O'Keefe by Lawrence Klingman
and Gerald Green

The extraordinary true story of an Irish-American sailing captain who for 30 years ruled a private empire in the South Seas, a story as fantastic and colorful as any novelist could invent. Vivid in its picture of Pacific customs, it is also filled with the oddity and drama of O'Keefe's career and a host of other major characters whose adventures are part of the history of the South Pacific. Made into a motion picture starring Errol Flynn.

$4.95   ISBN 0-935180-65-6

How to Order

For book rate (4-6 weeks; in Hawaii, 1-2 weeks) send check or money order with an additional $3.00 for the first book and $1.00 for each additional book. For first class (1-2 weeks) add $4.00 for the first book, $3.00 for each additional book.

1215 Center Street, Suite 210
Honolulu, HI 96816
Tel (808) 732-1709 Fax (808) 734-4094
Email: mutual@lava.net